Addy Russell

All My Life

All My Life

A MEMOIR

SUSAN LUCCI

WITH LAURA MORTON

itbooks

AN IMPRINT OF HARPERCOLLINS*PUBLISHERS*

———— ⟋ ⟍ ————

To Helmut, Liza, and Andreas—who are my world

Grateful acknowledgment is made to reprint the *Saturday Night Live* monologue from Broadway Video Enterprises and NBC Studios, Inc. Copyright © 1990 NBC Studios, Inc. Distributed by Broadway Video Enterprises.

HarperCollins books may be purchased for educational, business, or sales promotional use. For information please write: Special Markets Department, HarperCollins Publishers, 10 East 53rd Street, New York, NY 10022.

FIRST EDITION

Designed by Jaime Putorti

Library of Congress Cataloging-in-Publication Data has been applied for.

ISBN 978-0-06-206184-3

11 12 13 14 15   OV/RRD   10 9 8 7 6 5 4 3 2 1

CONTENTS

The Streak Is Over

T HE STREAK IS OVER!"

When I heard the very charming Shemar Moore utter those now-famous words onstage, my first thought was that he was announcing some play-off score for the audience. I had been to many charity events over the years where the MC kept the crowd up to speed on important sports scores, so I honestly didn't realize what was happening. The truth is, after my ninth Emmy loss, I couldn't hear the name of the person who won anymore. I would become numb as the winner was called out because, well, I had lost so many times. Was it self-protection? I think it must have been. But the way I always knew I didn't win was when somebody else stood up and made her way to the stage. Everybody in the audience, including me, was applauding and looking at her—not at me.

The Emmys that year were held at the Paramount Theatre inside Madison Square Garden because Radio City Music Hall, the usual location, was being renovated. Madison Square Garden is one of New York's great landmarks, so it was exhilarating to attend the awards there as a change from the usual venue. My husband and

I walked the red carpet, where we were greeted by the press and many dear, upbeat fans. I was invigorated by their enthusiasm but was doing everything I could to keep myself calm.

"Susan, who are you wearing tonight?" one entertainment reporter asked.

I was wearing a beautiful white silk Badgley Mischka gown. It had a tracing of platinum and a sprinkling of crystal beads. I also had gorgeous Fred Leighton chandelier earrings on and was carrying a matching Judith Leiber beaded bag.

My husband, Helmut, and I made our way into the theater, where we were seated in the front row next to Rosie O'Donnell, who was to my left. I had enjoyed appearing on Rosie's show a few times. She was always very warm and gracious, though I didn't know her that well. We greeted each other and then she leaned over to me and said, "Susan, when you go up onstage tonight to claim your Emmy, why don't you give me your evening bag. Otherwise, when they announce your name, you'll be very excited, you'll stand up, and you'll step all over that gorgeous bag and that won't look pretty on TV."

"Oh, thank you, Rosie," I said. "That is so nice of you, but history has taught me that I am probably not going up there tonight. I am a hopeful person, but past shows have proved that it's likely I won't win." Then we both nervously laughed at the obvious.

Even after Shemar shouted, "SUSAN LUCCI!" I remained seated. I didn't hear him call my name.

The only way I knew I had won was that Rosie reached over and grabbed my bag. It finally clicked that Shemar was referring to me when he said, "The streak is over." Of course, I was in total shock. This was the first time my name was mentioned after the envelope had been opened. I could barely muster up the strength to stand on my very wobbly legs or to hug Helmut, who had to literally pick me up by my elbow.

I leaned into Helmut and whispered, "Are you sure?"

"Yes," he said as he gallantly escorted me to the stairs leading to the stage.

I slowly walked up each step trying to remember what I thought I might say, you know, just in case. I rarely prepared an acceptance speech—it seemed unnecessary after nineteen nominations and eighteen losses. I was so weak in the knees as I walked toward the podium, I was worried that I wouldn't be able to stand.

Okay. I will admit that the night before the awards ceremony, for the first time in quite a while, I began to think there was a possibility that maybe *this* would be my year. The media certainly held out great hope. Plus, it had been a good year for the show. My story line was very strong. It primarily revolved around Erica's intervention with a then-eleven-year-old Bianca, my daughter on *All My Children*, who was struggling with an eating disorder. The scenes were wonderfully written and so many people were saying that they thought the performances and the writing were deserving. Yet I had heard that sentiment many times in the past, so I didn't want to get my hopes up too high. But if, for some reason, it was meant to be, I didn't want the moment to go by without thanking the people who mattered most. So, just before falling asleep the night before, I mentally created my list, you know, on the off chance.

By the time I reached the center of the stage, I finally had the courage to turn around and face the audience for the very first time. Everyone in the room was on their feet, cheering. I saw all of my peers in the industry crying and rejoicing in this moment with me. It felt as if it were a collective win for all of us. I watched in awe as Rosie O'Donnell, Marcy Walker, Leeza Gibbons, Gayle King, Kelly Ripa, Mark Consuelos, Peter Bergman, and my wonderful costar David Canary, and all of the tremendously talented women who were also nominated that night helped me soak in that unforgettable moment. I was so taken aback by their generosity, love, and support.

The standing ovation went on for what felt like forever, and in TV terms I suppose it was—it lasted four very long minutes. Dick Clark later told me it was some kind of award-show record. I was especially grateful that he, as one of the executive producers, had allowed that beautiful, wonderful applause to continue on because in that time, I was able to get over my cream-cheese legs, catch my breath, gain a little bit of my composure, and miraculously remember the thoughts I had collected for this very moment while in bed the night before.

"Thank you.

"Thank you very much.

"I can't believe it.

"You are so kind." I tried to start speaking even as I struggled to fight back my tears of joy, but the audience kept cheering. I took a step away from the microphone and looked stage right, where I caught a glimpse of Oprah Winfrey, who was standing in the wings jumping up and down, clapping and pumping her fists in the air.

"Oh, Oprah!" I said in total awe. I simply couldn't believe she was cheering for me.

Me!

I clutched my precious golden-winged statue against my chest like I was holding a newborn baby and I began to speak.

"I truly never believed that this would happen. First of all, I want to thank each and every one of you in this room. This is a roomful of such talented, hardworking people. And the fact that you have thought that my work was worthy of notice . . .

"NINETEEN times . . ." (this got a good laugh)

"It is something that I will treasure always.

"I thank God for the many, many blessings in my life. For parents that encouraged me to dream my dreams and who have been sitting in every audience of my lifetime including tonight.

"For my great teachers: Wynn Handman, the late Harold Clurman, Ron Weyand, and Inez Norman Spiers, who were so good at teaching and helped me to grow.

"Agnes Nixon: you changed the face of the medium we work in. I am so grateful to have been placed in your hands. Thank you so much

for creating the part of Erica Kane and for allowing me to be part of your writing full of so much humanity and passions and vision.

"I have so many people to thank and they're telling me to wrap it up."

The audience let out a loud "NO!" when I said that. I looked down and saw the beautiful Kelly Ripa, whom I worked with for many years on *All My Children*, shaking her head and saying, "Don't leave. Let her speak!" She was so adorable.

I continued without regard for the clock.

"I want to thank Joan D'Incecco, the legendary casting director at All My Children *who saw me for more than just an ethnic type and saw that I could play Erica Kane and for bringing me to Agnes's attention.*

"To the incredible acting company at All My Children *with whom I have the privilege to play these scenes every day. You inspire me. If I'm halfway good it is because I am afraid I won't be as good as you!"*

It was right about this time that the director began flashing all sorts of lights, signaling to me that I HAD to wrap things up. But I couldn't leave the stage without thanking the most important people of all.

"To my children: to Liza and Andreas. I wasn't meant to get this award before tonight because if I had I wouldn't have that collection of poems and letters and drawings and balloons and chocolate cakes you made all this time to make me feel better.

"To my husband: Helmut Huber, who has been with me EVERY . . . STEP . . . OF THE WAY.

"And to the fans: I was only supposed to be on every other Tuesday" (the audience laughed again) *"but thanks to you, I am here and I promise I will try my best never to let you down. I'm going back to that studio on Monday and am going to play Erica Kane for all she is worth! Thank you so very much!"*

I could hardly wait to get backstage to make three urgent phone calls. I had already told the producers of the show that if by some miracle I won that night, I would have to step aside before going to the pressroom so I could call my children. I knew they must have already heard the good news, yet I really wanted to hear their voices.

My first call was to my daughter, Liza, who was watching the show from her home in Los Angeles, having just started her own career on *Passions*. The Emmys show hadn't aired on the West Coast yet, so she hadn't heard the good news. When I told her I had won, she was beyond thrilled. Liza has been with me throughout my entire Emmy journey, ever since she was four years old. She had experienced all nineteen nominations, but up until that night, had never experienced what it felt like for me to win. She had only endured the many losses.

One year I came home to find that Liza had made letters from construction paper and had placed a word on every step of the winding staircase that leads up to my bedroom. The message read, "We love you, Mommy. You are the best actress in the whole wide world!" When I got to my room, I was greeted with a bouquet of balloons that she had tied to the bedpost. Liza would enlist her brother Andreas's help in any way that he could participate. He is five years younger than Liza, so he generally helped with decorating the many cakes, brownies, and other goodies they'd bake together so I would have a treat waiting for me when I got home. With all of the losses over the years, thanks to my children, there really were so many wins.

Win or lose, I always went back to work and continued to do my best to play this incredible character, Erica Kane—a role I was lucky enough to have been given, and the real reason why I've always persevered in the face of defeat, why I've pushed on time and time again.

I know it sounds clichéd, but the nominations alone really meant a lot to me. Whether or not I won, I never felt like I ever had anything to truly lose. Plus, it's not like the Emmy was mine to lose, because I had never taken the trophy home—at least not until 1999.

From my perspective, I wasn't relinquishing some title all of those years because the title hadn't been mine in the first place.

After so many nominations, I realized that I had to stop getting myself whipped into a frenzy every year around award season. It was easy to get caught up in the thunderous support I received from the press and the fans of *All My Children*, who were always so hopeful for me. Their never-ending enthusiasm was very moving. What was really amazing to me was that there were so many people who were determined that I get that award. And yet I was afraid that somehow, all of this attention felt unfair to those who did win each year. They were all talented, hardworking people who deserved the honor in every way. I certainly didn't want to take anything away from their achievements.

I'd heard rumblings over the years that some people thought I should be happy for not winning because an actress couldn't pay for the type of publicity I was receiving. There were many who thought I might even be in on it, like my continuous losing was somehow fixed. Naturally, that was absurd, but it didn't stop people from talking. I was astounded at these suggestions, because God only knows, I *wanted* to win.

I *really* wanted to win.

After Liza and I spoke briefly backstage, I immediately called my son, Andreas, who was watching with friends in New York. Lastly, I telephoned my mother, who was in Palm Beach and who is my biggest cheerleader. I just had to share my excitement with them all. By this time, my husband had made his way backstage. I am always comforted when Helmut is standing by my side. After I finished my calls, Helmut and I continued on to the pressroom to face the media and to do my much-anticipated interview.

As I walked through the door, the press and media backstage were all cheering for me. This was the hardened press corps who were all standing and applauding when I walked through the door. It was quite amazing—a completely joyous occasion. There was a lot of warmth and love expressed in my direction. Looking back, the whole experience was unbelievable. It was one of those rare occasions in life that I call my "Cinderella" moments. Those are the times where you have to pinch yourself because you cannot believe what you are experiencing is really happening.

When we finished with the media, Helmut pulled me aside. He had a very serious look on his face. Helmut has managed my career for many years, so I can usually tell what he is about to say, but this time I wasn't sure. I was hoping and praying that there wasn't some kind of mix-up—that they had made a mistake and called out the wrong name.

"I have a confession to make," Helmut said. "I made an agreement with *People* magazine that if you won, they could come to our house early tomorrow morning to do a photo shoot for the cover. I didn't want to tell you about this until I knew you had won." Helmut looked as relieved to share this news with me as I was to hear it, even though it meant that we could only stay at the Emmy afterparty for a short while. We gave and received hugs and kisses from so many well-wishers and then made the one-hour drive back to our home in Garden City, a suburb of Long Island, New York. Although I had wanted to open a bottle of champagne or dig into a guilty rich chocolate dessert to celebrate, we went right to bed. Of course, I strategically placed my Emmy on our dresser, where I could see it from across the room whenever I opened my eyes, which I did from time to time, just to make sure this wasn't all some crazy dream.

CHAPTER 1

Born to Perform

Over the course of the past fifteen years or so, different publishers and agents have reached out to me asking if I would be interested in writing a book. Each letter laid out the specific reasons why they believed people wanted to hear whatever it was I had to say. While I was flattered by their kind words, writing a memoir wasn't something I ever thought was in me. And, to be very honest, I didn't have the time it takes to sit down and write one. As a working actress, wife, mother, new grandmother, and a businesswoman, I live with a very full schedule. Most of the time I feel like I've been shot out of a cannon. I spend a great many days reading and memorizing scripts, creating the nuances that bring the dialogue and Erica Kane to life, and then I fill it all up with acting. On top of that, I'm attending design meetings for my products on HSN, I'm taking voice lessons, doing interviews, talk-show appearances, and trying to squeeze in my morning workouts somewhere between four and five in the morning! When I am not working, I am traveling for work or spending time with my family. I am always moving forward, so I wasn't sure that there would ever be a good time . . . or *any* time to look back. Those moments of reflection or "savoring the moment" have been few and far between for me.

There were many times when my makeup artist Robin Ostrow and my hairstylist Joyce Corollo, from the New York team at *All My Children*, also encouraged me to write a book, because people who knew we worked together always asked them questions about me. Robin and Joyce were constantly coming to me with different ideas about what I should write. They talked about fashion, health, beauty, and inspirational stories from my life. They were very encouraging, but at the time I still wasn't completely convinced that writing a book was the right thing for me.

In late 2009, I agreed to do a charity event for Francesca James, one of the legendary actresses of *All My Children*. She played the dual role of Kitty and Kelly. She auctioned off a handwritten letter from me answering whatever questions the winning fan wanted to ask. When I received the questions, I wanted to take the time to sit down and thoughtfully answer them. At first, it was just one of many tasks I had to do that day—something else on my already piled-high and overflowing plate. Much to my surprise, though, answering the questions was really fun and intriguing despite the tremendous time constraints. One of the questions this person asked was "What are some of your favorite things to do when you are not playing Erica Kane?" I love those types of questions because they allow me to be spontaneous in my response. I've always liked flying by the seat of my pants. Answering that letter opened me up, maybe for the first time ever, as I suddenly found myself thinking about the process of writing and what it would really take to someday author a book.

In early 2010, my son, Andreas, came to me and said that he really thought I should write a book, too. He had no idea we had received so many letters from various publishers and literary agents. I was curious to know why he felt I should, so I asked him to share his reasons.

"Once the girls I meet find out that you are my mom, they want to know how you accomplished your goals. They're eager to know your story." Andreas was very thoughtful, enthusiastic, and really heartfelt in his explanation.

Andreas mentioned writing a book to me a few more times. And then one day Helmut brought me a folder full of those inquiry letters he'd been saving over the years. I had no idea that he had kept all of them. We sat at our kitchen table and began to read some aloud. One by one, each outlined very clearly a singular message. People wanted the book to be about me from me. Everyone agreed that virtually anyone with a television knows Susan Lucci as Erica Kane, but no one really knows much about Susan Lucci. Rereading those letters, especially with the encouragement from my son and so many others, made me realize that maybe now I should make the time to share my story.

So here I am. After spending forty-one years in front of the camera playing the unstoppable Erica Kane while successfully shielding and protecting my privacy and the privacy of my family, I am closing my eyes and holding my breath as I begin to peel back the curtain of my life, hoping it is the right thing to do. It's a little bit scary and a lot intimidating. But if I am going to take you on this journey with me, then like everything else I do in my life, I am committed to going all the way—no limits and no self-imposed barriers holding me back. To be certain, this process has been different and challenging for me. But it is something I now fully appreciate and enjoy. I have never spent time in a therapist's office; nor have I ever candidly discussed my private life in public. I have spent many sleepless nights wondering why anyone would want to read my story, and to tell you the truth, I still can't say I know. I am a woman who pays attention to what those around me have to say, and for years, they've been asking me to share my story with you. So, with respect for those wishes and without further ado, here is my story.

My parents, Jeanette and Victor Lucci, referred to me as their "Christmas baby" because I was born on December 23, in Yonkers, New York. As a little girl, there weren't too many birthday cakes or parties for me because of the proximity of my birthday to the holiday. (I'm sure so many Christmas babies can relate to this!) Still, my parents always tried to make my birthday special. They put up our Christmas tree on December 22 so my birthday presents could be slipped under the tree and opened the next day, on my birthday. Much to my mother's credit, she always told everyone in our family that they couldn't combine Christmas and birthday gifts. After all, it wasn't my fault that I was born so close to the holiday.

My parents both grew up during the Depression era. Everything they did was about making life better for their children. Our family moved to Elmont, a suburb of Long Island in New York, when I was two years old. We spent five years there before settling into the picture-perfect enclave of Garden City.

My father's parents were Italian immigrants to America. His father died when my dad was only fifteen years old. His mother remarried, although I don't believe my dad was terribly close to his stepfather. When my brother and I were younger, my father occasionally took us to visit them, usually without my mother. I didn't understand at the time why she never came with us, but years later I would learn that my Italian grandmother didn't approve of my father's decision to marry a non-Italian girl.

My Italian grandmother only spoke a few words of English. When we'd visit, she'd smile, grab me by both cheeks, and pinch—hard. She showered me with lots of hugs and kisses, but we barely ever spoke. She always offered me a glass of milk—as *milk* was one of the few words she could say that I understood. Oftentimes, my father's other relatives, including brothers, sisters, aunts, and uncles, would be at his mother's home when we visited. They'd all sit around the living room telling big and boisterous stories, speaking only in Italian, gesturing with their hands, waving their arms, and laughing out loud. I didn't understand a word they said, but I always knew that whatever it was, it was hysterically funny. While they talked, I wandered around the apartment, exploring the knickknacks and family memorabilia my grandmother kept. I especially liked going into her bedroom, which was very dark except for the glow of the candles she'd keep lit for the Blessed Mother and the baby Jesus. My Italian grandmother was a devout Roman Catholic.

As a little girl, I remember thinking her home was very mysterious because I had never seen anything like it. I wasn't scared so much as intrigued by what it all meant. I had great curiosity about her bedroom in particular. Going to my Italian grandmother's home was all about mystery because I never knew what she and the rest of my relatives were talking about, yet I knew I liked the sounds I heard and the enthusiasm they had when they spoke.

I believe in mystery. I am drawn to it and am very comfortable being surrounded by it. Maybe that is part of why I chose to keep an air of mystery over my own life as I stepped into the limelight years later. Maybe.

My father was one of thirteen children. Although his older siblings were all born in Italy, my dad was a first-generation Italian American who wanted a better life for his children than he was given as a child. My father enlisted in the United States Army during World War II. He was a real patriot who considered it an honor to serve his country. Education was everything to him. He believed that there were no limits to what you could do in life with a good, strong foundation. Although he didn't finish college, he was able to put himself through school with help from his local steelworkers' union and the GI bill. He eventually formed a partnership in a construction business, which primarily helped build the steel infrastructures for high-rise buildings in New York City. My father's business allowed us to live a good but modest life. He worked very hard to provide all of the necessities—and then some—to our family. People often assume that because I have Italian features and have an Italian last name, I grew up in a large Italian family, but I really didn't. My father's family was my only touchstone to that heritage.

When we moved to Garden City, we didn't look like the typical Anglo-Saxon family living there. The community consisted primarily of Episcopalian families. I think ours was one of the few in the neighborhood with a vowel at the end of our last name. My father looked very Italian, with beautiful olive skin, jet-black hair, and big brown eyes. Although I resembled my mother more, I did inherit some of my dad's dark coloring, which made me feel like an outsider during my youth. I felt and looked different from the other children in our neighborhood and in school. There were so many times when people would see my father gardening out in our front yard or doing landscape work on our grounds and they would ask him questions as if he were the hired help. My father always laughed it off, without ever giving it a second thought. There was a certain amount of prejudice that existed in the 1950s, especially if you didn't look like everyone else. It hurt me deeply that people judged or looked down on my dad based on his appearance, especially because he was such a giving and generous man. If there was a blizzard or a hurricane, my dad would always be the first one out there after the storm blew over, driving around the community to see if there was any damage, downed trees, blocked drains, or if anyone needed his help. I'd sometimes get to go along for the ride. He'd sit me in the front seat with him and I felt so proud and privileged to be the one by his side.

My father was a very smart man, a voracious reader, and we all thought of him as an American history buff. In my family, we all referred to my father as the "walking encyclopedia" because of his vast knowledge on so many subjects. He knew everything about the great battles our country fought and took great pride in sharing his knowledge with my brother and me. Sometimes we'd take family trips to historical sites in upstate New York, including West Point and Fort Ticonderoga, so my father could teach us while showing us where these events took place. We'd sit around our kitchen table while he gave my older brother, Jimmy, and me impromptu quizzes or fun brainteasers to solve. Sometimes I'd figure out the answer before Jimmy. I could see the tickled look in my father's eyes—he was proud of me whenever I got it right.

On Sunday afternoons, we would take a family drive in my parents' car, something my brother and I loathed. Jimmy was six years older than me. He wanted to be with his friends on the weekends, not riding in the backseat of our car with his little sister. We'd usually end up having Sunday dinner at a family-style restaurant that my parents loved. As we stood in line waiting to be seated, my father often told anyone who would listen that I was the "brains" of our family.

My father always encouraged me to get a good education, to do the things I enjoyed most, and to never be afraid. We'd sit on a cushioned metal glider on the front porch of our brick house in Elmont, looking up at the stars together. He showed me the various constellations in the sky, explained the solar system, and reminded me to *dream big.*

"See that moon up there. You can reach that high. Keep your feet on the ground, and keep reaching for the stars, Susan. You can be anything you want to be," he'd say. "Never be afraid because you can be *anything* you want to be."

I know to some people it may sound clichéd now, because we've all heard that advice at some point, but I was only five years old when he shared those inspiring and encouraging words with me for the first time. They made an indelible impression, one I've never forgotten. My father was fantastic in so many ways. I was definitely "Daddy's little girl." In fact, that was his favorite song to sing to me for many years growing up.

I cannot imagine a daughter having a better dad than my father. He made it a priority to spend as much time with his children as he could. In the summertime, he rented a little cottage in Connecticut on the Long Island Sound where we took long walks on the beach, swam together, and talked about life. Although it might sound like

I was an indulged child, I wasn't. My father spoiled me with love and attention and with the luxury of his time, teaching me to draw, taking me horseback riding, ice skating, and years later, after he discovered golf, to the driving range.

Although he came from a very rough neighborhood, my father had developed an appreciation for the arts, especially drawing and music. My father and brother listened to opera. And with my mother, he listened to Frank Sinatra, Vic Damone, Tony Bennett, Peggy Lee, and Ella Fitzgerald. They were always on top of the latest entertainers. I remember walking in on my dad once while he was watching ballet on television. I was mesmerized by the image of him gazing at Rudolf Nureyev and Dame Margo Fonteyn dancing together.

And, my father loved to draw, especially with charcoals and pastels. He taught me to do the same when I was a little girl. I loved it, too. One of the first drawings I ever did was a portrait of Caroline Kennedy with her dog that I copied from an issue of *Ladies' Home Journal*. My father and I worked on that drawing for weeks. Sadly, there's been no time in my life to continue that pursuit, but I loved it so. I learned to play the piano as a little girl, too, and though I didn't love to practice and wasn't a great pianist by any stretch of the imagination, I loved to sing! When I told my parents I was no longer interested in learning the piano, my father decided to take lessons with me as his way of encouraging me to continue on. I think playing the piano was a secret dream of his. It was fantastic that he cared so deeply about me getting the best education I could—even piano lessons.

Although I appreciated my father's attempt to keep me interested, I wasn't. I had a friend who also took lessons from the same piano teacher and she hated them, too. One snowy night she and I concocted a plan to lock our teacher out of our homes. When he rang the bell, I threw myself under the bay window in the front of our house and lay flat against the wall so he couldn't see me. My friend kept to our plan and locked him out, too. We were so proud we pulled it off and happy we didn't have to have our lessons that night.

A few days later, the piano teacher called to say he wouldn't be teaching me anymore. Although I felt a little guilty about locking him out on such a snowy night, I was really glad I didn't have to take any more lessons.

My mother is and always has been a very beautiful woman. She has fabulous red hair, perfect fair skin, and a gorgeous sprinkle of freckles. Her father was from Sweden and her mother was born in Pennsylvania and was of French and German descent, so my mother's look is striking. My mother is very soft-spoken, can be very funny, is self-reliant, full of common sense, loves fashion, and has a real stubborn streak. She studied nursing in New York and was a practicing OR nurse for a number of years until my brother, Jimmy, was born and she decided to become a stay-at-home mom.

As far back as I can remember, I've had a definite and clear picture of what I wanted to do with my life. Although I was *painfully* shy as a child, I came out of my shell whenever I was acting, singing, dancing, and making believe that I was someone else. Playing games of "make-believe" was just the way I played. I loved to put my parents' musical sound tracks on the record player and listen to songs from Broadway shows and old movies so I could sing and dance along. I loved *Pal Joey, Oklahoma!, Golden Boy,* and *Damn Yankees,* just to name a few. In fact, the first song I can remember performing for my family was "Whatever Lola Wants, Lola Gets" from the original sound track of *Damn Yankees.* I was three. That's how we knew I'd grow up to play Erica Kane. To be certain, I was a totally different kid when I would perform. The stage was where I wanted to be, and when you're a little girl with a vivid and active imagination, *all* the world is a stage.

At church on Sundays I would fantasize about climbing the stairs to the balcony that overlooked the congregation where the choir sang from, standing on the rail, pushing off, and latching onto one of the many lanterns. In my mind, I'd swing from light to light, high above the ground, until I dropped down onto the altar, where I would regale the congregation (my audience) with my song-and-dance numbers. Yes, everyplace I went, I would create a vivid scenario where I could perform—because that's all I wanted to do.

I grew up in a neighborhood and at a time where most of the children were sent outside to play. But I preferred to be inside. When I was a very little girl, my mother finally convinced me to go outside and play with the other kids in the area. So one day I rode my tricycle down the street where we lived and some children pushed me off. I left my bike right there, went running home, and refused to ever go back out again. Whenever my parents tried to get me to play with the other children, I'd always find a way to sneak back into the house. One summer afternoon, my mother decided that I should spend the day outdoors. She sent me on my way to play and locked the door behind me so I couldn't get back inside. Thankfully, my mother's mother, whom I called Nana, lived with us. She came to the door and saved the day. I remember her turning to my mother and saying, "Jeanette, you cannot lock this child outside. She's just a little girl!" So they let me back in. I immediately ran up to my room and spent the rest of the day putting on a show with my favorite dolls and stuffed animals. Whenever I'd put on these shows, I'd imagine an audience the size of the Ed Sullivan Theater inside my bedroom. And let's be clear, it was standing room only. Later that afternoon my parents thought I'd had a breakthrough when they heard what they imagined were a couple of kids from the neighborhood playing with me. It turns out that the various voices they overheard were all mine. It was just me, playing and performing all by myself.

I adored my mother's mother—my grandmother Nana. She was very jolly and had a warm spirit. She was exactly what a grandmother should be—kind, loving, and affectionate. Nana had a very sweet fox terrier named Snookie, whom I also adored. But I must be perfectly honest with you. Until recently, the name Snookie has always meant so much to me because it reminds me of my grandmother. Now unfortunately, I can barely say the name without conjuring up thoughts of the Jersey shore. It just isn't right that such a precious memory has been tainted—make that tanned—by the association!

Nana was the first one up in the morning and the last to go to bed at night. She loved to laugh, play the piano for us, cook delicious meals, and bake the best cakes, pies, and even fresh bread! My most vivid memories of Nana revolve around music and food. My first exposure to the songs of George and Ira Gershwin, Cole Porter, and Irving Berlin was when Nana played them on her piano. I adored spending time in the kitchen with her every day while she made the most wonderful treats. Nana never used a mixer. She beat all of her ingredients by hand. I remember sitting with her while she put the finishing touches on a delicious apple pie or sprinkled cinnamon on baked apples, which I loved to eat. She taught me what it meant to be a great cook—something my mother and I never really came around to being ourselves, but both now have a wonderful appreciation for. Her family came from Alsace, the same region of France as Jean-Georges Vongerichten, one of my favorite chefs in New York. Apparently, good food is second nature to people from Alsace. She made great stews, chicken and dumplings, and other hearty dishes infused with a French and German influence. She always started with the freshest of ingredients and only used the best of whatever she could find. Every day when I came home from school, there was always something fantastic and yummy waiting for me—which made me very, very happy. When we weren't spending time together in the kitchen, she patiently let me create many hairdos with her hair. I could set part of it in curls and part of it in rollers. Nana never cared how it turned out, as long as we were having fun together, which of course we were.

I was so lucky to grow up in a home where there was always music playing and the smell of some delicious homemade meal. Since Nana lived with us, my mother never had to cook, and that suited her just fine. My mother preferred to do the cleaning. In fact, she kept a spotless and very organized home, something she tried to teach me to do, too.

I don't have a lot of memories of my Swedish grandfather because he divorced my grandmother when my mother was just five years old. My grandfather lived half the year in Sweden and the other half in St. Petersburg, Florida. Although I didn't see much of him growing up, I do recall that occasionally he'd write my mother letters asking how we were all doing. He didn't completely disappear from our lives, but we weren't close either. I don't know many of the details about why he left my grandmother other than that he went to Sweden on a vacation and never came back. He sent my grandmother a letter saying he no longer wanted to be married. Nana was a very proud woman. She refused to take any child support or alimony from him. Instead, she chose to play the piano, supporting herself and three children all on her own. She was a very good piano player. She started an orchestra and played piano in the local hotels in the Pocono Mountains near the small Swedish-German communities where they lived. She often accompanied the old silent movies that were shown in their local movie house as well. The Milford Opera House, which looks more like a quintessential Andrew Wyeth barn than a classic opera house, was a favorite spot for my grandmother to play her piano, too. I have always been very proud of my grandmother for how she persevered and managed to take care of her children as a single mother. She was so ahead of her time. She chose to take her talent and do something with it rather than sit around and wallow in her sadness. Divorce wasn't common back in those days. I am sure it was a challenge for the whole family because there weren't a lot of single-women role models then for my grandmother to look up to or emulate. Hearing these stories as a young girl gave me the eyes to see and the ears to hear so that I could relate to all sorts of situations growing up. These weren't my experiences, but they were poignant and important to the person I would later become.

I was eleven years old when my nana suddenly and unexpectedly passed away. I didn't like to sleep much when I was a little girl. I seemed to always have lots of thoughts dancing around in my head, especially at night. Sometimes I'd fall asleep then awaken for one reason or another. I didn't have nightmares very often or anything like that. I'd just wake up and was unable to fall back to sleep. The night Nana died was one of those nights.

I had just awakened when I heard a strange sound. It was a scary noise, unlike anything I had ever heard. I was in my bedroom on the third floor and the noise sounded like it was coming from our basement, where Nana lived. My father had finished our basement for her so she could have her own private quarters. He did a beautiful job on the space, making it very comfortable and beautiful for both Nana and Snookie.

I heard some sort of faint moaning. At first, I didn't know what it was until I was finally able to make out that it was somebody calling my mother's name.

"Jeanette, Jeanette." I knew it was coming from my grandmother because everyone else called my mother Jean. Only my father and grandmother referred to my mother as Jeanette. I was so scared. I had no idea what was going on. I was always afraid of the dark and lay there motionless, frozen by my fear. I didn't get up right away. In fact, I never got up to go to my grandmother that night. I stayed silent and still in my bed. Terrible thoughts were racing through my mind. I loved my grandmother very much. I was petrified at the prospect that she might die. That overwhelming thought was more than I could bear, so I pulled back the covers I'd been hiding under and ran into my parents' bedroom.

"Nana is calling you!" I said to my mother. She hadn't heard a sound. My mother dashed downstairs. Since she was a nurse, I knew she could help Nana get through whatever was happening that night. My mother called an ambulance right away. I overheard her tell the operator that she thought my grandmother Rose Granquist was having a heart attack.

"Come as fast as you can," she said.

The ambulance got to our home within minutes. They tried resuscitating Nana while getting her onto the gurney and loading her into the vehicle so they could race her to the nearest hospital. But it was too late. Nana died.

For years, I never told another soul this story. I was so ashamed of myself for being so paralyzed by my fear. My husband heard it for the first time as I was preparing myself to write this book. I have carried my guilt for not getting up sooner and helping my grandmother since that time. Could I have saved her that night? I don't know the answer to that. I will never know. Maybe she could have lived longer. I would have had my beloved grandmother with me for just a little more time if I had gotten out of bed sooner that horrible night. But the truth is, maybe I couldn't have saved her. She smoked and drank coffee for many years. Like my father, Nana smoked non-filtered cigarettes. Those certainly wouldn't have helped an already strained heart.

If either of my children had experienced a sudden and tragic loss like this, I would do my best to comfort and reassure them that what happened was not their fault. But my mother had no idea that I felt I could have possibly prevented Nana's death that night. And even though logic tells me that I didn't need to carry this weight on my shoulders for all of these years, I continued to feel terribly ashamed about the way my grandmother died, spending so many years wondering, *If only.*

Thankfully though, I have taken many memories of my grandmother with me throughout my life. Her love of food and zest for living along with her resilience, courage, perseverance, determination, and tremendous spirit are all traits I feel so lucky that she passed on to me. I can still imagine her in the kitchen wearing her housedress and pearls, whipping up something yummy. I'm so grateful that my mother gave me some of her jewelry and a green porcelain bowl Nana used all the time. I also have some sheet music from her days playing the piano in the Poconos. Maybe someday I'll choose one of those songs to work into my cabaret show as a way to honor the deep love I have for my nana. I know she smiles down on me every day. If you believe in guardian angels as I do, there is no doubt that Nana is mine.

Although my mother was a nurse by trade, she absolutely had a love and passion for fashion. Mother's love of style made her top dresser drawer a treasure trove for a young aspiring actress with an insatiable imagination like mine. She would allow me to play with all of her grown-up accessories. I was very big on wrapping her scarves around my head or turning them into different costumes. This was inspired by the old movies I grew up watching. Scarves and the sheer white curtains in our upstairs bathroom were magical to me because they allowed me to become virtually anything I wanted to be—a bride, an exotic princess, a first communicant. My mother often wore her hair pulled back in a chignon, with holders that were adorned with rhinestones. These were perfect for me to make a tiara out of. I'd slowly turn my head from side to side as I looked from every possible angle in the large mirror that hung over her dresser to admire the shiny sparkling headpiece I'd made. Once I had the tiara placed just right, I'd pull on her long white or black gloves and hold her ivory cigarette holder, which my uncle Leo brought back from Asia after World War II, between my fingers as if I were Ava Gardner or Gene Tierney. My mother always let me play and explore my creativity. And though she had no idea, she was inadvertently fostering what would later become my passion and calling in life.

As I got older, I began putting on shows with the other kids in the neighborhood. I was a one-girl operation, starring in, creating, writing, directing, choreographing, and costuming the entire production. By the time I was eight or nine years old, my parents knew I had developed a passion for singing, and they genuinely liked how I sang. I can't say for sure how their friends felt about it, but after dinner, they would have to endure another song from little Susan Lucci. Wherever we went, whether to a dinner or someone's birthday party, inevitably someone would ask me to sing a song or two. They'd clear off the table and lift me onto it, where I'd perform like a female Frankie Lymon. I was too ethnic-looking to be the next Shirley Temple. Plus, my older brother, Jimmy, listened to Frankie Lymon, a wonderful, soulful singer with a beautiful, sweet voice, so I had been influenced by his style. To our family and their friends, I was already a star.

My parents decided to send me to a parochial school from first grade until the time I went to high school. Although I enjoyed many aspects of its curriculum, the school was very strict. In fact, we were not allowed to talk during lunch hour. We were forced into silence for the entire time, which was very hard for me. We could laugh and scream outside in the school playground, but inside, it was mandatory quiet. There was always some boy who would break the silence by blowing up and popping a paper bag. Of course, he'd get into big trouble, but we secretly appreciated his attempt to buck the system.

One afternoon, my girlfriends and I were walking in the hall after lunch when I heard a couple of girls whispering and pointing at me. I wasn't sure what they were saying, but it was obvious they were talking about me. Finally, one of them asked if I was going to be in the local Girl Scout play. I hadn't heard anything about a Girl Scout play. I was stunned that I didn't know about it.

"Well, we are going to be in it!" they said. "We got our scripts and we are going to all be in the play." They were being so cavalier.

They told me the play was called *Cindy Ellen* and it was going to be a variation of the Cinderella story. Okay, maybe that's why I didn't hear about it. Everyone knows that Cinderella is a beautiful blonde. I was a brunette. Sure, all right. That made sense. I was certain that was why I hadn't been approached. When I was growing up, there were no brunette dolls to play with. There were no brunette angels for the Christmas tree and Cinderella was definitely a blonde! I tried to justify all of this in my mind, and yet I still felt very bad. I wanted to cry but I didn't want the other girls to see how terrible I was feeling. My girlfriend and I walked away. I was still fighting back my tears when we ran into Mrs. Morrison and Mrs. Smith, our local Girl Scout troop leaders.

"Susan! We've been looking for you." I could see Mrs. Morrison holding what looked to be a script under her arm.

"We want you to play Cindy Ellen in our play." It turned out that I was not only going to be in the play, I got the lead! I had no idea how the troop leaders knew that I wanted to be an actress more than anything else in the world, but I sure was glad they sought me out and that they thought I could do it. It was a wonderful turnaround to go from thinking I had been overlooked to being cast as the lead. I was absolutely thrilled because this was going to be my first legitimate stage appearance.

It was right around this same time that my mother handed me my very first copy of *Seventeen* magazine and my whole world changed forever.

"I think you will like this," she said.

And she was right; I did.

I believe the day she gave me that magazine, my mother was encouraging me to pursue my dream. The girls within the pages were all beautiful teenagers with such nice hair. I was mesmerized by all the posing and grown-up fashion. I began fantasizing about becoming one of the models I saw on the page. The only problem was, I was very petite and my hair, which is naturally curly, didn't look a thing like their perfectly straight and shiny hair. I spent my youth watching my mother take very good care of her skin and her health, which was a practice she passed on to me as well. The magazine was full of articles that helped me understand how important all of those things were, especially for a young girl. That was the day I realized there was a whole wide world out there to be discovered and it was mine for the taking.

When I was sixteen years old, I entered a competition to become an exchange student. It was sponsored by my high school and our local community. There was a required essay and several interviews involved in the selection process to become a student ambassador living abroad for the summer. After giving it some thought, I decided to focus on the program that was called Experiment in International Living. The program took place over three months during the summer between my junior and senior years of high school. It turned out that I was one of four kids selected from our community to participate. France and Sweden were my first two choices because I wanted to experience living in a place that I had natural ties to. Unfortunately, I didn't get either of those locations, and I was ultimately placed with a Norwegian family.

Living in Norway was a fantastic experience. This was the first time I really knew what it meant to think in a global way. When we got to Norway, I went through orientation with nine other kids from all over the United States who had come to live there as well. I had never before met anyone who lived in places such as Iowa and Indiana. Our teachers and chaperones were a married couple who were also professors from Yale. Shortly after our arrival, we met our respective families, who typically had a child around our age. The family I was placed with lived outside of Oslo, in an island community. They wanted to host an American exchange student because they wanted their children to practice speaking English. Many citizens of Scandinavian countries encourage their children to learn English as a second language, so although I didn't get to learn much Norwegian, I did get to experience their culture. It was interesting to talk to my Norwegian family, who asked me lots of questions about the Kennedys, American politics, and American opinions. This was an awakening for me because it was the first time I had stepped outside my own country as a "representative" of the United States of America. It was the first time I felt a responsibility for the way I spoke about America as an American. I wasn't sure I had all of the right answers. I hadn't spoken of these things to anyone else before this trip to Europe. But I knew the Kennedys were revered in our country, so I could easily speak to that. The world admired President and Mrs. Kennedy. It wasn't a hard sell.

I was very lucky because the family I lived with had the means to open many doors in their country, giving me the best possible exposure and experiences. My Norwegian father was a doctor, who was quite successful. His wife often took my Norwegian sister and me into Oslo to shop and sightsee. She actually knitted a beautiful Norwegian sweater and hat for me as wonderful souvenirs. She took me into Oslo to pick out the pewter buttons she later sewed on. I adored the sweater and hat so much that I still have them.

On weekends, we spent time at their home on a small island in the southern part of Norway, where dusk settles somewhere around one o' clock in the morning. Those long days of sunshine allowed for lots of outdoor living. We often took boat rides, walked around the island, picked bluebells and put them in a flower press, and enjoyed all the beauty this wonderful place had to offer.

Toward the end of my stay, I reconnected with the other kids from our program and our teachers so we could all spend a couple of weeks traveling around Europe together. We toured Norway for a few more days before taking a ferry from Oslo to Copenhagen. Most of us were running very low on money, so we decided to pool our funds and voted between staying in the sleeping quarters on board the ship or eating. It was unanimous. We would eat. It was a relatively easy decision for a few of us, especially one of the girls from Kansas and me, who were petite and could pretty much curl up and sleep anywhere. In fact, she and I spotted a luggage rack above some of the seats on the boat that we figured we could easily squeeze into. We removed the bags that had been stored there and climbed in. Unfortunately, the sea got very rough that night and we got thrown right out onto the floor of the boat. This was my first experience with seasickness—one I will never forget. Everybody on board was so sick. If you weren't holding your head over the rail, you were holding on for dear life. When we got to Copenhagen, we spent a week touring and seeing all of the sites before leaving for a week in Paris and then returning to the United States.

When I arrived in New York, I remember sitting with my parents so I could tell them all about my wonderful experiences overseas. I shared how much I enjoyed exploring my Scandinavian heritage and how appreciative I was for the opportunity to live abroad. The Cuban missile crisis was fresh in my mind, as it had been less than a year since that threat was posed to our nation. As a young adult, I was well aware of those tense days. After spending three months out of the country, I told my parents I thought every teenager should have the opportunity to be an exchange student. If they did, I believed it would have a big impact on the younger generation's global outlook, and could result in less war. I was living in an era where war was happening all around us. Although I was just a little girl during the Korean War, I was old enough to be aware of Castro coming into power in Cuba and of the Bay of Pigs invasion. And I realized that we were still living in uncertain times. I followed current events closely and with great interest. I was too young to become an activist, but I wanted my parents to know that I was aware of what was happening. Like most parents, my mother and father did their best to shield me from the horrors of the world, but we were living in a time when they were hard to ignore. And to be frank, I didn't want to put my head in the sand. I was sitting in French class on November 22, 1963, when I heard the news. A friend of mine went running past the open door to my classroom. This was a girl who was usually very upbeat and funny, but she had just heard that John F. Kennedy had been shot, and was running down the hallways of our school screaming to let everyone know. We weren't sure if we should take her message seriously at first though. It only took a split second to realize that no one would say something so horrible in jest. Everything came to a stop. How could the president have been shot? I had never experienced anything like this before. I didn't know what to do. I, along with the rest of our class, was in a state of shock. There was a great heaviness throughout the school for the rest of the day, week, and for many months to come. Our country was crying. Every one of us was in tears. I'll never forget—we were supposed to put on a school play that weekend. Of course, we were taught that the show must go on. Although it seemed wrong on so many levels, my drama teacher reminded us that it was the first rule of the theater, so we all got into our costumes and were standing backstage when the school decided this was one time the show would not go on.

As an aspiring actress, I would use the emotions I felt and witnessed others feeling during these types of tragedies and global events. I found inspiration in everything, the joyous as well as the sad. During my high school years, I was lucky enough to have a most enthusiastic and outstanding drama teacher as my first acting teacher. Inez Norman Spiers was legendary at Garden City High School. Mrs. Spiers gave our school the greatest gift by creating a drama department and theater group called Masquers that was one of the finest programs a public school could offer. Despite the fact that our school tended to focus more on academics and sports than the arts, the drama program was second to none. Mrs. Spiers had curly red Lucille Ball–style hair that was cut short and cropped close to her head. She wore green nail polish and was quite a colorful character in her presentation. As a teacher, she gave me such an incredible head start. I was thirteen years old when I took my first class with Mrs. Spiers and I continued to study with her until I graduated high school in 1964. She always had her students rehearse plays the way they do on Broadway and the way the protracted process works on television with a table read and blocking. She taught us to dissect scenes from beginning to end so we could understand not only the work but the meaning as well. Mrs. Spiers thought it was crucial to understand all areas of theater, so she taught us to apply theatrical makeup and to engage in role-playing, movement exercises, and character work. She also encouraged us to learn as much about the behind-the-scenes work of set design and construction as we could. Mrs. Spiers took no prisoners. She was tough and expected her students to comply with the high standards she set for us. She was a strict teacher who placed many demands on her students, but all of them were in line with what we would need to do as professional actors someday. I was very lucky that Mrs. Spiers took to me right away. She believed in me and encouraged me to pursue acting from the very start. I was always cast in the various productions, playing a variety of leading roles throughout high school, which was wonderful. Mrs. Spiers had us performing everything from *The King and I* to Noël Coward. The woman was incredible to offer that type of diversity in high school.

Doing all of those shows gave me the experience of being onstage and of working at an advanced level at such an early age. It was Mrs. Spiers who taught me never to upstage the other actors and to learn how to improvise when something goes wrong. She helped us discover how to turn every mishap into an opportunity. I remember hearing a story she told about an early Masquers production when a backdrop painting fell in the middle of a performance. Without missing a beat, the actor onstage said, "My, how the natives are restless tonight." My only dilemma was that while I was involved in the drama department, I was also involved in cheerleading. Because I cheered throughout the school year, I'd often have practice or games between play rehearsals. The only way I could rehearse and make it in time to a football or basketball game was to wear my cheerleading uniform to both. Mrs. Spiers hated that and wasn't shy about telling me how she felt. She explained that I didn't move the same way in a cheerleading outfit as I did in my costume—and she was right. So, sometimes, I would throw a dress rehearsal skirt over my cheerleading skirt, which made my hips look really wide, but at least I was doing the right thing. I didn't want to disappoint Mrs. Spiers, but I made commitments to both activities and I wanted to do both. Mrs. Spiers also didn't like the idea that I would finish rehearsals and then run off to the football field. Understandably, she wanted my undivided attention. I was told the year after I graduated that Mrs. Spiers officially banned rehearsing in anything but your proper attire. I am sure her heart was in the right place. It's not as if she didn't like sports because she was always trying to enlist the football players to be in her plays. But that *Glee* mentality hadn't quite sunk in at our school yet—at least not while I was there. Many years after I graduated, the school commemorated Mrs. Spiers by naming the auditorium after her. She deserved that honor and so much more.

My mother started taking me to New York City to see Broadway shows when I was a teenager. We mostly went when I was off from school or during summer vacations. Although New York City was only an hour's drive from our home, we hardly ever made the trip. My father thought New York was a very tough place, especially for women to go to on their own. Still, my mother and I loved the excitement of planning a special day together where we could have some important mother-daughter time and enjoy the experience of taking in the latest show and then dining at Sardi's, a place we had read about in the newspapers that was the most famous eatery in the theater district. It is a well-known hangout for the theater crowd, both actors and patrons.

We spent wonderful days together seeing everyone from Richard Burton in *Hamlet* to Sammy Davis Jr. and Lola Falana in *Golden Boy*. I hadn't yet been exposed to Shakespeare in school, so as a teenager, *Hamlet* was not easy to watch. Still, it was beautiful and spellbinding. I have never forgotten Richard Burton's massive presence on the stage. This was the first time I ever looked at an older man and thought he was sexy. Eileen Herlie, who I would end up working with years later on *All My Children*, played his mother, Gertrude. This particular production of *Hamlet* was done in all modern dress. I was speechless when Eileen crossed the stage in a full-length mink coat. She was an inspiration and so glamorous and elegant. On the way out of the theater, I somehow got swept away in the sea of people leaving the show. I was thrust up against a waiting limousine outside the stage door. My mother was trying to rescue me but was unable to reach my hand through the crowd. I turned to look into the window of the waiting car and there was Richard Burton sitting in the backseat with his arm around two young girls. I don't know why, but I thought one of them might have been Elizabeth Taylor's daughter Liza Todd. Mr. Burton looked so protective of those girls. He saw me peering through the window. We gazed at each other for mere seconds, but I was absolutely mesmerized by his very blue eyes. Although I wasn't so happy about being thrown up against his car, I was absolutely thrilled to have shared that moment with someone who was larger than life.

When my mother took me to see *Golden Boy* on Broadway, I begged her to let me wait outside the stage door so I could catch a glimpse of Sammy Davis Jr. Even as a teenager, I recognized Sammy Davis as one of the greatest performers of all time. I wanted to wait so I could ask for his autograph. We stood outside that door for hours, but he never came out. As I turned to my mother to say that we could finally leave, Miss Lola Falana was standing right in front of me. I remember watching her dance on *The Ed Sullivan Show*, and now there she was! It was thrilling. I don't know why I always remember what people were wearing, but she had on jeans, an oversize crisp white man's shirt, and sneakers. She was absolutely gorgeous.

"You're Lola Falana!" I said. "I've seen you on TV!" I was a giddy schoolgirl.

She just looked at me, like, "Yeah, so?" And then grabbed my Playbill to sign it. She wasn't rude, just quick. It was in that moment and exchange that I said to myself, *When I grow up and become a famous actress, I am definitely going to sign autographs!* I would never forget what it was like to be the wide-eyed girl full of hopes and dreams.

Our days of taking in shows on Broadway and spending time together in the city became a tradition that continued throughout high school and into my college years. My mother and I loved to see matinees and have lunch at Sardi's. The very first time we went there, Vincent Sardi, the owner himself, met us at the door. He was extremely pleasant to us, especially since he was used to more sophisticated patrons than we were. He personally escorted us to our table, which I thought was quite extraordinary—that is, until I saw where he was seating us. He stopped at the front table underneath a row of the very famous caricatures drawn of the celebrities who had eaten there. I didn't realize that this particular table in the front and center of the restaurant was a very sought-after place to be seated. At the time, I thought he didn't want his other guests to see the two of us. My mother and I were all too happy to be there, even if we thought Mr. Sardi was not. We had a very nice lunch. As we ate our meal, Mr. Sardi approached us and pointed to a table of well-dressed gentlemen who looked like Hollywood producers.

"I am sorry for the interruption. The gentlemen at that table would like to know who you are." He was talking to me. I was very flattered, although I had no idea why they thought I was anyone notable in this restaurant of notables. I was a mere "nobody" enjoying lunch in the big city with my mother. I wanted to be an actress. I was studying to be one, but at that time I was still a total unknown.

My mother and I continued to frequent Sardi's in the summers that followed. Every time we went there, we were greeted like old friends. Vincent Sardi was always so very nice to us. And, every time, people wanted to know who we were. One day, we were introduced to Marian Probst, who said she was one of the editors of something called the *Celebrity Register*, a chronicle of who's who in the world of entertainment made famous by Earl "Mr." Blackwell. Marian said she would like to include me in their next edition, which was amazing since I hadn't been professionally cast in anything yet.

I cannot explain what the draw was, but throughout my early life, it seemed that people had an instinctive sense that I was going to be famous. I can't say this with any authority other than my own experience, but from the time I was a young child, I always knew that performing was all I really wanted to do. I suppose there is some merit to the correlation between the image one projects out to the world and what the world sees. If you're lucky—*very* lucky—and you work hard, that portrayal can and often does turn into the stuff that dreams are made of.

CHAPTER 2

Marymount College

I graduated from Garden City High School in 1964, having had a great time for those four years. I was very excited that I had been accepted to Marymount College in Tarrytown, New York. As a way to earn some extra money before starting school, I got a summer job waitressing at the Garden City Hotel. This historic landmark was close to my parents' home and has been a favorite of the rich and famous for many years. It has housed the Vanderbilts, Astors, Kennedys, and Clintons. Charles Lindbergh stayed at the Garden City Hotel on the night before he embarked on his first transatlantic flight. Every summer, the hotel brought in twenty or so college kids to work as waiters, waitresses, busboys, and hostesses. The hotel got very busy during those few months, as there was outside dining in addition to the more formal dining room inside the hotel. They always needed more staff at that time of year. It was a wonderful place to work.

The executive chef was a tall, handsome Austrian named Helmut Huber. I was told by longtime staffers that he was once asked to be the chef at the White House, but turned it down because they didn't pay enough money and because he wanted to get out of the kitchen and into administration. The prestige was nice, but he wanted to move on in his career. The Knott Hotel Corporation that owned the Garden City Hotel at the time had promised Helmut that if he did two years there, they would promote him to become in charge of all the food and beverage operations for their chain, which included food services for the Pentagon and the United Nations among several other properties around the country. My first summer working as a waitress at the Garden City Hotel was Helmut's last as the executive chef.

One night, I went into the kitchen to place an order when I heard a bellowing voice with a thick Austrian accent say, "Young lady. Your skirt is too short. You are not a teenybopper. You're a young lady. It is too short! And you don't know how to hold a tray." When he finished scolding me, he wiggled his ears. I thought that was so funny and a little odd. Of course, he wasn't the first person to ever shake their finger at me. I had endured four years of Mrs. Spiers's drama club. If I could take it from her, I could certainly handle Helmut Huber.

I turned to one of the girls I worked with and asked, "Who is that man?"

"He's your boss!" she said.

I truly had no idea it was Helmut, the executive chef, standing in front of me even though he was wearing his tall white chef's hat and a double-breasted linen jacket with his name and title embroidered across the chest. When she told me his name was Helmut Huber, I asked her if that was one name or two. She said it so fast it sounded like "Helmuthuber."

At the time I was dating one of the boys who had been hired for the summer, too. RG was visiting from Colorado. He was the nephew of a family that lived in Garden City. I was crazy about him. At the time it never crossed my mind to think of Helmut as anything other than my boss. I eventually learned how to carry a tray, but I purposely kept my skirt short. That was the style of the time, and besides, I was about to start college and was working for tips!

By the end of the summer, I was very excited to start my freshman year at Marymount. The college had been established as an independent girls' boarding school in 1907 by the Religious of the Sacred Heart of Mary. Mother Marie Joseph Butler founded the institution to "create a place of learning where women could grow and where they could receive an education that would prepare them for positions of leadership and influence in the world." Marymount College at Tarrytown was the first of several colleges founded by the RSHM. Several of these still exist, including Marymount Manhattan, Marymount University, and Loyola Marymount. The school offered a great quality education for women, and had spectacular teachers. Their primary method is to teach you *how* to think and not *what* to think. My Catholic schooling as a young girl was all about indoctrination, whereas college became more about learning about all religions and the making of informed, thoughtful choices in every area of our lives. During theology and philosophy, we were required to read a variety of books so we could come to our own conclusions, examine controversial concepts, and not cop out. I learned to analyze things by breaking down information and figuring out what worked and what didn't. I didn't love that very painstaking and methodical aspect of discovery, but I am glad I had to do it because it became very helpful later in life. The Jesuits make you analyze everything. It's very painful but ultimately very good for you.

I met some wonderful women my first year at Marymount who remain my closest friends to this day. When I got to my dormitory on the first day of school, I was surprised to learn that I hadn't been assigned a roommate. There was another girl on my floor named Patty Depuy, who also had a single room. Patty lived directly across the hall from me. Although neither of us requested to have our own rooms, it was a very nice luxury. Our dorm was filled with all sorts of interesting women. Mary Anne Dolan lived in one of the corner rooms. She later became the first female editor for the *Los Angeles Times*. Mollie Beattie lived on our hall, too. She later became the director of the U.S. Fish and Wildlife Service. Joyce Brown also lived on our floor. She went on to become the president of the Fashion Institute of Technology in New York. These are just a few of the quality women who started Marymount College the same year I did.

I spent the first few weeks of school getting to know as many of these girls as I could. There was a tearoom in one of the buildings on campus where we gathered to talk and watch old movies. I grew up watching a lot of television. I always sat in front of the TV while my mother or grandmother prepared dinner. Even as a young girl, I was someone who read the opening and closing credits because I wanted to know who everybody involved in the making of the movie or show was. I learned as much about movies as I could, from the mainstream to the obscure. One night, at the beginning of my freshman year, I was watching a movie in the tearoom with the other girls when all of the sudden I heard someone from the back of the room shout out, "Oh, that's Oscar Homolka!" Now, for those of you who don't know Oscar Homolka, he was an old-time Austrian film and theater actor from the 1930s. He wasn't exactly a household name, so when I heard someone else in the room recognize him, I thought to myself, *Someone else knows Oscar Homolka? I must meet this person.*

When the lights came on, I looked around and it turned out that the girl who shouted Oscar's name was Patty Depuy, the girl who lived across the hall from me. We were kindred spirits from the very start. I figured that anyone who knew Oscar Homolka had to be a great girl. Patty told me she was from Milford, Pennsylvania, which was the "big" city near the small town where my grandmother was from in the Pocono Mountains. Although Milford is quite well known today for its summer theater community, back then it was just another small Pennsylvania town. Patty was the first person I had ever met outside my family who even knew of it.

Patty was an art major, so although we didn't have any classes together, we quickly became the best of friends. We ended up becoming roommates our sophomore year and remained roommates for the rest of college. When Patty and I were getting ready to decorate our dorm room together, unbeknownst to each other, she arriving from Pennsylvania and I arriving from New York, we had each picked out the identical bedspread, dust ruffle, and pillow sham. We could hardly believe the coincidence. That's when we knew for sure that our friendship would last a lifetime. Our schedules were very compatible. I was often out until all hours of the night building sets for a show or rehearsing and she would be in her studio painting. Patty was and still is a wonderful artist and is also one of the lucky ones who have been able to make a living doing something she genuinely loves.

As a performer, I always thought of Patty as the ideal audience member because she is the most enthusiastic observer I have ever met. I discovered this the first time Patty's mother took us to New York City to see *Fiddler on the Roof* starring the great Zero Mostel. Throughout the show, Patty laughed the loudest, clapped with great passion, and cried with tremendous emotion. She was on the edge of her seat for the whole time. I remember watching her that day and thinking everyone should have a Patty in their life—or at the very least, in their audience. Lucky for me, I did and still do have her in my life. Today Patty runs her own interior design company called Patricia Johnson Interiors.

Patty was friends with a girl from one of her art classes named Linda DePalma, who I then became friends with, too. Linda was a spectacular girl. She was smart and very hip. I always thought of her as our "Cher" because she was and still is the epitome of cool. Today Linda is a prominent artist in Baltimore and is the director of education for the Creative Alliance.

Pat Murphy was another girl I became very close to. Although she was not an aspiring performer, she had a great love and interest in theater. She eventually went on to become a very talented and beloved theater teacher and chairman of the drama and theater department at Piedmont High School in San Jose, California.

When I first met Cathy Gasperina, I was completely intimidated by her. Cathy was chic, smooth, smart, tall, and a beautiful redhead. She was also very sophisticated. I'd heard she had gone to the International Marymount in London and Rome before coming to New York to attend Marymount. From the outside looking in, Cathy represented everything I had dreamed of as a little girl. Much to my surprise, Cathy also turned out to be a lovely human being. She was just a wonderfully interesting individual who went on to teach English literature and become the head of the English department at Hamilton-Wenham Regional High School in Hamilton, Massachusetts.

These four women became my closest friends. I hold each of them very near and dear to my heart. We all grew up together and have shared so many wonderful and, yes, painful moments throughout the years. Patty Depuy was definitely the glue that held us all together. It was really Patty who taught me the value and importance of being a good friend. Although I always had a strong sense and appreciation for family when I was younger, I never understood what being a good friend meant. I was so intent on becoming an actress, going to New York, and getting my career off the ground that I didn't make the time to nurture those relationships. I was like a horse with blinders on. All I could see was what was in front of me, and at the time that was strictly pursuing my education and a career. Patty called me out one day, saying I was so . . . independent! That comment really made me stop and think. It affected me to my core, so much so that I've never forgotten it. Patty wasn't paying me a compliment. She had grown exasperated by my inability to treat our or any friendship well. I am so grateful to Patty for her persistence and desire to hold us all together as friends over the years. I didn't want to be perceived as so independent that I was excluding people or to appear as if I didn't care about my friends, because I dearly loved them all. I never even realized that I was somehow letting any of them down. It wasn't intentional or conscious. Patty shook me up and helped me come to my senses. And I am so happy she did because I have cherished all of the good times we've shared together over the years since we all met in 1964.

I was very fortunate to pursue my studies in acting at Marymount College because the faculty was truly accomplished. I studied with Mr. Ron Weyand, the head of the drama department, who had graduated from the Yale School of Drama and was part of the Lincoln Center Repertory Company; Judith Propper and Wendy Guillou, both of whom, like so many of the other teachers I met, had studied theater in London; and a host of other faculty members who were affiliated with the William Shakespeare Company, the Alexander technique, and Martha Graham Dance. There were many more rare opportunities to study with wonderful professors who were on staff or came to Marymount as guest teachers and lecturers during my four years at college, too. In addition to being fantastic teachers, all of my professors were still working in their field of specialization. To study acting at Marymount was to pursue the finest education from the very best in the business. To them, acting was all about the art.

As students, we were expected to learn the process and techniques that turn good actors into great ones. We delved even deeper into the inner workings of staging a show than I had before, from building the sets to striking them at the end of every run. We learned a variety of acting techniques that I use to this very day. Mr. Weyand had his class go through one particular exercise that I'll never forget. He made an entrance onto the stage and then impersonated each of us through movement and actions. The class had to guess who he was. I knew right away when he was me. He sauntered onto the stage, shaking his hips from side to side with a wide smile across his face. Yes, that was definitely me.

Mr. Weyand wasn't just a great teacher—he was also sensitive to us as people. He impressed upon all of his students that pursuing acting could be a very devastating career choice. He explained that the rejection could be demoralizing, as could the work. He said, "If acting is making you miserable as human beings, then the pursuit is not worth it. And, if you are one of the lucky few who do make it out there, don't go into that bubble. Don't allow yourself to become so out of touch or removed from humanity that you can no longer experience and express humanity." I've never forgotten those poignant and impactful words. His stellar advice became my mantra in life and throughout my career.

———— ❧ ❧ ————

CHAPTER 3

You're Too
Ethnic-Looking

By February 1967, RG and I had become engaged. Needless to say, my parents were less than thrilled with the idea. I was just a junior in college and had so much life ahead of me. I was so young and headstrong that when he proposed, I said, "Yes!" I loved him very much and thought that was all we needed to make things work.

Despite their concern, my parents decided to celebrate our engagement anyway. They hosted a lovely dinner party at the Garden City Hotel with friends and family in attendance. As luck would have it, Helmut happened to be at the hotel that night. He was visiting colleagues and having drinks with some friends as well. My mother and I were walking through the hallway when we unexpectedly spotted him. My mother was so delighted at the chance meeting that she invited Helmut to come have a drink to celebrate my engagement. He said he'd be delighted to join us, but he would have to make it dessert since he was meeting people for dinner. By the time he arrived, most of our guests had left. It was just our immediate families sitting around the table. My father was seated at the large round table; my mother was directly across from me with an empty seat between her and my then-future mother-in-law. Helmut walked into the room and confidently sat between the two ladies. When I looked across the table, I noticed a very different man sitting in front of me than the one I had met in the kitchen of that hotel a few years back. For the first time, I saw Helmut in a different light. I suddenly thought he was very attractive. I also thought there was a problem because I shouldn't be feeling that way about another man. There I was, engaged to be married, and all I wanted to do was get to know Helmut better. That's when it occurred to me that my parents were right. I probably wasn't ready to get married. I didn't call off the engagement, though. No, I let myself ruminate for a while. *Maybe this was a fleeting moment,* I thought.

Sometime during coffee, Helmut leaned over to my mother and whispered into her ear, "You know, this thing between Susan and this boy is never going to last."

"You know, Helmut, I think you are right," my mother replied. "I actually hope you are right. But I can't say anything to Susan because she is so headstrong."

Neither said a word to me about that exchange until many years later. As far as I was concerned, I was still engaged and making wedding plans.

While I was studying at Marymount, RG was attending Colorado State University and working as a ski instructor during the winter months. I visited him there whenever I could get away from classes. He'd teach me to ski, which I absolutely loved. I thought it was very glamorous to get on a plane and visit a handsome boy I was in love with, just as I thought it was truly romantic when he would come to New York to visit me. During one of his last visits to see me, he and I were headed into Manhattan for a dinner date. He came to Garden City first to pick me up. It was a typical Saturday night on the Long Island Expressway. Even though there was a lot of traffic, it was moving along well. There were sporadic stops and starts along the way, but nothing of any concern. As we made our approach toward the city, I pointed to the twinkling lights of the spectacular Manhattan skyline.

"Look at how beautiful those buildings look framed in between those two bridges!" I said.

As one might expect, my fiancé turned to look. He must have become captivated by what he saw because he didn't turn back to the direction in which we were driving. I noticed that the car in front of us had stopped and I thought RG would surely turn around in enough time to avoid crashing into that car, but he didn't.

I don't remember a lot of the details about the crash itself, but I do recall the moments right after impact. I could see the windshield of the car had been shattered although I wasn't exactly sure how it happened. I was a bit dazed and confused, if not in total shock. I felt something dripping down my face. I turned to RG and asked, "Is it raining?"

My fiancé said as carefully as he could, "No. You went through the windshield."

"Am I okay?" My fiancé was tentative answering my question.

"I think so" was all he could say.

He wasn't very convincing.

Since there was a lot of traffic, it took awhile for the police and ambulance to show up. When the first police officers arrived on the scene, they shined their flashlight into the car. I was practically blinded by the brightness, but I remember one of them flinched when he saw me.

I overheard him say, "I think she *used to be* a pretty kid." They were speaking about me in the past tense. That's when I knew something was terribly wrong.

The emergency medical team arrived just a few minutes later. They got me out of the car and into the ambulance, then proceeded to take me to Elmhurst Hospital in Queens, apparently the nearest hospital to where we were. The thing I remember most is that no one would look at me during the entire ride. I kept trying to catch someone's attention, but the EMTs refused to make eye contact with me. When we arrived at the emergency room, everyone inside was speaking Spanish. I had no idea how I was going to express myself because I didn't understand a word they were saying. I only knew a few basic words that I learned back in high school, none of which felt appropriate under the circumstances.

Thankfully, I was met by a big, warm-spirited English-speaking nurse who immediately put me into a wheelchair and assured me that I was going to be all right. One of the other nurses must have noticed my engagement ring because she turned to me and said, "Oh, honey, I am sure he will still marry you." I know she was trying to be comforting, but after hearing that comment, I was beginning to panic. It seemed no one wanted to tell me how badly I had been hurt, but I could tell by everyone's reaction that my wounds were severe.

The doctor on duty came in to see me. He was direct and to the point.

"You're going to need stitches—a *lot* of stitches," he said.

Since my mother had been an OR nurse, I didn't want to make any medical decisions about stitches or anything else without her being present. If I was going to be scarred for life, at the very least I wanted my mom to be with me and assess the situation before they started sewing. I called my parents to tell them what had happened. I no sooner hung up the phone than they arrived at the hospital in what felt like a flash. My mother boldly came into the treatment room just as the doctor was threading his needle.

"You haven't even cleaned her wounds, let alone taken out the shards of glass in her face, and you want to sew my daughter up? What is the matter with you?" My mother scolded the doctor for his lack of professionalism and care. My mother, who also had red hair, pulled a real Shirley MacLaine from the movie *Terms of*

Endearment. No one was going to mess up her kid. She had a loving look of concern for me as she blasted the doctor and then helped me out the door.

"We're leaving, Susan." That's all she said.

She and my father drove me as quickly as they could to Nassau Hospital, a private facility near our home in Garden City. My fiancé was sitting in the backseat with me, holding my hand while my mother and father were in the front. Every now and then I caught a glimpse of my mother turning around and looking at me with tremendous worry in her eyes. I still hadn't looked in a mirror, so I was oblivious to my real condition. Strangely, I wasn't in any pain. I don't know if I was in shock or if the trauma had been so severe that I was just numb. I kept saying, "I'm fine. I am going to be fine." And I believed every word I was saying. Something kept telling me that I would get through this. I wasn't worried or upset. I was calm and oddly at peace. I remember trying to make everyone else stop worrying, too.

Thankfully, when we entered the emergency room at Nassau Hospital, it wasn't very busy. I was taken immediately to an examination room. A very kind doctor spoke with my mother for a few minutes and then quickly began to examine the wounds.

"You are quite right, Mrs. Lucci. There are a lot of shards of glass in her skin, very close to her eye and under her chin. And it looks like your daughter has fractured her nose, too," the doctor said.

My nose had blown up and swelled to more than twice its usual size, to the point where my face was beyond recognition. I never loved my nose in the first place, but now I was sure it was going to be a mess. My entire face was already black, blue, and green from the bruising. The doctor explained that I was going to need reconstructive surgery. He offered to call a plastic surgeon. In those days, plastic surgery was still a very scary and unknown proposition. The only images I had ever seen were in the movies of people coming out of the operating room wrapped up in bandages, looking like mummies. Although my mother probably knew better, she declined his offer to call the plastic surgeon. I'm sure she reasoned that it was better to act fast than to wait for his arrival, since enough time had already passed getting me from one hospital to another.

I ended up on the operating table for four and a half hours so the doctor could remove even the tiniest pieces of glass and take his time meticulously stitching me up. I don't recall exactly how many stitches I needed, but I ended up with several above my right eye and under my jaw, too. As luck would have it, my surgeon that night was a resident in plastic surgery. He was young, fearless, and caring— three traits you want in a skilled surgeon. Perhaps it was divine intervention that I ended up on his table that night. If I hadn't, I was told the glass could have traveled and cost me my eyesight. I know I would have been permanently disfigured and left with ir-reparable scarring. I was told that I would probably lose part of my right eyebrow from the damage and that it would never grow back. And, although I still have a scar just above my right eye, thankfully it's only visible to those who have ever done my makeup or can get close enough to see it.

I am most grateful to that doctor for the way things turned out. It took me more than two months to recover from the accident. I spent the bulk of that time recuperating at my parents' home in Garden City. Whenever I'd get a bout of cabin fever, my mother usually offered to take me to our local Lord & Taylor for lunch. Everyone knows that a little shopping is always a good prescription when you're feeling off, right? When we ventured out, I occasion-ally forgot that I had still had bandages on until I'd notice someone looking at me or a mother telling their child not to stare. I must have been a pretty scary sight and probably should have stayed home, but I felt cooped up and wanted to get out. We'd inevitably bump into someone from our town and they never quite knew what to say. It was uncomfortable for everyone.

I remained bandaged for most of my spring semester at school my junior year, so I didn't attend any of my classes until the end of that semester. One of my school chums told me that Mr. Weyand was doing his best to prepare the other girls in my class for my eventual return. He reminded them that when I did come back to class, it was surely going to be an adjustment for us all. I think Mr. Weyand was trying to warn them that I might not be the same girl I used to be and they should only be pleasant and supportive.

When I finally returned to class, I had started to heal better than anyone expected. My scars weren't as noticeable as we anticipated. I believe wholeheartedly that it was all due to the wonderful and meticulous attention I received from the resident surgeon who stitched me up.

I spent the summer of 1967 working as a waitress at the Garden City Hotel again. I began bumping into Helmut on a fairly regular basis. He had a German girlfriend who was one of the hostesses at the hotel. I loved to stand off in a corner and listen to the two of them speaking German to each other. Even though I didn't understand a single word they were saying, I thought they sounded so sophisticated and smart. By this time, RG had moved to New York. Once we started living in the same city, we spent a lot more time together and I realized we really weren't suited for each other. A girl knows when something isn't right. I loved RG, I adored his family, but we weren't meant to spend the rest of our lives together. I was convinced that it was time to break off our engagement. It wasn't just because I was so attracted to Helmut. There were lots of men I was meeting whom I found myself attracted to. Also, I realized that I wanted to be free to pursue my career after I graduated. The more I thought about it, the more I realized it would be a lot harder later on to get out of a marriage that wasn't working than it would be to call off the engagement now. It would be better to bite the bullet and let us both go free rather than potentially be miserable or make a truly regrettable mistake. Although I knew it would hurt RG, it was the right thing to do. I gently broke the news to him that things were not going to work. He accepted what I had to say and we each went our own way.

When I returned to Marymount that spring, I jumped right back into my studies as if nothing had happened. I enrolled in an acting class that was all about getting us out of our comfort zones. This class presented the opportunity to work with professional actors from New York, which I thought was very exciting. One of the actors I met called me to see if I would be interested in auditioning for the New York State Miss Universe Pageant. I thought it might be fun to see what this was all about. I went to what was described as a press breakfast at a restaurant on the Upper West Side of Manhattan. Other than the occasional trips I had made to the city with my parents, I hadn't spent much time there, and especially not on my own. A few friends from school and I had ventured there a couple of times to attend a lecture or to see a show at Café La MaMa, where Mr. Weyand had also performed, or at Lincoln Center, where he was a member of the Lincoln Center Repertory Company and where he shared a dressing room with Philip Bosco. Still, Manhattan was an unfamiliar place. My greatest impressions of life in New York City had primarily been formed from watching all of those wonderful old movies on *The Early Show*, *The Late Show*, and *Million Dollar Movie*. I remembered scenes of places like the Stork Club and the party scene in *Breakfast at Tiffany's*. I thought all of the chicest women in New York dressed like Audrey Hepburn, so I always showed up in Manhattan wearing a little black dress and pearls, looking like my own version of Holly Golightly.

I didn't know a single soul when I took the train in that day. Talk about getting out of my comfort zone! I was relieved when I met other aspiring actors and models at the restaurant. Most were professionally way ahead of me, so I used the opportunity to pick their brains about how to get started as an actor in the Big Apple. Almost immediately, the owner of the pageant and two very kind girls I met took me under their wing. They told me how to pull my portfolio together and about the *Ross Reports*, which provided names and addresses to various agencies around New York. They explained how to get a good professional head shot, how to create a résumé, and all of the other "must-haves" if you are going to make it as an actress in New York.

When I went back to class the following day, I shared my exciting new findings with my classmates and with Mr. Weyand. He was very understanding and encouraged me to soak in everything I was learning. But he also reminded me that his job was to educate me. His hope was that I would graduate from Marymount and go on to pursue my master's degree at the John Houseman School of Theater, a part of the famed Juilliard School, one of the most prestigious performing arts conservatories in New York, or go on to audition at the Yale School of Drama. Mr. Weyand fully believed that I had the talent to become a very fine actress. He was always supportive of me even if he didn't always agree with my choices. I told him I didn't have a desire to attend graduate school. I just wanted to find my wings and go to New York and act. I was through studying in school. I wanted practical and real-life experience. I knew he was disappointed with that decision, but he agreed to help me write my résumé. It was clear that he felt I should have a career in film or in the theater. Television was certainly not in his game plan. And daytime television? Well, that never even came up.

Back in the 1960s, television was considered by many to be a lesser form of entertainment—but not by me. As a little girl, I would often take my pillow and lie on the floor of the hallway outside my parents' bedroom and watch their television when I was supposed to be asleep. I watched the *Armstrong Circle Theatre* and *Playhouse 90*, and saw all sorts of things I wasn't supposed to see. I especially remember watching *For Whom the Bell Tolls* with Maria Schell, particularly the scene where she shared a sleeping bag with a man. That was the first time I had ever seen anything like that, and was completely fascinated. I really don't know what it was about that movie that stayed with me all of these years, but I have never forgotten watching it. Those amazing shows are what kept me glued to the television set and piqued my interest to watch even more. I was hooked from that point on. So, every time one of my professors would talk down about television, I knew in my heart that I loved it, and as it turned out, someday, it would become my destiny.

The father of one of my girlfriends from Garden City was very good friends with Robert Dale Martin, one of the top executives at CBS. My friend's father asked if he could help me get a meeting with Mr. Martin. Luckily, and for reasons I will never know, he agreed to see me. When I went to his office, Mr. Martin offered me some of the best advice I was ever given. He said that if I wanted to be an actor in New York, I needed to give myself a year before taking a job out of town. He explained that a lot of young aspiring actors make the mistake of taking the first job they're offered, which is usually some national touring company of a Broadway show. While it's great work and can mean really good money, once you're out of the loop, it is extremely difficult to find your way back in.

"If it's New York that you want, Susan, then stay here and work," he said. And he was right. It was excellent advice that I have never forgotten.

"And, there's one more thing, Susan. You may run up against some issues because you might be considered a little too 'ethnic-looking' for television, as you don't have blond or red hair and you don't have blue eyes."

Ethnic-looking? I knew I didn't look like everyone else when I was growing up, but I had never heard the word *ethnic* applied to me before. When I was a little girl, my mother and I would watch the Miss America pageants together on television. My mother always pointed out the brunette contestants to show me how beautiful and exotic-looking they were. She always picked one of them to be the winner. I never forgot her descriptive words. Her comments helped me maintain my self-esteem throughout my early years, and now, for the first time, as an aspiring actress, I would pull confidence from those memories to help get me through the inevitable challenges.

While it may seem a little odd to talk about ethnicity in today's more liberal world, back then Mr. Martin had a valid point. We were a nation tuning in to watch color TV. No one wanted to watch a brunette when they could watch a fiery redhead or golden blonde. Not since I was cast as Cindy Ellen had it occurred to me that my looks would be a detriment to my career. After all, many brunettes such as Sophia Loren and Raquel Welch had made wonderful careers for themselves. I shared my views on the subject and then asked Mr. Martin what he meant by ethnic-looking.

"Those women are exceptional and few and far in between," he said.

It was strange because I didn't take his comment to be negative or as a setback. I don't know if that was because I was young and naive and simply didn't know any better or if I just didn't believe that he was right. I probably didn't take it to heart because I didn't think he was necessarily talking about me. And besides, I believed in myself. I understood what he was saying, but deep down, I just knew it wouldn't matter. There wasn't a doubt in my mind that my "look" would become my calling card.

I ended up getting involved in the New York State Miss Universe Pageant, but only for a while. My father never wanted me to become a professional actress. He didn't believe that it was a wise career choice. Of course, my parents knew nothing about show business. Everything they knew was based on the sensationalized stories they read about in the newspaper. Still, my father was proud that I was asked to be in the pageant, so I went ahead with the competition. I made it to the finals, which was the bathing suit competition. That round of the competition was set to take place in the Catskill Moun tains in upstate New York. When I gave my parents the good news, my father didn't share my happiness. You see, the final round of competition took place the same week as my comprehensive finals and oral exams for school. My father made it utterly clear that I needed to finish school and graduate. Plus, he didn't love the idea of me parading around in front of a bunch of "dirty old men" in a bathing suit. Of course, he didn't know any of the men who were judging the competition, but in his mind, they were a bunch of old guys staring at his daughter, and that made them dirty old men. Deep down, I knew my father was right, so I quit the competition and finished school.

Although my academic grades were very good, in order to graduate I was required to take a series of oral exams. Mr. Weyand administered these tests. His first question was posed as an analogy I had to complete:

He said, "Iced tea is to a glass as . . ."

"A painting is to a frame," I responded.

"Very good, Miss Lucci," he replied, expecting things to go as smoothly as I did.

I thought, *Okay. This is going to be a breeze.* These types of questions went on for four hours. His final question was about a certain character in a play. He wanted to know what "type" I thought this person was.

Type?

I've never been one to put labels on people. I vividly remember meeting one of my dad's coworkers, an ironworker, who had the thickest New York accent I had ever heard. These men were in construction and sounded very rough when they spoke. "Dis, dat, fuhgedaboudit!" That's what I heard when they bantered with one another. But one afternoon, when my father and his friend picked me up from college, I sat in the car and listened to the two of them discuss everything from free will to dance and art. My expectation was that they would talk about sports or news, but certainly not ballet or opera. That experience taught me never to put labels on people because they just might surprise you.

So when Mr. Weyand asked me about "type," I was reluctant

to answer. I certainly understood that he wanted me to give him a sound bite that would put the character into a box. I refused to do it. I thought about my response for a minute because I wasn't sure I wanted to risk not graduating over taking a stand. But I had to. I recalled something one of my philosophy teachers had taught me about the concept of both/and. He made it clear that we don't have to live in a world of either/or because things can be both/and. We have the ability not to choose exclusion. We can also choose inclusion. Yes, it was deeply philosophical, and certainly arguable, but to me, it made perfect sense. I have always wanted to live in a world where both/and was possible. I'd resisted having to make a definite choice since the time I was a little girl playing my favorite board game, the one that required I choose between "Money, Fame, and Love." It's not a generational thing, thinking I could grow up to have everything. I really didn't think one had to make choices that involved sacrificing something else you liked or loved. That was the philosophy of both/and—so I expressed what I felt.

"There are just too many surprises about people. I cannot say that this person is one type or another. The character may be both. This character may embody all types. We don't know the answer. It's something to explore." I held my breath and my ground. Mr. Weyand was frustrated. It was meant to be a simple question. I had made it complex. I didn't want to be combative. I never want to be argumentative, but I felt I needed to say what I was thinking.

Mr. Weyand refused to pass me. He was so upset about my answer that he stopped the exam and threatened not to graduate me. When the word got out, some of the other department heads spoke to him on my behalf. I was carrying a 3.9 grade point average in my major. The other department heads said there was no real reason for me not to graduate other than the personal opinion of this one man. Thankfully, he compromised and allowed me to take the exam over. This time I passed. I received my bachelor of arts degree in the spring of 1968.

Nineteen sixty-eight was one of the most volatile years in American history. These were tumultuous and changing times for our country and for the world around us. It was a time when nearly everyone my age was examining the establishment. College campuses all over the country were exploding with protests over the Vietnam War. Robert Kennedy and Martin Luther King were assassinated within two months of each other, and after Lyndon Johnson decided against seeking another term, Richard Nixon was elected president. Women's rights movements were making strides, but were nowhere close to where they needed to be. I'd heard stories on the news about students at Columbia University burning their books. And women in Manhattan were burning their bras. Things had changed quite a bit since I had started college. When I first got to Marymount, the nuns were in habits and we had to attend a mandatory charm class. We were required to wear white gloves and pearls to mass. By my sophomore year, the nuns were out of their habits and in miniskirts, with dangling earrings. I was rather conservative when I began attending Marymount, but by the time I graduated, even I was different. I remember making the rounds in New York City right after college. I wore a green jersey halter-style dress and no bra. I was so moved by Gloria Steinem and the message she was spreading that I decided to forgo wearing one. So much of what she was saying made complete sense to me. Equal pay for equal work. Hello? How could anyone not get that? Still, it was a different time, where men were the sole breadwinners and therefore made more money. That night, I walked into a restaurant wearing a green halter and no bra. There was a table full of men who stood up and applauded when I walked by.

I spent the summer of 1968 running around New York City and trying whatever I could to land a job. When I wasn't making the rounds, I was continuing my studies, having enrolled in more acting classes. I studied with the wonderful Wynn Handman, the artistic director of the American Place Theatre, which he cofounded with

Sidney Lanier and Michael Tolan in 1963. His role in the theater had been to seek out, encourage, train, and present new and exciting writing and acting talent and to develop and produce new plays by living American writers. Wynn's classes were very accessible and easy to get to because they usually took place in the afternoon. He taught at a small studio across the street from Carnegie Hall. Someone had told me that Wynn was an excellent drama instructor for women, whereas Uta Hagen, the legendary actress and teacher who was an inspiration for generations of aspiring actors who studied with her at HB Studios in New York City was known as a better teacher for men. As teachers, they followed the studio's interpretation of the Stanislavski Method. The Stanislavski Method of acting involves a set of techniques meant to create realistic portrayals of characters. The major goal of the Stanislavski Method is to have a perfect understanding of the motivations and objectives of your character in each moment. The technique is most often used for realistic plays, where the goal is to create an accurate idea of normal life.

Now that I was out of college, my parents insisted that I get a real job to earn some money while I pursued acting. I primarily worked as a temp because I knew employers wouldn't have high expectations of a girl who was there for a day or two. I also knew I would have the necessary flexibility to audition. I worked in offices all over the city, including a grout company. I didn't even know what grout was, but I did whatever they wanted me to do. I mostly sat in an empty office and waited for someone to ask me to type a letter or answer the phone. A few people called and asked me about grout. I'd have to put them on hold and find someone in the office who could answer their basic questions because I surely didn't know what I was talking about.

My first professional job was handed to me through Robert Dale Martin. I was asked to be the color girl at the Ed Sullivan Theater. I'd sometimes go there in the afternoon while they put the cameras on me and adjusted their lights. Ironically, I got the job because I *didn't* have red or blond hair. My dark eyes, olive skin, and brown hair made it easier for them to set their color codes.

Being allowed to experience the inside of a television studio for the first time at the Ed Sullivan Theater was absolutely thrilling. I grew up watching *The Ed Sullivan Show,* so it was very exciting to be a part of its production, even if it was only as a color girl for lighting. The opportunity allowed me to understand how the lights are hung, how a studio is wired for sound, and all of the behind-the-scenes nuances it takes to put on a show. The stage manager was very experienced and I could tell he was highly regarded by the crew. He took his time explaining all of the details to me, from cameras and props to sets and show breakdowns. It was a once-in-a-lifetime experience for a young girl dreaming of someday being on TV.

CHAPTER 4

Hello, New York

Have you heard the news about Susan Lucci? She broke off her engagement." Helmut was meeting with a friend at the Garden City Hotel who casually offered this update over lunch. Even after Helmut left his position as executive chef, he occasionally stopped by the hotel since he was now responsible for the operations side of the properties his company owned.

Helmut excused himself from the table, went to the nearest pay phone, and called me. I was in New York making the rounds when he phoned, so I missed his call. When I got home, my mother gave me the message. I had a feeling Helmut was calling to ask me on a date. There was definite chemistry between us, but there was also a ten-year age difference. The slogan for my generation was "Don't trust anyone over thirty!" I could only imagine my parents' shock and horror at the thought of me dating a man who was over thirty. Once in a while even my mother would repeat the slogan to me.

It's true, when I looked at Helmut, I saw a man. I knew he had been married and divorced and that he had children. He was unlike anyone I had ever gone out with, let alone set my sights on. There was so much that was appealing about Helmut and lots that scared me just a bit, too. He was incredibly secure and self-assured. I loved that. He is a man who doesn't readily take no for an answer. If he asked me out for dinner on a Friday night and I said I was busy, he'd ask me to lunch. If lunch didn't work for me, he'd say, "Okay, Saturday it is, then." You get the idea. I was single, out of college, exploring my options, and in pursuit of a career. I wasn't playing a game. I wanted to enjoy my freedom. It was pretty clear that he wasn't going away without a fight or making a valiant effort.

None of my rejections seemed to sway his interest. He continued to be funny and charming, and the more he tried, the harder I was falling. Helmut knew I liked to play tennis, so he made arrangements for us to go to the U.S. Open. He knew I adored going to the theater, so he'd set up tickets for the hottest shows. He took me to see Marlene Dietrich at Radio City Music Hall, and what a treat that was. She had the chutzpah and showmanship to come onstage in a flesh-colored beaded gown with a twenty-foot white fox stole dragging on the ground behind her. That woman sure did understand the stage. She worked everything she had and sure knew how to use it. She was fabulous. After the show, Helmut bought me the album of her show. I played it constantly. Even though she wasn't the greatest singer of our time, she was a tremendous performer.

I was being wined and dined in the most fabulous way. Helmut and I would meet at a restaurant for what I always thought would be a quick lunch and then he'd say, "Let's take a walk." I'd agree to go for a stroll, thinking we'd part ways after a few blocks, and then Helmut would suggest going for a cocktail.

"Call your mother. See if you can stay in the city for dinner," he'd say, fully aware that he had parlayed a quick lunch into spending most of the day and evening together. Although my parents liked Helmut from the very start, they certainly were aware of how persistent he was being. Deep down, I believe they were worried he'd end up whisking me away to Austria and that I would be too far away from them. They knew how much I enjoyed my experience as an exchange student, so I think their concern that I could be persuaded to live abroad again was valid. I knew my parents thought I was too young to be married when I was engaged the first time around and I don't think they planned on me marrying someone ten years my senior. Still, I believe they thought Helmut would make a very good husband. My father often joked with my mother that if I continued to date Helmut, he was going to make me marry him.

It's true that Helmut was ready to settle down and get serious in a relationship. But I wasn't. I was uncomfortable about the ten-year difference in our age, especially in the beginning. At the time it felt like an awfully big gap. I admired Helmut and adored being in his presence. I thought we could, at the very least, remain friends. Although he proposed very early on, I didn't accept; nor did I think it was right to lead him on. In all honesty, I had just gotten out of a relationship that I knew wasn't right. I didn't want to start another one. And more than that, I truly wanted to pursue my career. Helmut, ever the gentleman, took the news with great dignity. "You never know what will happen in the future," he said. I agreed with him, thinking I'd never see this man again. After that night, he left me alone for several months.

Since I was getting serious about becoming a professional actress, I thought the time had come to find myself an agent. I was told by some friends that if I wanted an agent, I should look in the *Ross Reports*. I thought the agencies listed in all capital letters were the best and most important. The two girls I met during the Miss Universe pageant had told me that if you showed up to certain agencies unannounced with your picture and résumé in hand and spoke with the receptionist, you could hand them your package, and with a little luck and charm, you might get an appointment to see one of the agents on the spot. If the receptionist thought the agency could make some money with you, she would open the gate, so to speak. Sure enough, that is exactly what happened to me.

I am generally a very shy girl, but if I want something, I will always find a way to get through my discomfort and make things happen. (Like writing this book.) I was driven to succeed, so I cast that shyness aside and stormed through the doors of every agency in town holding my head shot and résumé in my hand while introducing myself to the receptionist like I was seeing an old friend. I had made up my mind early on that I wouldn't sign with an agent until he actually got me work. If you were new to the industry, that was the usual arrangement. Don't get me wrong—some agencies wanted to sign me on the spot, but if they didn't put you under contract, they were fine with you going freelance until one of them got you work.

The first agents I met were a team named Bob LaMonde and Bill Tesch. They were considered good agents and they seemed to think I had something going on. We spoke for a while, then one of them turned to me and said, "You're a gorgeous girl, Susan, but take a look around. Do you see how people are dressed? Kids your age are wearing jeans and love beads, not black dresses, white gloves, and pearls!" And they were right. That's when I tuned in to what was really happening all around me in New York City. I created a look that was my own, but was still comfortable and easy for me to slip into every day.

I did a lot of freelance work for the Michael Hartig Agency, too. They kept me busy with auditions, but not a lot of work. Like Mr. Martin had predicted, I had been offered a couple of jobs out of town, but I remembered his advice, so despite the opportunity to earn some money and gain valuable experience, I turned them down.

A couple of months had passed since I had last spoken to Helmut and I will admit that I had come to regret my letting him go. I actually missed him. I'd heard through the grapevine that he had gone on an extended trip to Europe to visit his family. I had no idea how long he'd be away or when he was coming back.

Much to my surprise, Helmut phoned one day out of the blue.

"I know you like to eat," he said.

That was such a funny way to start a conversation because most people don't think that about me—but Helmut sure did. He'd been out to dinner with me enough times to know that I truly have a love for food and fine dining.

"There's a black-tie hotel industry dinner and dance at the Waldorf Hotel coming up. I think you will enjoy it. I would love for you to be my date," he said.

"I'd be delighted," I said. And I was. I was very happy Helmut called that day. When he came to pick me up, Helmut stood in the doorway of my parents' home looking so handsome in his tuxedo. I had borrowed my mother's long white fox stole, which I wore over my shoulders. The event took place in the grand ballroom of the hotel. There was a large orchestra playing as Helmut escorted me into the room. I loved to dance, but I didn't know how to do a proper waltz. When the orchestra struck up a Viennese waltz, Helmut took me by the hand and taught me to waltz—Austrian style. It was very romantic. Sometime during that dance I looked up at him and thought, *Maybe I need to reconsider.* It was a spectacular evening that left me smitten as a kitten from that point on.

The next morning, Helmut called my home to say he had white fox hair all over his black tuxedo. He wanted to know if I could tell him how to remove the hair. He laughed as he told me he actually tried to vacuum it off. My mother got on the phone to tell him to go out and buy a lint brush. Before he hung up, Helmut asked if he could take me to the Jones Beach Theater to see *South Pacific.* He thought I'd enjoy seeing that show. Although we had spent a lot of time together, I considered *South Pacific* to be our official second date and the evening at the Waldorf to be our first. Much to my surprise, Helmut told me he loved me that night. He is very much his own man, someone who is clearly very decisive and self-possessed. The man knows what he wants and isn't afraid to let you know, too. He has always told me how he feels. He had already made up his mind that if he ever got married again, it was going to be to me. I wasn't quite as sure. He'd hand me baby-name books in English and in German so I could pick out our children's names with him. He'd bring them out and talk about the day we'd be married at a stone chapel on a cliff he once saw while vacationing in Kennebunkport, Maine. He always thought that church would be where he'd get married, if he ever got married again. Helmut was relentless as he continued proposing while wining and dining me for the next several months. The more time we spent together, the deeper in love I fell. As time went on, I knew that he truly got me in a very real way.

Helmut took an interest in everything I was doing. He'd take me to one acting class and pick me up from another. He took me to places all over the city where he would shine and where people knew him by name. And he also took me skiing, at which he could showcase his extreme finesse and expertise while helping me learn and grow on the slopes, too.

There was one memorable evening that Helmut and I will never forget. He picked me up for dinner at a restaurant in New York City. I was wearing a red knit pantsuit that was composed of red pants and a matching tunic and thin belt. When we got to the restaurant, the maître d' looked at me in horror and said to Helmut, "No pants allowed!" Such strict dress codes weren't uncommon in the 1960s—even the late sixties—but overturning them had become a challenge for some. With more and more women entering the workplace, women began to feel like they should have more flexibility in the way they dressed. They no longer wanted to wear only skirts and dresses in order to be accepted in public. Still, it wasn't until Yves Saint Laurent began designing more gender-neutral clothing in the late sixties and early seventies that many restaurants eased up on these restrictions. One of the main reasons this was happening with more frequency was that on more than one occasion, women wearing pantsuits would simply take off their pants and walk into a restaurant dressed in only the upper half of their suit. They were protesting the fact that other people were allowed to dictate what they could and couldn't wear out to dinner.

I didn't know about any of this at the time, but I looked at Helmut and instinctively said, "It's not a problem." I excused myself and headed to the ladies' room to remove my pants. I looked in the mirror, pulled the tunic down, and voilà, I was wearing a mini-dress. I walked back to the front desk wearing my "dress" and a big Cheshire-cat grin, and said, "I believe we can now be seated."

Years later, I remember reading a story about a well-known New York socialite who had done the same thing. I don't recall what she was wearing at the time, but she had also removed her slacks. When I saw the article, I thought to myself, *I'll be darned. I was just a kid out of school, but at least I was in good company!*

It took me three months to tell Helmut I would marry him. He'd been asking me to think about it for so long. I knew he was the right man for me the night we were at my parents' house sitting on their sunporch in the middle of January. My mother and father had gone to bed, while Helmut and I decided to stay outside and talk. I was barefoot and very cold. When I mentioned that my bare feet were a bit chilly, Helmut took off his socks and put them on my feet to keep me warm. He was such a good man and I was so incredibly touched by his gesture. I know it probably sounds a little foolish to a worldly person, but to me, it was romantic, caring, warm, and real. These were the qualities I wanted in a husband, and Helmut had them all. That's when I turned to him and said I would marry him.

"You are the slowest woman I have ever met!" That was his response when I finally said yes.

When Helmut gave me my engagement ring, it was a very spontaneous moment. He had picked me up from an acting class in Manhattan to drive me back to Garden City. We were on Ninety-sixth Street, headed for the Triborough Bridge. I knew he had something else in mind, but he just couldn't wait, so he told me to press the button to open the glove compartment. When I did, there was my ring—a two-carat pear-shaped diamond set in platinum. We picked September 13, 1969, as our wedding date, leaving me a little more than eight months to plan the event.

As my mother and I attended to all the details, I continued to go on general go-sees and auditions. In July of 1969, I received a call from Larry Masser, one of the agents from the Hartig Agency, who phoned to tell me about a new soap opera one of the networks was thinking of doing. He wanted me to go on a general interview but made it clear that they wouldn't be making any decisions for at least six months. It was a very hot and muggy summer day in New York City. My hair is naturally wavy, and on this particular day, it was supercurly from all of the heat and humidity. Since I had been told many times that I was too ethnic-looking to work in television, I thought this meeting was going to be a total waste of time. After all, I had dark skin, dark eyes, and unmanageably curly dark hair. I was pretty sure that I was not the girl they were looking for. I told Larry I didn't want to go, but he insisted. I did what any enterprising girl would do when having a bad hair day—I found a scarf and tied it around my head Gypsy style to hide my frizzy hair. It was 1969, so this look wasn't too out there. It may have even been chic by some standards. For me? It was a quick solution to tresses in distress.

I was supposed to meet with the executive producer, line producer, and casting director for the unnamed start-up show at a studio on the west side of Manhattan. When I got to the meeting, I only met Joan D'Incecco, the casting director, who told me this new show was called *All My Children*. It turned out that Joan was extremely influential in making the final decision to cast Erica Kane, the character I was there to talk to them about. Our meeting was only a few minutes long. It was a quick look at me and a short conversation about the character. Joan described the young girl they were looking to cast as fifteen years old, full of herself, and unafraid to speak her mind, especially when it came to her mother. That was all I heard, but it was enough to leave me curious and wanting to play this part. Joan confirmed that it would be at least six months before they got the show up and running and that she would call me back when the time was right. I was hoping she would remember me because I really liked what I had heard. Before leaving, I made sure Joan knew that I had studied with the finest teachers, trying, as I always did, to set myself apart. I knew she would have good things to say about me to the others in charge of hiring, but I still wasn't convinced I was what they wanted.

Helmut and I were married shortly after that meeting. Even though he dreamed of a small ceremony at that chapel in Maine, our ceremony took place at St. Joseph's Church in Garden City. Although September is a lovely time of year in New York, looking back, I would never recommend getting married in early September if you don't have to. Anyone who has children knows how hectic that time of year can be for families because kids are just starting school and life around the house and in careers are just beginning to get back into the regular swing of things. We took our vows in front of 125 of our closest friends and family. I carried a bouquet of gardenias, Nana's favorite flower, as a way of having her close to my heart that day. My best girlfriends from college were my brides-maids, and Helmut's friends from work were the groomsmen and best man. During the ceremony, the theme from Zeffirelli's *Romeo and Juliet* played and a soloist also sang "Let There Be Peace on Earth." When it was my turn to slip Helmut's ring on his finger, I was so nervous that I accidentally picked the wrong hand. I tried to gently slide the ring over his knuckle, but I couldn't get it all the way on. I kept trying and trying to get the ring on before Helmut took it from me and forced it on his finger. But following my lead, he, too, put the ring on my wrong hand. We didn't realize our mistake until after the ceremony. The bishop assured me that despite the mix-up, we were definitely married. When we tried to switch Helmut's ring to the correct hand, we couldn't get it off his finger. The first thing Helmut did when we got to the reception was go to the men's room to run his hands under water with a lot of soap so he could make the switch.

My parents planned a lovely reception at the Garden City Country Club, where they were members. Since Helmut is Austrian, as we exited the church we chose a recessional from *The Sound of Music*. We chose "Live for Life" for our first dance. It was from a movie we saw together when we were dating. It meant so much to us. It's funny because neither of us can remember what movie it came from, but we sure do remember the song.

We spent our wedding night at the St. Moritz hotel in New York City. One of Helmut's friends was an executive there who graciously surprised us with a beautiful suite. The next day, we flew to St. Thomas, where we enjoyed our honeymoon for six glorious days and nights.

As any young respectable actress would do upon returning to New York, the moment we arrived, I called my answering service to see if I had any messages. The operator told me that a Ms. Joan D'Incecco from ABC had called. It had only been a few months since she and I met. "Clearly," Helmut said, "I am your good-luck charm."

My heart was racing with excitement and joy. When I phoned her back, she asked me to come in to meet with Doris Quinlan, the executive producer; Bud Kloss, the producer; and Felicia Minei, the associate producer of the show. I was very excited to be called back in because acting is a very competitive business, especially when you are just starting out. I was told that hundreds and hundreds of girls of all shapes, sizes, and coloring had walked through their door. Sometimes agents will send in actors they know aren't right for the role just to give them the experience of auditioning. To be called back was a very good thing. I thought I would have an opportunity to read for them this time around, but they only wanted to take another look at me. I wrapped my head in a scarf like I did when I first met Joan, figuring there was something she liked about that style or look.

I only spoke with the producers for a few minutes. As I turned to leave, they asked me if I had any questions. I paused for a moment and then asked if they wanted to see my hair. Much to my surprise, they said no.

I was called back for the third time a few weeks later. This time, however, I blew my hair out so it was very long and straight. I wanted them to see me as I usually am. I was not only asked to read for the executives in charge, I was told they were going to film a screen test with me the following week. From the first audition, Frances "Fra" Heflin and I were paired up as mother and daughter. Unfortunately, she wasn't able to be at the screen test, so I played the scene with someone else.

I was handed my sides and given only a few minutes to prepare. As I was reading and memorizing my lines, I noticed a woman breeze by me. I will never forget that moment. She was a petite blonde wearing a cappuccino-colored Yves Saint Laurent pantsuit that I recognized from a recent issue of *Vogue* and she was holding a brown alligator bag.

Bud Kloss, the producer, must have seen me look up and stare at her.

"That's Agnes Nixon. She is the creator of the show. She is going to be watching your screen test," he said.

Agnes Nixon didn't look like anyone I had ever met before and she certainly didn't look like what I had expected. She was from my mother's generation. Like my mother, she was very pretty, but she was also such a dynamic stylish powerhouse. She was the first "professional" woman I had ever seen in action. Despite her petite frame, I was mesmerized and completely taken by her gigantic presence. I was impressed from the moment I saw her.

I watched *One Life to Live* every day after class at Marymount. Agnes Nixon created that show and was and still is considered daytime royalty. She set what is the gold standard for the medium to this day. I actually read about Agnes Nixon in college, so I was aware of her many accomplishments. Knowing she was there to watch my screen test really put the pressure on.

The scene was about a fifteen-year-old Erica Kane who was waiting for her math tutor to come over. It was eight pages long and contained dialogue between Erica and her mother, Mona. I was told that Erica's father had left her mother when she was just nine years old. He was a famous movie director who went to Hollywood. Although he spoiled Erica with money and material things, he never wanted to see her.

Mona was a single mother. In the early days, the character of Mona used to drink and she wasn't a great housekeeper. She and Erica lived in a very modest home, full of dirty ashtrays and empty bottles, while Erica continuously waited for her dad to come home. Despite the rest of their humble surroundings, Erica's room was as glamorous as a fifteen-year-old girl's room could be.

Erica's way of getting ready for her math tutor, of course, was to look in the mirror and apply another coat of mascara. Mona was supposed to be Erica's constant voice of reason. She kept asking Erica why she was getting so dolled up for her math tutor.

"Don't you think you should be studying your math instead of putting on makeup?" she asked.

The math tutor turned out to be the very cute boyfriend of another girl in Erica's high school class. Erica's way of self-soothing was to collect boys like trophies, preferably by breaking up their relationships with other girls.

"You don't understand, Mother! This is Phil Brent, and he is very handsome and smart. He doesn't care if I know math." That was Erica's response to Mona's reasoning.

In those few pages, Agnes Nixon had established character, relationships, and history, all of which she did with tremendous humor—something you never really saw before between a television mother and daughter. It was written in a very real style, one that was fresh for television back then. I remember thinking that if Mr. Weyand could read this scene, he would know why I was so interested in playing this character. Erica was like a young Scarlett O'Hara. Remember, this was before the Brat Pack and here was a very well-written major part for a fifteen-year-old character. Somehow, I thought Mr. Weyand might just understand that the part was full of possibilities.

When I finished my screen test, I will say that I felt pretty good about it. I always enjoyed the audition process, no matter the outcome. I thought I had done well, but there really is never any way to tell until you get that call. I loved the part and thought I was right to play the character. Even though I was already out of college, I looked young enough to portray a fifteen-year-old. Plus, I was close enough to that age to understand what a real mother–teen-daughter relationship would look like. There was a lot of role wrapped up in the character, and even more—there was fiery oil and water between Erica and Mona.

After my screen test, I waited in the lobby of the Reeve Studio on the corner of Sixty-seventh Street and Columbus Avenue for my husband to pick me up. It was a rainy November day. I was staring out the window when I noticed the producer of the show, Bud Kloss, out of the corner of my eye.

"We'll be calling your agent in the morning," he said.

Did that mean I got the part?

What else could it mean?

I was beyond thrilled because I really liked the part. I could hardly wait to tell Helmut the good news. I am one of the luckiest women in the world to have married a man who supports my every move. It is not easy to be the husband of a woman who has a public career. It takes a strong sense of self and a lot of security in your relationship to make it work in the long term.

Something I always found attractive about Helmut is that he is very much his own man. He is very secure and extremely confident. He has a wonderful sense of humor and has always taken great pride in my talent and career. From the very start, Helmut wasn't just supportive; he would pitch in. He always did whatever it took to help me be prepared. If that meant he had to cook us dinner or clean the house, he would do it. It was really about who got home first.

Helmut didn't believe it was right for one human being to stand in the way of another, especially when the other is your wife. I was so young and naive, and thankfully, Helmut was older, with more life experiences under his belt, so I never once felt like he was anything except loving and supportive, especially when it came to my career. When I told Helmut that I thought I got the part of Erica Kane, he was as happy for me as I was for myself. Naturally, we had no idea what this all meant. In the beginning, it was merely a job.

The next day my agent called to confirm the wonderful news that I was being offered the role of Erica Kane. They were giving me a three-year contract. My heart just about sank. Three years? I didn't want to commit to doing a show for three years. My only frame of reference for that period of time was four years of high school and four years of college, both of which had felt like an eternity. I was only twenty-one years old, newly married, and just starting my career. There was so much I wanted to do. If I were tied down to the same show for three years, how would I ever accomplish my goal of becoming a serious actress? I told my agent that I absolutely loved the part, but I didn't want to commit to three years.

He explained that contracts can be negotiated, but it was a good offer that he thought I should take. He promised he'd get me out of my contract if I absolutely ended up hating the role. It sounded reasonable enough, so I reconsidered and accepted the part. I desperately wanted to reach out to Mr. Weyand to share my good news. I was certain that if he could read the material I'd been given, he would approve of my decision to pursue television and forgo graduate school. I never did, but a year later, *TV Guide* did a profile on me and contacted him to ask his thoughts on my work. He said very positive things, so I eventually knew that he approved of my decision, even if I didn't know it at the time.

I am so lucky that I had been given the eyes to see and the ears to hear because I knew, without a doubt, that Erica Kane was "the part of a lifetime." But I had no idea that this expression would end up being so literal in my case. Looking back, it's practically comical that I was worried about being locked into the part of Erica for three whole years. Forty-one years later, I am still playing Erica Kane and loving every minute of it.

CHAPTER 5

— ᥫ᭡᭫ —

The Early Days of *All My Children*

Many years after being cast as Erica Kane, I heard a story that Bud Kloss, the original producer of the show, hadn't been sure if I was right for the part. Apparently, he went to Agnes to suggest that I read for the part of Tara as well as Erica. I was told that Tara was the good girl who was dating the math tutor who was coming to see Erica, and Erica was the naughty girl in town. When Agnes saw my screen test for the first time, she turned to Bud and said, "There's no way she would be Tara. This girl *is* Erica. Her eyes are Erica's eyes."

Looking back, it was clear that Agnes had a vision from the start. The mere notion that my eyes were Erica's is so interesting to me because, as I mentioned earlier, color televisions were just becoming all the rage. Blond hair and blue eyes were what America saw as mainstream. Other shows played into that appeal, but Agnes wasn't concerned about it. In fact, Agnes wanted something different for the part of Erica Kane.

Agnes had worked as the head writer for *Guiding Light* for many years. NBC was about to cancel the show, when Agnes offered to take a crack at it to help salvage it. *Guiding Light* quickly became the most popular show in daytime, which is how Agnes began her remarkable track record. Agnes wanted to do stories that were timely, topical, and had meaning. But at the time Procter & Gamble, the owners of *Guiding Light*, weren't interested in doing anything that could be construed or perceived as controversial. Agnes wanted to write with purpose, so when she was asked by Michael Eisner to come to ABC and create a new show for them, her only concern was whether or not she would be allowed to write about relevant social issues. They told her she could, and so in 1968, she created *One Life to Live*. Her first major story line revolved around Carmen Gray, an African-American actress who could pass for white—a courageous and titillating story for the times.

Soaps were huge moneymakers for the networks and *One Life to Live* became one of the biggest for ABC. Legend has it that Agnes already had the original script for *All My Children* sitting in her desk drawer when network executives came to her to create another daytime drama. She had pitched the show to Procter & Gamble and NBC a few years prior, but they rejected the idea. After her success with *One Life to Live*, ABC said they were looking to do a soap opera that would bring in young viewers. She had the right show, and in 1969, Michael Eisner gave her the green light to move ahead with *All My Children*. I did an interview with Michael in 2008, during which he shared with me for the first time that he was the executive in charge not only of green-lighting *All My Children* for the network, but of approving the cast, too, which, at the time, meant my fate was very much in his hands. Thankfully, he liked what he saw and I was able to take on the most delicious role in daytime.

Agnes once shared a wonderful story with me about the inception for the show and where her inspiration came from. She visited a psychic who told her that she saw Agnes as a teacher and that millions of people would listen to whatever she had to say. The psychic told Agnes that the story she had to tell was coming from an Irish ancestor on the other side. Agnes absolutely believes that a dead relative had given her the story that ultimately became the foundation for the show. As a writer, she took whatever inspiration she had been given and created the most wonderful and exceptional daytime drama in the history of television.

When *All My Children* made its debut on January 5, 1970, Agnes became the first writer to create a realistic story line that involved teenagers as main characters, including my character, the young troublemaker and bad girl in town, Erica Kane. Erica was only supposed to be on once a week, but within months of the show's debut, a major story line was given to me. There were lots of other actors on the show who had paid their dues before me, but rather than encountering jealousy, I was given love and support.

Although I was somebody who had grown up watching soap operas, I had never seen anyone like Erica Kane before being cast to play her. I thought she was great, mostly due to the tremendous writing of Agnes Nixon. Agnes understood the challenges in the mother-daughter relationship and knew how to convey them with ease, humor, and sensitivity. She knew that Erica and Mona loved each other in spite of their fights and their differences. Maybe it was because Agnes had children of her own that she was able to connect with the material in such a real way. Whatever the motivation, Agnes simply got it, and as a result, the viewing audience fell in love with Erica for all she was worth.

For a young actress just starting out, it was wonderful to be surrounded by so many caring and appreciative adults who had already been there and back. They encouraged me to grow, stretch, and become the actress I always dreamed of being.

I was paired with the actress Frances "Fra" Heflin, who was cast as Erica's mother, Mona Kane. Mona had divorced her philandering husband, Eric, after he deserted her and Erica when Erica was only nine years old. While he found fame in Hollywood as a film director, Mona dedicated her life to raising Erica the best she could. Erica was a true "Daddy's little girl," so in spite of all of the attention and things Mona showered her with, she blamed Mona for her father's leaving. His absence left Erica feeling extremely insecure about herself and on a never-ending quest for love. No matter how beautiful Erica thought she was, she was always worried there would be a prettier girl. She was consumed by her need to be loved and went out of her way to make herself better than everyone else. Erica's only goal was to be somebody. She always believed that she was meant for more than what her dull life in Pine Valley could offer, and she frequently reminded Mona of this by telling her how unhappy she was living there. Erica was often quoted as saying, "This is just a small town. This is not the corner of Hollywood and Vine! I'm going to be somebody. I'm going to get out of this small town someday."

Erica was extremely vain and yet very popular. In today's world, she would definitely be considered a "mean girl" or "queen bee" by her peers. She considered herself to be the prettiest girl in her school. She couldn't understand what the object of her affection, Phil Brent, saw in her nemesis, plain and frumpy Tara Martin. She was out to destroy their relationship and take Phil for herself. Erica often played the damsel in distress to get Phil's attention. Although Phil was a chivalrous gentleman, he only had eyes for Tara. Mona did her best to protect Erica from Phil's rejection, but her attempts to spare her daughter heartache only ignited Erica's rage and increased her feelings of insecurity and rejection. She demanded that her mother stay out of her life, which set up the roller-coaster relationship Erica and Mona endured for years.

Working with Fra was spectacular in every way. The chemistry between us was undeniable. I loved her very much. She was warm, smart, and very talented. Fra had fair skin and very blue eyes. I thought to myself that although we didn't really resemble one another, in many ways she reminded me of my own mother. I was so excited and truly blessed to be paired with such a lovely soul.

Fra came from a show business family. She was the sister of Academy Award–winning actor Van Heflin. She herself had studied at the Actors Studio with Marlon Brando and appeared on Broadway with him in *I Remember Mama*. She worked with Charles Laughton in London, where she lived for many years before returning to New York. Prior to working in soaps, most of her acting experience was stage work in New York and Europe.

Fra and I shared a dressing room for sixteen years. We ordered and ate lunch together in our tiny cubby every day for those years. Over time, she became extended family to me. I often confided in her and asked for guidance in acting and in life. I got to know her three children, including her son, Jonathan, who became a well-known director for such films as *The Accused*, *White Line Fever*, and *Brokedown Palace* as well as for several episodes of *ER*. Her daughter Mady went on to become a daytime actress as well, playing roles on *The Edge of Night*, *Texas*, and *As the World Turns*. And I got to know her other daughter, Nora, who has many stage and films credits to her name, too.

I was a very lucky young actress to be able to observe Fra and have her for a role model. She impacted my life both personally and professionally. She taught me not to be too sentimental, meaning I shouldn't allow myself to get too self-righteous in my role. Through her stories and experiences, Fra let me know that all of the trappings of fame should be avoided. From the very start, it was apparent that I was surrounded by good actors and not foolish people.

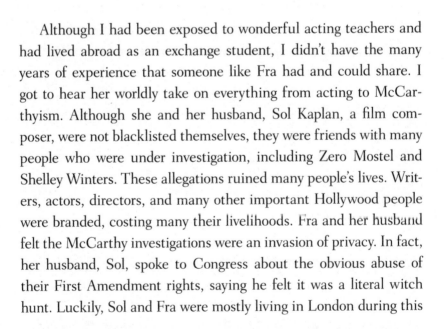

*T*here were two very funny scenes I did with Fra Heflin in the early days that I've never forgotten. The first was a scene in which Erica was trying on a dress that Mona was going to hem for her. I was wearing a black slip under the dress, which Fra inadvertently ended up sewing the dress to. When I tried to slip the dress off, it was caught and wouldn't come down past my knees. We tried to continue with the scene, but I was tripping all over the place. Fra and I both fell down from laughing so hard.

The other memorable scene with Fra happened while Erica was telling Mona about a doll she really hated from her childhood. There was a fly in the studio that kept landing right between Fra's eyes. I saw it and she felt it. We tried to keep it together, but we had to do several takes until the fly went away.

Although I had been exposed to wonderful acting teachers and had lived abroad as an exchange student, I didn't have the many years of experience that someone like Fra had and could share. I got to hear her worldly take on everything from acting to McCarthyism. Although she and her husband, Sol Kaplan, a film composer, were not blacklisted themselves, they were friends with many people who were under investigation, including Zero Mostel and Shelley Winters. These allegations ruined many people's lives. Writers, actors, directors, and many other important Hollywood people were branded, costing many their livelihoods. Fra and her husband felt the McCarthy investigations were an invasion of privacy. In fact, her husband, Sol, spoke to Congress about the obvious abuse of their First Amendment rights, saying he felt it was a literal witch hunt. Luckily, Sol and Fra were mostly living in London during this time, so they were only slightly involved and therefore only slightly impacted. I remember Fra telling me how loyal she thought Shelley Winters and her husband were for defending people's rights and for not snitching on anyone. They had a lot of integrity, which I greatly respected and admired. I have no firsthand knowledge of both sides of the story, but I do know that for many artists of the day, the McCarthy investigation equaled career death. The whole McCarthy era was a blight on our national history and certainly on our industry and artistry. As a young actress starting out, none of that made a whole lot of sense to me.

When *All My Children* was first televised, the show was a half hour long. We aired from one to one-thirty five days a week until 1975. We had to finish taping the show by two o'clock in the afternoon because the local news station used our equipment. We'd have just enough time to do a run-through and then tape the show. When we finished taping, we'd all gather at an apartment that the show rented near Lincoln Center to do a table read for the next day's episode. Since we shot the shows in sequence back then, everyone was required to go to the table read regardless of whether or not their character was in the show that day. These table reads were more like protracted rehearsals. Those of us playing the younger characters on the show would be required to put our scenes on their feet the same day by blocking and rehearsing. I don't recall any of the seasoned actors having to do that, only the younger, less experienced of us. I welcomed that process, as I was one of the few actors on the show who needed the extra time to get the scene right; remember, this was truly my first professional on-screen credit. There were a few other young actors on the show with me, including Karen Lynn Gorney, who played Tara, and Jack Stauffer, who played Chuck Tyler, but they had other credits to their name by the time *All My Children* went on the air. I had done work on a couple of movies that were shot in New York and a few other things here and there. I even did a day on another soap—*Search for Tomorrow*—before landing *All*

My Children. At the time my mother and I thought all of the soaps aired live, but *Search for Tomorrow* was taped. I knew my mother was at home watching the day I did that show and I knew she would be panicked when she didn't see me on that day's episode, so after I finished the taping, I ran to the nearest pay phone to let her know I'd made it to New York safely. I was certain she would think something had gone terribly wrong if the episode ended and I wasn't in it.

All My Children currently uses an old photograph of me during the opening credits that is actually my original head shot from 1970. The show took it for publicity and marketing purposes. It was shot on a hot summer day, when my hair was naturally wavy. I was on my way to rehearsal when someone told me to stop to have it taken. It was a casual request, so it never occurred to me that photo would resurface. It turned out to be one of my favorites.

All My Children's first action took place in the fictional town of Pine Valley and revolved around the lives of several families and characters. Phoebe Tyler, who was the matriarch of her family and was undoubtedly the queen of Pine Valley, was played by the incomparable Ruth Warrick. Ruth's first big break in acting occurred when she was hired by a young Orson Welles to play Emily Monroe Norton in *Citizen Kane*. When she auditioned for the part, she read with Welles. She said that because she was so new to the acting business, she was not aware that it was very rare to actually read with the star. What she also didn't realize was that this was also Welles's first film role. *Citizen Kane* proved to be a major moment in her life and the long-term success of the film would follow her for the rest of her days. She also starred in several television shows, including *Father of the Bride* and *Peyton Place*, two shows I remember watching like it was yesterday.

I respected Ruth from the first moment we met. I looked at her with great admiration because she appeared to have a very full life. She somehow balanced her obligations on *All My Children* with other endeavors, whether outside projects, charity events, social gatherings, or her family life. She inspired me because I knew what I wanted to do with my own life and here was Ruth, someone who was actually doing it all.

Ruth came to the set in the morning looking a lot like Katharine Hepburn. She wore no makeup, a jaunty newsboy cap, sneakers, and kind of slouchy pants. She looked supercool. She would rehearse, do the show, and dash out of the studio to catch a plane at least once a week to go wherever she had to be next, whether Los Angeles, Chicago, or Denver. Somehow she'd be back in the studio the next morning without missing a beat. She was always glamorous, even when she was dressed down.

Ruth was also quite the practical jokester. You never knew what she would come up with next, but you always knew it would be memorable. There was one absolutely unforgettable day in the 1970s that became a legend on the set for years to come. We used to get our notes from the director as a company. Notes are essentially professional criticism to help get the scene right when we went from rehearsal to tape. These sessions were referred to as "Red Chairs" because the crew would set up a slew of red director's chairs in the middle of the studio floor so everyone could meet and get their notes. Basically, we'd all assemble to be told how bad we were.

One day, at the end of dress rehearsal, Ruth was in one of the final scenes, which called for her to wear a long mink coat. When she finished rehearsal she sauntered over to a nearby set flanked by two cameramen, who were, oddly, wearing long jackets, too. All of a sudden Ruth and the cameramen dropped their coats and streaked . . . naked past us. That was Ruth! She was funny and elegant all bundled together.

I continued my education in acting during the first several years I was on *All My Children*. I had the privilege of studying with Harold Clurman, who has been heralded as "the Elder Statesman of the American Theater." He embodied the passion, the fervor, the inspiring voice of an entire generation. Harold Clurman was the cofounder of the famed Group Theatre along with Lee Strasberg and Cheryl Crawford. The Group Theatre of the 1930s was considered by many to be the most significant ensemble art theater in the history of American theater. It revolutionized not only the American theater but every facet of American acting, too. I took his midnight classes, which were well known and difficult to get into. They were primarily for actors who were working on Broadway. When the curtain came down at ten or eleven o'clock at night, those actors often dashed to Harold Clurman's midnight classes so they could continue developing and practicing their skills. Just being seen there was spectacular. Mr. Clurman would hold us spellbound as he told stories of all he had done throughout his marvelous career. It's not easy to hold the attention of a roomful of actors, especially after midnight, but Mr. Clurman could do it with ease. I think that says a lot about the man and the respect we all shared for his talent. The fact that I had studied with so many terrifically talented professors at Marymount opened a lot of doors for me, but it especially helped when it came to getting the audition for Mr. Clurman. My education separated me from the other new kids on the block and kept me from being perceived as just another hopeful wannabe with some talent. It was clear that I had credentials as an actress. All these factors gave me a definite leg up. I was very lucky to have the training and the opportunity to keep perfecting my craft after college and while I worked on *All My Children*. I continue to use the skills I learned in these early days all the time.

Adhering to the advice I received from Mr. Weyand about staying grounded in humanity, I kept things simple during those first years of working at *All My Children*. Helmut and I were living in an apartment in Forest Hills. I went to work in the morning with three dollars; I took the bus to work for one dollar, ate a yogurt for lunch, and returned home on the bus for another dollar, which still left me with change in my pocket. After we moved to Garden City, I continued taking the train and subway to work for the next ten years. Although I had never had any kind of incident using public transportation for all of those years, apparently there was a study released by the Metropolitan Transportation Association that rated the subway line I traveled as the most dangerous in New York City. I always dressed down on the train, wearing jeans and sweaters as my main staple. One day, some kids I often saw on the same train recognized me from the show. They came over to talk to me.

"You've got to get out of here," one of the kids said to me. I didn't understand what he was really saying.

"What do you mean?" I asked.

"We know who you are. We love Erica Kane. You look like a grown-up teenager. But you can't ride the train anymore. You'll get hurt." I thought it was very sweet that they were so concerned for my safety.

"I haven't had any problems. I am sure it'll be okay." I was trying to reassure them that I was fine.

"It's time. You can't keep taking the train." It was the early eighties. Things were happening in New York City that have since been cleaned up. I liked taking the train and enjoyed the people-watching, so I didn't stop.

A few weeks later, I bumped into that same group of kids again.

"We're really afraid for you. You've got to get out of here, okay?" For whatever reason, this time I was more convinced by their warning, so I stopped taking the train to work. I took cabs when I could, but eventually my schedule got to be so unpredictable that even that no longer worked. In all my years on the show, though, I have done my best to remain humble in my approach to work and life because I didn't want to find myself in that isolated bubble Mr. Weyand spoke of. I never wanted to lose touch with the small things in life that most of us take for granted along the way.

I made up my mind very early in my career to avoid the trappings of the business that were inviting for so many, yet scary to me. I didn't want to get labeled a prima donna or diva. Unfortunately, those two titles seem to come with the territory when you convincingly play both five days a week on TV. When those two words were first used in reference to me, I thought to myself, *I don't have temper tantrums. I'm not demanding. I certainly don't act like I'm entitled.* I couldn't understand where those blanket titles were coming from. It took me a while to figure out it really had nothing to do with me at all. Fortunately, *diva* has taken on a slightly different meaning than it used to have, and I can only say thank God for that. Today I think the word is more synonymous with glamour girl than it is with bitch. And *that*, I can live with.

CHAPTER 6

Being Erica Kane

A year and a half after *All My Children* made its debut in January 1970, *TV Guide* did a feature story on the character of Erica Kane and me. This was the first time a daytime actress was featured in the publication. That story was the very beginning of the unexpected social acceptance my character would continue to receive for more than four decades. Once Erica took off, fans of all ages wanted to know more about her. In the early days of the show, my mother frequently received phone calls from young girls and women pretending they went to school with me or knew me from somewhere. Once they engaged her in conversation, they'd begin asking all sorts of questions about how her "daughter" gets away with *everything*.

"I tried that on my boyfriend, and it didn't work," they'd say. "What did I do wrong?"

"My husband wants to leave me. What should I do to keep him?"

The calls and questions were constant. Unfortunately, my mother didn't write for the show, so she had no idea how to answer the callers. It got so bad that we eventually had to change her phone number and remove her name from the local listings. People often ask if I am similar to Erica as a person. Although we do have some common traits, the one thing we *really* share is our love of fashion, especially our taste in clothes and shoes. The biggest difference between us, though, is that what I would choose to wear to a cocktail party, Erica wears to go to Starbucks for her morning cup of coffee, to catch a plane, or to give her child a bath.

Playing Erica Kane is fun—and I mean *lots* of fun. She is the ultimate fantasy girl living the ultimate fantasy life. I have met so many young girls and women named Erica, who, yes, were given their names by mothers who wanted their daughters to be just like my character. In fact, I met one woman in Boston who told me that her daughters were named "Erica Kane" and "Susan Lucci"! As flattering as that may be, I must admit that I thought it might be a little difficult for the girls as they grow up . . . just a bit.

What has always made Erica so much fun for viewers is that you never know what she is going to do next, but you can guarantee there will be a man involved. Her whole existence is based on collecting men and searching for the love she never got after her father abandoned her and Mona. It is for these reasons that she became the kind of woman she is—a woman who absolutely needs a man in her life.

I'd like to think there's a little bit of Erica in most everyone. It may depend on what day of the week it is or how much sleep you got—or didn't get—how determined you are or whether there's a full moon, but I think everybody is capable of being like Erica. Of course, not everyone will be lucky enough to avoid paying the consequences that are clearly missing from the pages of my scripts (except for an occasional trip to prison or a short coma in Pine Valley Hospital).

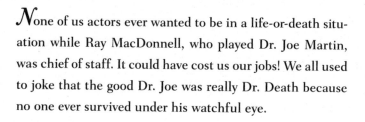

*N*one of us actors ever wanted to be in a life-or-death situation while Ray MacDonnell, who played Dr. Joe Martin, was chief of staff. It could have cost us our jobs! We all used to joke that the good Dr. Joe was really Dr. Death because no one ever survived under his watchful eye.

Erica is the girl every girl wishes she could be. She is passionate, tempestuous, and drives men wild. She gets away with saying and doing things that other women only wish they could say and do. Men want to either kiss her or kill her. Or both.

What makes Erica Kane such a one-of-a-kind character is that she is the result of a truly collaborative effort between Agnes Nixon and, as she so generously says, me. Agnes has told me many times over the years that Erica is as much mine as she is hers, but I must confess that I've always thought that Erica and I were extremely lucky to have been put in Agnes's very fine and caring hands from the very beginning. Day after day, what I see on the page takes my breath away. Agnes once described Erica's spirit as a phoenix rising from the ashes. She cannot be kept down for very long. With Agnes's writing and a tremendous amount of trust and camaraderie among the cast, I am able to continuously take risks as an actress and really spread my wings and fly. After forty-one years, that's a gift.

Playing Erica Kane has been a joy from the very start. She was so fresh and exciting, especially for the times. Everyone was taking notice—from the press to seasoned television executives. Shortly after I started on *All My Children*, I attended a network Christmas party where I was introduced to Fred Pierce, the president of ABC Television at the time. Fred was a television legend for his part in helping build the success of the ABC network. He introduced me to the gentleman standing next to him, who happened to be Fred Silverman, the head of ABC Entertainment. Fred Silverman was highly respected in the industry for his ability to turn shows into franchises by taking a hit program and spinning it off into others. Some of his shows were *Happy Days, Laverne & Shirley, Mary Tyler Moore,* and *All in the Family,* just to name a few. We chatted for a few minutes when Fred Pierce very graciously turned to me and said, "I think there should be an Erica Kane on every show. She is an amazing character!" Those were kind words, to say the least. And it turns out, they were visionary in a way, too, because Erica Kane was the first of "the most beloved and despised" women on television, the kind that you just love to hate. She was the model upon which so many great characters would later be based.

History has shown that great writing and creativity underlies the progression and evolution of our culture. Someone always paves the way for other greats. Agnes Nixon credits Shakespeare for writing everything there was to write. Without Madonna, could there really be a Lady Gaga? And without the Brat Pack, would the kids from *Jersey Shore* or *Laguna Beach* have been, well, just kids?

Agnes gave me the tools needed to turn Erica Kane into a full-blown diva—one whom I am very proud to be a part of creating and shaping. A diva that perhaps inspires others to follow. In 1981, ABC aired a new evening soap drama called *Dynasty.* At the beginning of its second season, the producers of that show introduced a character named Alexis Carrington, played by the wonderfully talented and beautiful Joan Collins. When the Alexis character took the show by storm, many people drew comparisons between her and Erica. And while they were both larger-than-life divas who loved men and who lacked certain scruples, there was one significant difference between them: Alexis was driven by a lust for power, whereas Erica has always been driven by her desire for love.

People often ask what I think made and has kept Erica and the show so appealing all of these years. For me, the answer is simple. Agnes Nixon's daytime dramas are interesting, real, thought provoking, inspiring, and original in so many ways. She is one of the only writers in the forum who successfully blended reality with scripted drama. Her well-thought-out and highly developed characters represent people we know, work with, want to be like, or love to hate. Agnes has always done her homework and has great humanity herself. She draws her characters with dignity and complexity, and keeps the storytelling character driven. Her writing is never preachy; it is simply portrayed. By writing this way, she gives her audience the opportunity to connect with the characters—and her diverse point of view—and encourages them to sort out their feelings about the various stories for themselves.

I remember coming home from classes at Marymount and watching episodes of *One Life to Live*. There was a powerful story line at the time, which dealt with drug addiction. Throughout those episodes, there was information scrolling across the bottom of the screen about how to contact the Odyssey House hotline if you needed a place to go for help. I had never seen anything like this on television; it blended reality with fantasy. I thought it was impressive and socially responsible to offer help to viewers who might be in need of counseling. It didn't surprise me that Agnes would continue to develop these types of informative story lines when I started working on *All My Children*. It was always important to her that she be free to write stories that informed audiences by shedding light on various human conditions. I think that mandate is a secret to good writing, whether in film, television, or plays.

There is a tremendous responsibility that comes with that type of writing, however. Agnes was always able to accomplish her goal of informing viewers in an entertaining way by telling a complicated story through the eyes of complicated characters. Agnes's style is to show that no one is lily white and no one is chalkboard black either.

Everyone has a point of view and Agnes makes sure to give the show's fans a well-rounded perspective. Because that point of view is always authentic to her characters, the stories are very rich and instructive and have resulted in some great people-watching—if only on TV. I think this is part of the secret of why there is so much ongoing interest in *All My Children* and Erica Kane. Is it chemistry? Alchemy? The magic Agnes creates with her writing? Looking back, I don't think everything can be reduced to a formula, and our show is a great example of that. I love that there is so much more to *All My Children* than some formula because otherwise there wouldn't be that magic. I am often asked about what makes our show work and why it has lasted so long. The truth is, I'm not sure I know the answer, because I don't believe there is one answer. It's a harmony of many elements, which come together and somehow just works.

While I believe that some people develop into perfectionists over time, I was definitely born one. My perfectionist behavior has never been about pleasing anyone else—it has always been about living up to the very high standards I set for myself. This extends as far back in my life as I can remember. My teachers always told me that they could correct my homework with a blindfold on because they knew I was going to turn in perfect work. I learned to read and memorize things at a very early age. At first, I learned by looking over my brother Jimmy's shoulder while he was reading his comic books; later, in first grade, I learned while reading in school, then by reading license plates on passing cars, telephone numbers, and ultimately through scripts.

Not long after being cast as Erica, I went on an audition to play Miranda in an off-Broadway production of *The Tempest* with an up-and-coming director. I thought I was totally prepared for the audition. When I got to the theater, the director was committed to working with me to help me nail the part. He was trying to get me to change my tack so I could bring something different to the role, something particular that he was looking for. He thought I had it in me, so he kept pushing and pushing, hoping that I would get it right. We worked on one monologue until he thought I was ready. But when it came time to do the audition, I didn't deliver. I didn't get the part.

I left the theater, hopped into a cab, and headed back to our home in Forest Hills. I spent the forty-five-minute ride (and subsequently much of my life) going over all of the mistakes I made, asking myself why I couldn't get to that place where the director wanted me to go. If I had been able to find it, I know the part would have been mine. I appreciated all of the time and work he put into my audition and felt I had let him down. I was so frustrated with myself because I had always been a very quick study, but this time, that just wasn't the case.

About two blocks away from the theater, something suddenly clicked and I knew what I needed to do. I wanted to tell the cab-driver to turn around and go back to the theater so I could try again, but I didn't have the courage or the nerve. I was too shy to go back and ask for a second chance. My shyness has always been the elephant in the room and has, at times, held me back from performing in my freest, most authentic way and from getting whatever it is I want. It's something I have always struggled with and is an area where I wish I could be more like Erica. To this very day, I regret my decision not to return because I know I could have landed that part and I would have loved to play Miranda.

Since I am a trained Method actress, I draw from my personal experiences and recollections, whether it's sense memory or the memory of an actual event. I always wanted to do well and enjoy the work I chose to do. There are many times when I wish I wasn't such a perfectionist because that drive often hampers me. I get so disappointed when I don't meet my self-imposed expectations. Not only do I feel like I've let other people down, I feel as if I've let myself down, too. Even now, I sometimes think that maybe I'm kidding myself—that I'm not a very good actress and that what I've really been is lucky all these years. I've been told I'm talented since I was a little girl, but I still question myself all of the time.

Can I do this?

Am I kidding myself?

Maybe I can't . . . These are just some of the thoughts that still sometimes go through my head. But then I remember to breathe, reassess, and let those thoughts go. I remind myself that I've been well trained and have learned my craft from the very best in the business, so I try to hold on to this whenever those negative thoughts creep into my head. I have a tremendous amount of pride in my work because I love acting, and I especially love playing Erica Kane.

Thankfully, Erica was perfectly written from the very beginning, so understanding her and matching her drive to have and be the very best, and not to settle for anything less, were traits that were already a part of who I am to my core. Soap opera scripts are brand-new, full-length, ninety-plus-page plays you get to act out five days a week. It's the blessing and the curse of the medium. We get fresh material every day, but that is *a lot* of material to memorize, especially if you're in many scenes a day. Still, memorization is only half the battle. Once you've got the words down, you must bring them to life.

For a while I didn't realize that Erica had special mannerisms until my daughter, Liza, was around the age of two or three and she sashayed into my bedroom one day, flipped her hair from side to side, and said, "Like you, Mommy!" I had to laugh because, like Mr. Weyand did back in class at Marymount, my toddler child had perfectly captured Erica's (or was it my?) head toss. This was definitely a sign that acting was in Liza's future, too.

A good actress will bring slight but relevant gestures to her characters, which define who she is without ever saying a word. Although my character has evolved over the years, she has always been excitable and full of expression. Yes, Erica has always been known for her fiery temper and her irresistible diva behavior. By comparison, it takes a lot to rile me up, but very early in my career, my feistier side had a tendency to rear its head from time to time, too. I have never been one to lose my cool at work, but there was a moment when I was around twenty-four years old that has become something of a legend on the set of *All My Children*.

There was a fantastically talented director working on the show at the time by the name of Henry Kaplan. When he first came to the show, I had never met another human being quite like him. He was downright frightening to me. He used a wand while directing, like he was conducting an orchestra instead of working with actors.

Henry was a man who was very comfortable in his own skin. His sense of humor was incredibly biting. He wasn't especially careful with the words he used or how his message was being conveyed. He was notorious for saying something very jarring to actors moments before they were set to do a scene.

"You have no timing!"

"You're as funny as a fish!"

These were not words of encouragement, especially to a young actress just starting out. His comments were meant to cut, rattle, and disarm—at least that's how I saw things from my very naive and green perspective. I didn't understand that Henry was just being sarcastic. I took his statements very seriously, so much so that after a couple of weeks of his poking, I began to feel physically sick. I was tied up in knots over the things he was saying to me.

The final straw came during a very emotional scene where Erica and her mother have a big fight. Erica had packed her bags and was leaving. At the end of the scene, I was supposed to pick up my suitcases, walk to the front door, open it, turn, and then give a long final look to Mona before walking out and slamming the door behind me. This was not a complicated scene. However, during the first rehearsal, the suitcases that were placed on the set for me were hard-shelled. They were so heavy that I could barely pick them up and accomplish what I was supposed to do.

I don't know how it is on other shows, but on *All My Children*, the actors are responsible for checking their props. It was obvious they weren't working for me, so I spoke to the head of the prop department to ask if he had any soft-sided suitcases I could use instead. I figured those would be easier and lighter to carry. He assured me that it wouldn't be a problem to swap the cases. When we did our final dress rehearsal, the soft cases weren't that much lighter, but they were better and easier to handle than the hard cases. I was feeling okay about the scene. I knew it wasn't perfectly smooth, but it was a lot better than the last time we'd run through it.

Just before we began taping, the director called us to "Red Chairs" so we could get our notes. There was no time for lunch that day, so I brought a cup of yogurt with me to eat while we sat and listened to Henry. The entire company was there as Henry proceeded to yell at me. He called me the most unprofessional actress he had ever encountered.

"You have no business being an actress. How dare you go behind my back and speak to the prop department about changing suitcases. How dare you do that scene with soft suitcases!" Henry was in a rage. Even if I wanted to explain myself, he never stopped yelling long enough for me to get a word in edgewise.

I was seeing red because he wouldn't let me speak. I remember shaking on the inside while furiously stirring my yogurt. I was frustrated as he continued to cut me down.

"You will use the hard suitcases, got it?" he commanded.

I kept stirring and stirring until I'd finally heard enough. I was afraid that if I stayed, I'd throw my yogurt right at Henry, so I got up and walked away. I had a scene to play and needed a few minutes to compose myself. I left the studio floor and went into the hallway. I was infuriated. Perhaps I let my own insecurities get in the way— perhaps I was being hypersensitive, but I was really upset. Still, I was young and too new to the show to think I could tell anyone how I felt. I figured I just had to get over it, go out there, and do my best.

I stomped down the hallway until I came across an empty control room. I stood in the dimly lit cubicle, still stirring and stirring until, on impulse, I suddenly threw my yogurt against a wall of television monitors. At that very moment, Felicia, our associate producer, came into the room. I wasn't known for being a troublemaker on the set, so she knew something was terribly wrong.

"Susan, what is it?" she asked

I told her what had happened. I didn't like being in that position, but what else could I do? There I was standing in a room with yogurt dripping down the walls—it was raspberry.

"Don't worry about this, Susan. Go to your dressing room. I will take care of *everything*."

I was very grateful for her kindness and understanding. I walked across the hall to my dressing room, where I suddenly realized after looking in a mirror what she meant by "everything." I had been wearing my costume—a brown velvet jacket—the back of which was covered in yogurt. Even my hair was doused in it from the windup to my throw. I was desperately trying to wipe the mess from the jacket when Fra walked into our dressing room.

"Oh, honey. What happened?" She had been on the floor getting her notes, too, but I don't think she knew how upset I was after receiving mine. So I told her what I was feeling.

"Oh, dear. Don't take Henry's words to heart. That's his sense of humor. He's just pushing your buttons." Fra always had an aura of calm that I found comforting.

I hadn't realized Henry was just being, well, Henry. I felt so embarrassed for having blown up like that. The wardrobe department, being the miracle workers that they are, salvaged the jacket in ten minutes' time. Henry was none the wiser about what had happened as I made my way onto the set to do my scene. When I got there, I noticed that the soft suitcases had been left for me to use. Sure enough, and just like Fra said, he was only pushing my buttons.

A couple of days later, Henry knocked on my dressing room door. "Do you have a minute?" he asked.

"Sure, come on in." I was nervous.

"I heard what happened, Susan. I want you to know that I never meant to hurt your feelings." I thought it was very nice of Henry to stop by and offer an explanation. He most certainly did not have to do it. It was very much appreciated, though. It turned out that Henry and I forged a wonderful relationship after that incident. Not only was he a tremendously talented director, he became a good friend. He continued to go after me for many years, but now I knew where he was coming from. Although I hadn't noticed it before my blowup, Henry had a gleam in his eye that let you know he was being a little bit of a devil whenever he was trying to get a rise from you.

When I was pregnant with my daughter, Liza, he must have overheard me talking about finding an antique christening gown for the baby. We didn't have a special gown in our family, but I really wanted one. A few days later, Henry, who also happened to own an antiques shop, called me to say he had found the perfect gown for my baby. I will never forget working with Henry, but more important than that, I will always treasure our friendship.

I only had one other meltdown on the set after that incident. This second event involved a wooden hairbrush and a mirror. I don't recall what happened, but I do remember how thankful I was that the industrial-strength mirror didn't shatter. If it had, there would have been glass *everywhere* and the fallout would likely have been much worse than it was. After that outburst, I realized there is no real payoff to these types of meltdowns. There is no place for them on the set or in life. We work in pretty tight quarters, so if someone is acting like a full-blown diva, it affects everyone. I have learned it is far better to take a giant step back and breathe before reacting. If you do, I assure you, things won't seem so bad when you finally calm down. Of course, it is only fair to point out that as Erica Kane, I do have lots and lots of opportunities to use my emotions and get them out in a safe and effective way. You can bet there have been plenty of times when I've channeled personal frustration into a scene where Erica can say and do all of the things I'd sometimes like to as Susan Lucci. There's an expression in acting—"Use it!"—which means use your emotion in the scene you're about to do—if you can. That outlet is a great perk of the job. The work is demanding enough. Keep the drama on the stage.

CHAPTER 7

Blended Lives

I was told early on that many writers prefer not to have any interaction with the actors they are writing for. They would rather watch the nuances that the actors bring to the parts they are playing in the context of the show. Apparently, how we interpret their words further feeds and inspires what they write. I had been told that Agnes Nixon preferred this kind of distance. She liked to create a character and then see what each actor brought to the part. I understood the process and respected it.

The first time I ever spent one-on-one time with Agnes outside of the studio was during a train ride we took together to an event in Princeton, New Jersey. I met her on the train and sat next to her for the entire ride down from New York. Over the course of our trip, Agnes turned to me and asked if I believed in spirits and the Ouija board. I told her my only experience with the Ouija board had been at slumber parties with friends when I was a little girl. At the time I felt like we were the ones who manipulated the pointer to move around the board. Agnes said she had been skeptical, too, but now totally believed in it. She shared a story with me about going to a party with some friends who decided they wanted to use the Ouija board after dinner. One of the men at the party was a complete skeptic. He refused to sit at the table, choosing instead to watch the action from behind everyone else. All of a sudden the pointer went haywire, spelling out what appeared to be gibberish. Agnes said she was disappointed because she wanted to prove to the man that the Ouija was real.

"There must be some type of problem here," she said.

"No! Wait!" the skeptical man cried out. "That's not gibberish. It's spelling out the name my father called me in Lithuanian."

After that, the man was a complete believer.

When we finished the event in Princeton, Agnes invited me to join her for a late lunch at her home in a beautiful suburb of Philadelphia. Her house was a beautiful historic home that used to be a stop on a Pony Express route. It was very much a family home. It was warm, elegant, and inviting all at once. I watched Agnes interact with her four children and realized she wasn't just a businesswoman. She was a mother, too. She created a lovely environment for her children to grow up in, inspiring me to want one day to do the very same thing. Although Helmut and I did not have any children, we were definitely planning on starting a family.

After lunch, Agnes asked me if I would like to work the Ouija board with her.

"Sure," I replied. After hearing her earlier story, I was curious to see what might happen.

"Do you have any questions?" Agnes asked.

"Yes. When will I have a baby?" The answer came back, *Sometime in the distance.* I was a little disappointed because at the time, I was secretly hoping I might already be pregnant.

"Will it be a boy or a girl?" The answer came back, *A girl.*

"What month will she be born?" The answer came back, *February.*

Honestly, I didn't know what to think about the experience. I've never forgotten that day, though, because it was the first time

I realized just how "in touch" Agnes Nixon really is to things and how "in tune" she is to people. Agnes is quite spiritual and deeply intuitive. I've come to believe that there was never a "coincidence" to those story lines on the show that mirrored events in my personal life. Although I'd rarely shared intimate information with Agnes before she wrote these scripts, she somehow always knew exactly what was happening with me.

There have been a number of story lines on the show over the years that blurred the lines between Erica's reality and my own. Although the timing didn't always correspond, the experiences often did. Sure, there were also lots of stories revolving around events that were the complete opposite of events in my life, too, but those were the stories that gave me even more of an opportunity to push myself and grow as an actress because I had to dig deeper to find the right responses.

Although Erica eventually turned into an independent and powerful businesswoman who was much more capable than she ever thought she could be, she surely didn't start off that way. She was left with a large gaping hole in her heart after her father abandoned her at such a tender age. So many young girls feel that type of early loss and then grow up feeling some sort of responsibility for their abandonment, as if they somehow weren't lovable enough to keep their father home. Erica spent years blaming her mother, lashing out at her for not stopping her father from leaving. Deep down, she grew up believing that she herself was the real reason he left. Although her father lavished expensive gifts, clothes, and cars on her, he never spent *time* with her. He never came just to see her. And, he didn't want Erica to come visit him either. It wasn't until Erica's fourteenth birthday, after much begging and pleading, that he finally decided to invite her to Hollywood so they could celebrate her birthday together—or so she thought. Her father supposedly sent the invitation because he thought Erica might enjoy meeting some of the famous movie stars he worked with and knew. It turned out, however, that his career wasn't quite what it seemed. He was trying to lure a popular movie star to commit to his next project. He also knew this actor was a known pedophile.

Erica's birthday came with a cake, fourteen candles, and hours alone in the house with the actor. Her monster of a father thought that if this man could score with her, he would likely agree to star in his project. Erica wound up being raped and became pregnant. Although Erica had the baby—a little girl—her mother, Mona, decided she should give it up for adoption. Erica was still a child herself and was incapable of raising a baby without it impacting her life in unimaginable ways. So she agreed to relinquish the baby without ever seeing her after she was born. Many years later that daughter would be brought back to the show and introduced as a new character, Kendall. Kendall is played by the beautiful Alicia Minshew. Alicia has brought so much to the part and is an absolute joy to work with every day.

Agnes Nixon is a wonderful storyteller who isn't afraid to take risks. Although the rape story wasn't revealed on the show for many years, it was quite controversial when it did air. This type of conflict was typical of the subjects Agnes was willing to tackle. She made it a point to bring complicated issues to the forefront, which was very cutting edge for the times. When Agnes is involved in the writing of a show, the story feels so natural and real.

Before *All My Children* made its debut, no daytime show had ever dealt with the Vietnam War in depth. Agnes chose to write about Vietnam at the height of the war, making it every bit as controversial on the show as it was in our country. Agnes perfectly chronicled how the town of Pine Valley, like the rest of the country, was divided between those who supported the U.S. position and those who protested it.

When Agnes decided to bring the war into *All My Children*, she did it with dignity and grace. She made sure that all the people filling out the humanity in those scenes—whether they were extras

or the "underfives" (meaning actors who had less than five lines)—
spoke Vietnamese so there was authenticity for the viewer at home.
Whenever Agnes took on a controversial topic, it wasn't done for
self-aggrandizement or superfluous reasons. It was done because
these topics were organic to the show and because Agnes feels a
deep responsibility to share and spread her knowledge and awareness to others. She included these modern-day issues and concerns
in order to draw in a larger audience but also to speak to that broader
audience about what issues she thought were relevant to their lives.

One of the most talked-about stories in our show's history unfolded in 1973 when Agnes made the decision to have Erica get an
abortion. I never realized how big that story would become. I knew
we would take some flak from people who didn't agree with that
point of view, but I hadn't understood just how important it was
while we were doing it. My sole focus was to play the scenes strictly
from my character's perspective. In the thick of things, and from
Erica's point of view, it all felt so right to me.

Agnes started writing the story on the day after *Roe v. Wade* was
decided. The Supreme Court had just declared that women had the
constitutional right to choose, which became front-page news all
over the country. When it aired, the story made television history
because it was the first *legal* abortion ever portrayed on television.
The television show *Maude* aired a controversial abortion episode in
November 1972—two months before the passing of *Roe v. Wade*—
but Maude's choice was to have an illegal abortion, whereas Erica
was free to make the decision without breaking any laws.

The story began as Erica discovered she was pregnant while
married to her first husband, Dr. Jeff Martin, played by Charlie
Frank. Charlie was very clean-cut and had the bluest eyes I had ever
seen. He very much fit the part of Jeff Martin, a young doctor in the
making. Jeff was the older brother of Erica's high school rival, Tara
Martin, and Erica wanted to marry him. She was somehow able to
convince Jeff to leave Stanford, where he was studying, and finish

his medical education at Pine Valley University. Erica was absolutely determined to marry him. She saw him as a means of escape from her mother's house and from her horribly boring existence in Pine Valley. She believed that Jeff was going to become a great doctor and thought that when she became "the doctor's wife," other people would have to accept her as *important*, too—a recognition she very much longed for. Even though Erica was just sixteen, she and Jeff eloped across state lines in a snowstorm so they could get married without anyone interfering with their plan.

Their wedding scene took place in the middle of a faux blizzard. This was my first encounter with fake snow. I wore a beautiful coat and matching fur hat that looked like something we borrowed from *Dr. Zhivago*. The "snow" was made from what appeared to be tiny plastic shavings. Although it stuck to my hair, ears, and eyes like real snow, it didn't melt.

News of Erica and Jeff's wedding was very upsetting to both of their families. Erica's mother, Mona, thought Jeff was a very solid young man, though she had tremendous apprehensions about her daughter being married at such a young age. Jeff's parents, Dr. Joe Martin and his wife, Ruth, had many reservations about their son's decision to marry Erica, too. The Martins were one of the most established families in Pine Valley. They were well liked and highly respected, as Joe Martin was the chief of staff at Pine Valley Hospital. Joe Martin was an elegant and sensible man who was played with such finesse by Ray MacDonnell.

On the set, Ray had a mischievous glint in his eyes at all times. He was very funny and made it nearly impossible for actors to look him in the eyes because he was always ready with a joke to make you double over with laughter. Ruth was played by Mary Fickett, who was one of the original stars of the show. Mary was always very kind and down-to-earth, and quite welcoming of me as a young actress just starting out. Grandma Kate Martin, played by Kay Campbell, was also lovely and dear. Grandma Kate was always baking and offering Erica cookies, pie, and such. In many ways, she reminded me of my nana.

The Martins intimidated Erica because they represented everything she longed for in a family but didn't have. She never expected to fit in with them because they were all so well educated and refined and she was street-smart and self-taught by comparison. Although they reluctantly accepted her into their family, it didn't take long for everyone to see through Erica and realize her ulterior motives, which were to live a better life.

Jeff didn't have a lot of money since he was still working as a resident in the hospital. He worked long hours for very little pay. Erica was terribly unhappy in the small, cramped apartment they lived in. She had fantasized that her life would be far more idyllic and comfortable than it had turned out to be. Soon after the marriage, Erica realized that she was even more uncomfortable in her new life than she'd been at home with her mom. Bored and with too much time on her hands, she was growing restless and wanted something more out of life than being a stay-at-home wife. She found the perfect job working at Anne Tyler's boutique as a clothes buyer, which allowed her to make several trips to New York, where she also started to do some modeling. Her new career set Erica on a path that would open up her world in ways she never imagined.

Although Erica had been taking birth control pills throughout her marriage to Jeff, she wasn't taking them regularly, which was a risky thing to do. Jeff and Erica had talked about wanting someday to have children, but when she found out she was pregnant, she feared the baby would interfere with her thriving new career. Erica began justifying reasons not to keep the baby.

1. They didn't have a lot of money, so having a baby wasn't a terribly responsible decision.
2. Jeff was busy at the hospital and away from home most of the time.

3. She was on the verge of breaking through as a top fashion model.
4. She wasn't emotionally prepared to give a baby the love and attention it would require.

After she listed her reasons, the only conclusion she could possibly come to was that she had to have an abortion. Erica tried to keep her decision from her husband and his family because she knew they wouldn't understand or support her choice. When she got to the abortion clinic, however, the doctor informed her that she would need her husband's consent in writing before he would perform the procedure. Erica used her charm and skills of persuasion to convince the doctor that her husband was very busy at the hospital and couldn't be reached. She assured the doctor that they had discussed all of their options and had agreed that terminating the pregnancy was the best choice for them. Despite her pleas, the doctor insisted on having Jeff's signature before performing the procedure. Knowing she would never get Jeff's consent, Erica forged his name, thinking he would never discover the truth.

A few days after this, she developed an infection. She tried to ignore it for as long as she could but wasn't able to hide her pain. She eventually collapsed and was hospitalized. At first, Jeff believed her illness was due to overworking, but then his father, Dr. Joe Martin, discovered that Erica's infection had been caused by an abortion. Jeff was surprised to discover that his wife had been pregnant and even more shocked by what she had done. When Erica was well enough, he confronted her. While she insisted she'd had the abortion in order to save their marriage, Jeff knew the truth. She had done it for herself and for her career.

Erica felt abandoned by everybody, as no one took her side, not even her mother. Even though Mona was angry about Erica's decision to terminate her pregnancy, she also knew that much like the first time Erica became pregnant, she was still too much of a child herself to take care of a baby. Mona was able to talk to Jeff about Erica's logic, even if she didn't agree with it and convinced him to give her daughter a second chance.

Erica's decision to terminate her pregnancy was extremely controversial. The country was very divided on the issue of abortion and our show was the first to openly tackle the topic, which brought about a lot of discussion. Pro-lifers and Pro-choicers both criticized the story line. As someone who was a part of it all, I had my share of challenges, and the biggest one was that I was actually pregnant when the story began to unfold. I didn't tell anyone because it was too early to share the good news. I wanted to wait until I was past the first trimester.

Early in my fourth month, Helmut and I decided to take a vacation to the Bahamas for a few days. When we arrived, I felt like I might be coming down with the flu. My whole body ached and I was gradually developing a lot of pain in my abdomen. Unable to do much of anything, I encouraged Helmut to play a round of golf while I rested.

By the time he returned to the hotel, I was doubled over in pain and the only place I wanted to be was lying on the cold tiles of the bathroom floor. Helmut could see that I had to get to a doctor, and fast. He called the front desk to ask for the address of the nearest emergency room. They sent us to a private hospital in Nassau that wasn't too far from the hotel. I remember the outside of the building was pink stucco and the bars of soap in the facility came from the various hotels on the island.

It was obvious that I was having a miscarriage. I was in terrible pain, but I didn't want to show it while we sat in the waiting room. I did my best to put on a brave front, but Helmut and I both knew what was happening. We didn't need to talk about it. The doctors immediately performed a D&C, which was a very uncomfortable procedure. The worst pain, however, was in my shattered heart because I had been very much looking forward to becoming a mother.

We caught the next flight back to New York, where there was a terrible ice storm pounding the metropolitan area. As the plane began its approach into JFK, it made a sudden and unexpectedly sharp drop. I had never experienced anything like that before. When it happened, I was walking back to my seat from the bathroom. As the plane quickly dipped, my head hit the ceiling and I was thrown to the ground. I remember thinking that if I hadn't had a miscarriage in Nassau, I most likely would have had one on the plane from the impact of that fall. When I made it back to my seat, I noticed a pretty flight attendant sitting next to my husband. The turbulence was so bad that she'd grabbed the first available seat— next to Helmut. I took one look at her and thought, *If this plane is going down, I'm the one who's going down with Helmut—get out of my seat!* There wasn't an ounce of Erica in that thought—*that* was all me!

Thankfully, we landed safely. My mother met us at the airport to help in any way she could. A few days later, I saw my personal physician, who told me the pregnancy had been fine, but he thought I wasn't getting enough folic acid in my diet, which may have caused the miscarriage. Of course, today most pregnant women take a folic-acid supplement along with prenatal vitamins, but back then, we didn't have this knowledge. I had no way of knowing that I could have prevented the loss.

In an ironic twist, after leaving my doctor's office, Helmut and I were walking down Fifth Avenue in New York City when a woman approached us. She looked at me and then turned to Helmut and said, "What's the matter with you? This woman just had an abortion! She should be back in the hospital, she's sick!" Of course, she had no idea what we had actually just been through. She was referring to Erica and the story she obviously was watching unfold on the show.

I felt a great sense of loss for our unborn child that seemed to linger for months. At home, Helmut and I privately mourned, while

I did the best I could at work each day, shooting the emotionally charged scenes surrounding Erica's abortion.

I never shared the details of my miscarriage with anyone on the set, including Agnes. I made a decision very early in my career to leave personal baggage at home and to use that emotion only when it was essential to my work. I always closely guarded the private details of my life, which meant no one ever really knew what was happening behind my closed doors.

I have been asked many times in interviews and by fans if I had a problem doing the abortion story line. I didn't. First and foremost, when I read the script, I really believed that those words, in the context of the character of Erica Kane, were exactly right. I never thought about how *I* felt—only about whether or not the story was right for Erica. Still, there were many times after the story aired that I remember going places where people stared at me in judgment.

"There goes that Erica Kane! Imagine, she had an abortion!" The tsk-tsks were audible everywhere. The ongoing comments followed me from the sidewalks of Manhattan to elevators in office buildings. I wasn't even safe in church. I remember going to confession one day in my hometown. I was seated in the pews saying my penance and there were people down the row and in the pew in front of me. As I continued, they were whispering loud enough for me to hear.

"Oh my God!"

"Can you believe she is praying?"

"I'm disgusted."

I wanted to remind those women that *I* didn't have an abortion— my fictitious character did. They weren't judging the character I play—they were judging me, the actress. I always thought there was no safer place to be oneself than in church. Their judgmental comments didn't stop me from going, but they didn't make it easy either.

Interestingly, during the writing of this book, Agnes told me that at the time there was an additional controversy surrounding this story line that I knew nothing about. Many fans thought Erica was the wrong character to have the abortion because she was already the bad girl in town. It wasn't all that far-fetched for her to have made such a decision. Thousands of people wrote in saying that they thought it made more sense for Nurse Mary Kinnecott, the resident good girl who had grown close to Jeff when Erica had deceived him, to be faced with such a big decision. This angle certainly would have been very compelling, but it didn't end up playing out that way. I was glad to have had the opportunity to be a part of this landmark story line, as it set a precedent for many more important stories to come, all of which I would gratefully and fearlessly take on and make my own.

Aside from the abortion and miscarriage stories, there were other story lines over the years that mirrored, to some degree, and even paralleled things that happened in my life. For example, Agnes didn't know that I had gone through a windshield at the age of nineteen when she decided that Erica would suffer a terrible disfiguring accident. She was bandaged similarly to how I was bandaged during my many months of recovery. My experience served me well, because once again, I could draw upon very personal events and bring those emotions to the character.

I was told very early in my training that the biggest secret to Method acting was that you can't remember an emotion per se, but you can remember the circumstances surrounding all of the things that happen in your life. This can include songs, smells, places, words—anything the mind retains—because those details are what help bring the memories and emotions flooding back. Look, life happens, so we may as well place those events, good and bad, somewhere that eventually helps us get through whatever else life brings in the future. This is just as good advice for an aspiring actor as it is for the rest of us who like to live life to its fullest and greatest potential every day.

*E*rica got to do so many fun things over the years. Since many were done in real time, I had the chance to experience these amazing events, too. When Erica landed her talk show, *New Beginnings*, for instance, she learned to pitch a baseball in Yankee Stadium and shoot hoops with the New York Knicks, all while wearing high heels! She rang the opening bell at the NASDAQ, which was simulcast on their giant electronic billboard in Times Square, and was hoisted on the shoulders of the players on the New Orleans Saints, including Archie Manning, after shooting a commercial in the Superdome for her Enchantment cosmetics line.

CHAPTER 8

From *All My Children* to All of *My* Children

It was mid-1974 when I joyfully discovered that I was once again pregnant. This time I wanted to let the producers of *All My Children* know as soon as possible so I could be extra cautious with my and the baby's health. I wasn't sure how they would take the news. But before I could phone the proper people, I received a call from Agnes. She told me she was getting ready to write a story for Erica in which Erica suffers a miscarriage after becoming pregnant with her soon-to-be second husband, Phil Brent.

I was stunned when Agnes delivered this news. She didn't know about my actual miscarriage and had just been made aware that I was newly pregnant, so naturally she was concerned about how this story line might impact my emotional state. I was very touched by her thoughtfulness but assured her I could do it. At first, I didn't think I would have any issues playing this story line. I had great faith and respect for Agnes's work. I knew she would examine some of the same emotions I had gone through, and thought maybe it would speak to other women who have suffered a miscarriage. In many ways I was the best person to take on this challenge. I also trusted in my skill as an actress to compartmentalize Erica's emotions from my own enough to do the job and still see my new pregnancy through.

My original audition scene for the role of Erica revolved around the very handsome and desirable Phil Brent coming to Erica's house to tutor her in math. Erica didn't care the least bit about math, but she definitely had eyes for Phil, who was dating Tara Martin, Erica's nemesis throughout high school. The rivalry between Erica and Tara went on for years. In fact, it wasn't until Karen Lynn Gorney, the actress who played Tara, left the show that Erica and Phil were finally free to begin dating.

Phil was originally played by Richard Hatch. In the early days, Phil and Tara were the show's fabulous young ingenue couple. When Karen left *All My Children*, Richard was written out of the show by sending his character off to Vietnam to fight in the war. When Phil returned from Vietnam in 1973, he came back to Pine Valley as a severely injured soldier. His whole head and face were bandaged so no one could see what he looked like. Of course, when his bandages were removed, it was evident that Phil was being played by a new actor, Nick Benedict.

This Phil looked very different from the original. He was taller yet still very handsome. It would have been a challenge for any actor to replace Richard Hatch, as he had made quite an impression as the originator of the part. Somehow, though, Nick was able to fill those shoes and get audiences to accept him as the new Phil. That was not an easy task, but he accomplished it with ease and loads of talent. Nick was a sweetheart to work with and very kindhearted. In the end, I think Erica married Phil because she saw him as the "one who got away." Unfortunately, he was more of a trophy for Erica than a husband.

In the beginning, Phil didn't take the relationship quite as seriously as Erica did. He was flattered by her attention and was very attracted to her, but he wasn't in love with her. As for Erica, she was merely on a never-ending quest to collect men. When Erica realized that she and Phil weren't really meant to be, she was pregnant with his child. Despite her condition, she ended the affair without telling Phil about the baby. She contemplated another abortion, thinking that was the only sensible choice for her. But before she could terminate the pregnancy, Phil somehow discovered that she was carrying his baby. Much to her surprise, he was ecstatic over the good news, so much so that instead of leaving, he convinced Erica to marry him.

Ever in search of true love and a perfect family life, Erica got swept up in the fantasy of what their life together could be. Sadly, Phil seemed to want Erica to be something she couldn't be—domestic and in the house at all times—so their happiness didn't last very long. Shortly after their wedding, Erica suffered a miscarriage. She became so distraught by her loss that she had a nervous breakdown. Phil committed Erica to a mental hospital so she could properly heal from her loss and broken heart.

Although Erica lost her baby early on in her pregnancy, I continued to grow with every passing month of mine. I gained thirty-three pounds, which isn't a lot for most women, but on my nearly five-foot-two-inch frame, it was significant. With this particular pregnancy, the additional weight was distributed all around my body, which made covering up my growing belly, bottom, and hips on the show a real challenge. The director did whatever he could to have me sitting in bed during my shots. He cleverly cut out a hole in the bottom of the mattress so my rear end could rest inside, making my tummy look flat. The prop department strategically placed pillows all around me under the covers to even out the whole look. They often gave me a half-eaten box of chocolates (the crew was happy to help me out with that!) to make it look like Erica was "stuffing" her emotions and therefore gaining a little weight. When I wasn't in bed, I was shot holding an oversize clutch purse, and then an open menu, and finally seated behind a chair and wherever else they could creatively hide my expanding profile.

Clearly, I had a lot of personal experience to draw on for the miscarriage story line. As we got deeper into the plot, things became more emotionally demanding. I instinctively put up a protective wall around my baby and was willing to go only just so far with the emotions because my unborn baby was my priority. I tried my best to do a good job, but only in ways that I was sure wouldn't hurt the baby.

When I was pregnant with my firstborn child, my father came to talk to me about something very serious. It was a hot summer day, so we decided to sit outside, but in the shade.

"Maybe it's time to settle down, Susan," he said.

The words *settle down* have always made me cringe a little, especially since I knew my father was speaking about giving up my career. He made it clear that although he supported me in my desire to be a professional actress, his preference was for me to stay home and have lots of babies. If he had his way, I would have gotten married and filled up the pews in church with children. He made no secret about those wishes. I often told my father that acting was all I had wanted to do for as long as I could remember. All of those times I sang, danced, and made up stories as a little girl and acted out all of the parts, I was being who I was right down to my toes.

My father and I talked for a while before I said to him, "What if this baby is a little girl, Daddy?" I chose not to know the gender of my unborn child, so I had no idea if I was carrying a boy or a girl when I said that. "Am I going to tell her to dream her dreams but only until she's twenty-five?" I was hurt and confused by my father's wishes because they were so inconsistent with my own. My dreams were to have it *all.* I didn't want to give up my career to have children and I didn't want to give up having children for my career. That is my both/and philosophy in a nutshell. And although my children would always be my priority without question, I always felt I would be able to do both.

Regardless of how my father felt, I chose to follow my dreams, something I would not have been able to do without all the love, care, and encouragement I received from my parents as a little girl. Their love gave me the spirit to go ahead and pursue my dreams even if they weren't their dreams for me, too.

Thankfully, all of my efforts to preserve and safeguard this pregnancy paid off. After twenty-two hours of labor, it was decided I'd have to have an emergency C-section because the umbilical cord was wrapped around my baby's neck. I gave birth to my beautiful daughter, Liza, in February 1975. Suddenly that day with Agnes and her Ouija board made complete sense to me. I had a baby girl in February, just as it had predicted.

Before we go any further, since I have never really spoken about my children in public, I ask you to please indulge me while I shout my true feelings about both of my kids from the rooftops. I am so proud of them, and while I've always let each of them know how I really feel with abundant—maybe even overabundant—hugs and kisses and words of praise, so that they would always know how much I love and treasure them, this is the first time I am being so overt outside of our circle of family and close friends. While I know Liza and Andreas will probably cringe when they read this, what's a mother to do?

Becoming a mother was the most wonderful gift I have ever received. I had no idea what an impact this would have on me. Only a few days before I went into labor, I sat on the sofa at our home in Garden City and told my husband with a straight face that the baby was not going to change our lives. We were still going to go skiing, travel to Europe, and see our friends.

After Liza was born, I did a complete about-face—and I mean a *complete* about-face. The moment I laid eyes on that baby, I instantly became a different person. I just wanted to be with her morning, noon, and night. I ran to the mailbox to get all of the invitations to events and parties before Helmut could see them so we wouldn't have to attend any of them. It took me three months to finally agree to leave the house without her.

Before Liza was born, I hired a wonderful baby nurse named Irma, who came to stay with us for three weeks to help with the baby when we brought her home. Since I delivered Liza via a C-section, I needed time to recuperate. Irma had come extremely highly recommended. I had friends who planned their pregnancies around her availability, so I felt very lucky to have her. Irma's calling in life was to take care of newborns and help their parents make the transition with ease. I was the youngest child in my family and I never spent any time working as a babysitter growing up, so I had very little experience with infants.

Irma was very nice, extremely experienced, spoke fluent German, and was a tremendous help in so many ways. When I came home from the hospital, she had set up a small table and chairs in our bedroom so Helmut and I could have dinner together after he got home from work without my having to walk up and down the stairs. She thought of every last detail to make my recovery easier and my first few days and weeks at home comfortable.

At the time Helmut was a three- to four-pack-a-day cigarette smoker. He did everything with a cigarette in one hand or held between his two front teeth. He skied with a cigarette, played tennis with one, and even swung his golf club while smoking. Of course, this was at a time before our collective consciousness about the dangers of tobacco and smoking was raised. Still, he was a heavy smoker and had never been able to successfully give up the habit.

Helmut came home from work each night ready to share a meal and catch up on each other's day. At the end of dinner, the routine was for Irma to bring Liza into our bedroom so we could spend some quality time with her together as a family. Liza was so small that Helmut could easily hold her in one of his hands. He'd stare into her eyes while making silly adorable sounds and faces to amuse her. Irma cleared our dishes as Helmut did what he always did after a meal—he lit up a cigarette.

The first time Irma saw him do this, she took one look at my husband, carried Liza back to her room, and then came back and announced, "Mr. Huber. If I ever see you smoke in this house again while I'm here taking care of this baby, I'm leaving!" Helmut got her message loud and clear. He realized she was right and quit cold turkey.

Irma was also a wonderful cook and baker. She, too, reminded me of my nana in that way, which was a lovely feeling to have during this very happy time. Since I was nursing, Irma told me that I needed to drink a beer or a vanilla bean milk shake every day because both provide all of the nutrients a baby wants and needs. I am not a beer drinker, so I opted for the vanilla bean milk shakes, which were fabulous. She also made coconut macaroons that were delicious. After a week or two I had to tell Irma to stop feeding me so well or I'd return to the show as "Fat Erica"! She told me not to worry because nursing would take care of all of those extra calories. It turned out she was right!

After Irma left and I went back to work. Helmut and I took turns putting Liza to bed. One evening I came home to find him sitting at the top of the stairs with Liza in his arms, singing her a lullaby he'd made up. He was getting ready to put her down in her crib for the night. I heard him singing, so I quietly went to the bottom of the stairs to listen, being careful not to disturb that moment. I'll never forget that sight, that moment between father and daughter. The lullaby became one of Liza's favorites, so much so that I eventually began singing it to her, too.

For the first several months, my mother came to stay with Liza whenever I had to leave. She helped out until I could find a proper nanny, which took some time.

Although Helmut and I lived in Forest Hills for the first few years of our marriage, we moved back to my hometown of Garden City just before Liza was born. We thought about living in New York City, but Helmut helped me see that there was something special about the place where I grew up that we should pass on to our children. I found great comfort in Garden City because it was a community of family and familiar faces. Garden City is a very multigenerational town. It is common for parents to live there and for their grown children to return to raise their children there, too. My parents lived close by, making it easy for them to drop in and visit whenever they wanted.

I loved being back in Garden City. People all over town knew me as Susan Lucci, the girl who grew up in that town, and not "Susan Lucci," the actress who plays that Erica Kane woman on TV. I could go to the dry cleaner, butcher, supermarket, and nail salon as myself. I never had to worry about putting on a front because Garden City was my home, too. When we moved back, we finally had a home where I could do the gardening, create seasonal displays, and give my daughter the type of home environment that I grew up in. I made all of her baby food from scratch and did my best to be a good mother.

When Liza was a baby, it was a wonderful blessing that *All My Children* was only a half-hour show because that meant I could be home by three o'clock in the afternoon every day to spend time with my precious little girl. Thankfully, my schedule only called for me to go into the studio about three days a week. On the days that I had to work, I could hardly wait to get home to see her. One day, when she was around four months old, I went over to pick Liza up from her blanket on the floor. I rushed to her so fast and furiously that she looked at me and cried. I was so excited to see her that I scared her!

My mother phoned me one day at the studio to say that she thought Liza was on the verge of taking her first steps. This was a monumental occurrence I didn't want to miss. I had seen the signs that she was getting close, so I held my breath and hoped that she would be able to wait until I got home before taking that first leap. Lucky for me, my mother held her off. Not only did she wait for me, she waited for her father, too. Later that night, we both had the absolute pleasure of watching our daughter take her very first steps.

Liza was quite a verbal child. She is extremely smart and was speaking in full sentences before she was two years old. She could also count to twenty in both English and German, which I thought was amazing. She was very creative, even then, and like me, she loved to put on performances. She and her best friend, Katie Howe, a little redhead born on the Fourth of July who lived down the street, would play with my hats, clothes, costume jewelry, and shoes. They'd put on fashion shows, jump on the furniture, and do all of the wonderful things my mother encouraged me to do at her age.

When Liza was just a little girl, she came twirling into my room one day. "When I grow up, I am going to be an ice-skater. Since you're an actress, we can visit each other in our dressing rooms and we can share costumes." I thought that was adorable. When she first began taking skating lessons, she was really good and she really liked it. She took her music with her everywhere we went so she could always practice her choreography routines. I even brought Liza to the set of *All My Children* with me when we were shooting ice-skating scenes. Erica was skating in Rockefeller Center as part of a "photo shoot" for some modeling job she had.

*E*rica Kane got to do something that I never had a real shot at doing myself professionally—she became a fabulously successful fashion model. I knew from the start that her foray into this field was going to be the only chance I'd ever get to do this type of work, which proved to be very glamorous and fun. Although I was approached to be a "head" model when I first started acting in New York, I turned it down. I'm only five foot two on a good day, even standing up tall, so that certainly prevented me from walking the runway, but it never stopped Erica from doing it (because she is five foot eight!). I accepted that modeling was never really in the cards for me, but I loved wearing all of Erica's glamorous costumes while shooting at the Metropolitan Museum of Art, twirling around the fountain at Lincoln Center, where I posed on a cold marble slab outdoors in the middle of December in nothing more than a chiffon strapless dress, standing precariously on top of the fountain at the Plaza hotel, and cruising on a Statue of Liberty–bound ferry, which I almost blew off of when the director told me to get closer to the rail!

The Met shoot was supposed to be a very high-fashion editorial piece for Erica's magazine. I wore gorgeous hair extensions and Asian fan headpieces. For me, playing a high-fashion model for a full editorial layout was really fun. It was at the Plaza shoot that I discovered that sometimes you have to suffer for the sake of art. The crew were all dressed in down parkas as the temperatures hovered somewhere around thirty degrees before a steady wind kicked in, and I, of course, was dressed in a little spaghetti-strap dress. There were men selling roasted chestnuts on the street and I was frolicking in my skimpy day wear. Let me tell you, it's really hard to be glamorous in the cold! That was some of my best acting.

It was wonderful to have Liza there on the ice with me, skating around as I shot my scenes, but it was such a cold day that I worried she might get frostbite. The director asked everyone to stay on the ice to do another take, although one of the producers came over to me and said it would be okay if Liza wanted to go inside. When I told her she didn't have to stay with me in the cold, she turned to me and said, "No, Mommy. The pernouncer said we have to stay on the ice." And that just about sums up my daughter, who is and always has been so independent, capable, and strong. She was such a trouper and always has been.

It felt like it was just a blink of an eye between then and the day I found myself driving Liza to college in 1993. She was attending the University of North Carolina in Chapel Hill. Liza and I are as close as mother and daughter can be. I was very sad that she was going to be living so far away. Helmut and I drove her from our home in New York so we could help her get settled. As we were leaving, Liza stood in front of her dormitory waving good-bye to us. There was my darling girl, so smart yet vulnerable at the same time, getting ready to start the next phase of her life. I continued to look at her as we drove away until her image faded in the distance.

It broke our hearts when we had to return home without her. Helmut and I both felt like we were in mourning. I knew at that moment that I needed to stop and see my best friend and the godparents to both of my children, Patty, and her husband, David. Thankfully they live in Washington, D.C., which was on our way home. I called from the road to say we were coming. When Patty opened the door, I fell into her arms and broke down into tears. I don't remember her walking me to the sofa, but I sat there and cried for hours.

Patty's daughters Emily and Katie are a little younger than Liza, and they are my "fairy God-daughters." When they saw me so distraught, they turned to their mother and said, "We will never go away to college, Mommy. We will go to school right here in Washington." Those girls, Emily and Katie, made me smile as they distracted me from my otherwise broken heart.

I often imagined what Liza was going to be when she grew up. I knew from an early age that she had loads of talent. I thought she might become a dancer or choreographer because she was a natural and that's how she played. She was always putting together shows for her friends to be in. She was especially unique for her age because she had the ability to see the larger view of things, even when she was as young as eight years old. She would see more than the dance, the word on the page, the lyrics to a song, or the music that was playing around her. She instinctively got the big picture. That is the trait of a born director. She enjoyed every part of the process of performing, so I knew she'd want to do something related to it. I had no idea what it would end up being, though.

When she was eleven years old, she began to show a strong interest in acting. She had a wonderful drama teacher at her school who agreed that Liza had something special.

Liza set her sights on auditioning for her school production of *Annie*, which is not an easy musical to do because the lead character, Little Orphan Annie, sings throughout the show and the music isn't easy. Liza hadn't done anything like that before. The audition process lasted for nearly a month. She practiced every day on our sunporch, teaching herself the songs from the show so she would be ready.

Liza's teacher was very smart in guiding her throughout the process. She didn't want there to be any prejudice for or against Liza because she was the daughter of an actress. She had each little girl put on a red wig and anonymously sing to the people who were casting the part. Liza did a great job and had tremendous natural instincts. She had rehearsed standing on a platform, pretending it was the stage. When it came time for her audition, there was no platform present. But she instinctively knew where to stand without missing a beat. We were absolutely thrilled when she was selected to play Annie.

I sat in on her rehearsals whenever I could. I wore dark glasses so she wouldn't see me tearing up. One day she finally said to me, "Mom, even though you are wearing those glasses, I can see the tears!" I was so filled with joy and appreciation for her talent. It was heartwarming to watch my daughter blossom into a fine actress.

She subsequently did many plays in community theater and at her school. She ended up studying communications in college, where she continued to learn about acting on both sides of the camera, and about writing, too. My interest has always, and only, been in performing. Even when I was forced to direct at Marymount, I had to exercise every ounce of self-control within me to focus on the entire creative process and not the acting. I enjoyed it, but not nearly as much as I did performing. But Liza was spreading her wings much wider than I ever did so she could test the waters to see where she wanted to swim.

Liza made her official television debut in the 1995 Lifetime original movie I starred in called *Ebbie*. The movie was a loose remake of *Scrooge*, where I played a woman who, like the original Ebenezer, didn't have an appreciation for Christmas or the holiday season. Liza also appeared with me in a Ford car commercial. It was about that time that Liza made it clear she had been bitten by the acting bug. In 1999, she was cast as Gwen Hotchkiss on a new daytime soap called *Passions*. In 2000, Liza was asked to be Miss Golden Globe, an honor the Golden Globes gives each year to the daughter of a celebrity. This is an honor that is usually extended to second- or third-generation actresses, and usually to someone who is from the Hollywood film community. We were completely shocked and delighted that the Hollywood Foreign Press Association decided my daughter would receive this title, because my career had only been New York–based. I was so proud that she was asked and extremely proud of how she conducted herself throughout that show and in everyday life. Liza chose her own gown for the awards ceremony, a pale green halter dress, and she looked like a tall, blond Greek goddess. She wore her hair pulled back and looked absolutely gorgeous. Liza's job was to escort everyone who came on and off the stage. She walked with dignity and grace as she showed tremendous warmth to each person she came into contact with that night.

Five years after giving birth to my daughter, I became pregnant once again. My due date was February 29, 1980. Yes, it was a leap year. Recalling how difficult it was for me to deliver Liza naturally, my doctors suggested that I have a planned C-section for this delivery, which they thought would be less traumatic for both my baby and me. They gave me the choice of delivering on February 28, February 29, or March 1. Helmut and I discussed the options and decided to wait until the date got closer so we could be certain that the baby's lungs were fully developed and that there would be less chance of complications. I wanted the baby sooner rather than later, but like my pregnancy with Liza, I didn't want to know if I was having a boy or a girl. I wanted the element of surprise. When the baby was tested, its lungs were healthy and strong, so on February 28, 1980, I went into the hospital to give birth to my second child, a bouncing baby boy we named Andreas.

Initially, everything seemed fine. He was a little sleepier than Liza had been, but other than that, he was perfect. Thirty-six hours after Andreas was born, the nurses came to me and said, "Mrs. Huber. Do not be alarmed, but we will not be bringing the baby in to see you this evening."

Needless to say, I *was* alarmed. Every warning bell in my body went off. The nurses explained to me that Andreas was being held in the "A" nursery just down the hall and I could go see him if I wanted to. Thankfully, I was recovering more quickly from my delivery than expected, so I was able to get out of bed and make the walk there with an IV on wheels. I ran—no, I flew—down the hallway so I could look through the window and see my son. When I arrived at the nursery, there were several doctors standing over Andreas, examining his tiny little body. I asked one of the nurses what they were doing. She explained that when my son had been in the main nursery, one of the other nurses noticed that he was turning blue around his mouth while drinking the supplementary water they often give to newborns. It's not uncommon for babies to have an uneven complexion, but this particular nurse saw something more, as if something was wrong. I am eternally grateful to her for her astute observations, as she literally ended up saving my son's life.

The doctors on duty weren't sure what was causing the discoloration, so they ran every test they could to help provide an answer.

"We want to do a spinal tap on Andreas," they said. These were not the words I had been hoping to hear.

I looked around, trying to make a decision about what to do when I noticed Dr. Greensher standing in the main nursery. He was the pediatrician I used to take Liza to before he left his practice to become the head of pediatrics at the hospital. I went into that nursery to ask him if he would look at my baby and what he thought I should do. We didn't know what was wrong with my son and I didn't know the doctors who were treating him, so I asked if he would consider taking a look at Andreas. Dr. Greensher immediately agreed. When he came out of the nursery, he said he thought Andreas should have the spinal tap. I wasn't allowed in the room while the doctors did the procedure, but I am sure it wasn't a pleasant experience for my little boy. I was assured he wouldn't feel a thing, but I knew that the staff was just trying to comfort me in any way that they could.

When they finished, they put Andreas in something that resembled a space capsule so they could take pictures of his heart from every angle. From there, Andreas was placed in an oxygen tent called an isolette and kept in intensive care until we could get some conclusive answers. I was told it could take as long as three weeks to get the viral culture results. As you can imagine, that was an eternity to have to wait.

When my daughter was born, everything was picture-perfect. We spent a couple of routine days in the hospital and then took her home. I had no idea that just down the hall from the blissful nursery where she rested there existed a whole different world for parents of children with complications. I didn't know anything about this other side of childbirth until Andreas was born.

The hospital staff was exceptionally caring and understanding. Parents were allowed to visit their babies anytime of the day or night. I was required to scrub like a surgeon, put on a surgical mask, and wear a gown over my clothes before entering the unit. I also wore special gloves so I could reach through the tiny porthole in the isolette Andreas was in. I wanted him to feel my touch. Every time I reached through the hole, he grabbed on to my finger and held it tight. I talked to him for hours at a time so he would know I was there. It was awful to see my baby with wires attached to his tiny little body. I ached with worry that his first impression of this world was of plastic and metal.

I will never forget the sound of the beeping and buzzing machines that he was wired to during those horrible weeks. Five-year-old Liza drew pictures for her new baby brother that we hung up around his isolette so he could see them whenever he opened his little eyes. I put a music box pillow inside with him so he could hear music, too. I did everything I could think of to keep my son comfortable in his otherwise very scary and uncomfortable world.

The doctors administered antibiotics just in case his infection was bacterial and gave him several shots a day to keep his immune system strong. It was heartbreaking to listen to my little baby boy cry. In my desperation, I would fantasize that if I pulled off all of his wires, wrapped him in a cozy blanket, and took him home, he would be okay. Of course, I knew that would have been foolish, but it was how I really felt. In an effort to alleviate unnecessary pain for my son, I asked the doctors if there was another way to administer the antibiotics. They told me they could give him the shots through something called a Hepburn lock. This entailed inserting a device in the baby's heel so he would be stuck with a needle only that one time. All subsequent doses of medicine would be given to him through that device so he would only feel the pain of the initial insertion and would be spared further pain from daily injections.

I was so grateful that Andreas was at Winthrop Hospital, a facility that not only specialized in, but was at the forefront of, the care of newborn babies.

A few days after Andreas's situation began to unfold, I met Dr. Paul Twist, a neonatologist who specializes in treating ill or premature newborn babies. Dr. Twist was a tall lanky man who looked more like a basketball player than a doctor. As I spoke to Andreas in his NICU isolette, Dr. Twist came up behind me and whispered in my ear, "Never underestimate the power of what you are doing for your son." He told me the sensation of my touch and the soothing tone of my voice had tremendous healing power. As fate would have it, a few weeks before Andreas was born, I saw an article in the *New York Times* science section about how babies in orphanages who aren't touched enough or don't have their gaze returned often don't make it through diseases such as measles the way other babies do. Dr. Twist explained to me that babies get their self-esteem through our gazes and touch, and that is what gives a baby the strength to fight whatever it is he's fending off.

When he left the nursery, I remember thinking that Dr. Twist was a man of science who was giving credence to a mother's intuition to make her presence known. I was very grateful he told me all of those things, but I was also in tremendous emotional pain. I couldn't understand where I had gone wrong. I didn't drink caffeine or alcohol, didn't eat the wrong foods, and did everything within my power to give my child the best start in life. Why was my baby so sick? I cried because I felt so bad for somehow letting my baby down. I knew it was typical and quite normal for mothers to blame themselves. You can't help feeling guilty when you're watching your newborn struggle.

With no conclusive answers, Andreas was put through a second spinal tap and then subjected to all of the same tests he had already had. When the viral culture finally came back, Andreas was diagnosed with a terrible strain of the flu. Nineteen eighty had been a year when the flu was at epidemic proportions. Quite a few babies who were exposed to the virus that season actually died.

I had continued working throughout my pregnancy, right up to my ninth month. I was completely healthy until the very end. Just before delivering Andreas, however, I remembered that I'd just had a bout with the flu. I nursed Andreas for his first thirty-six hours; if I was still sick, I could have passed the virus on to him. Luckily, my son's exposure was minimal, and now that we had answers, it was treatable, too.

The nurses who looked after my son were spectacular in every way. They loved and cared for him as if he were one of their own. I don't know how they do the work they do. I imagine there must be a tremendous rate of emotional burnout because they are caring for very ill newborns. They took care of my son and all of the babies in the nursery because the babies were in need of their love and attention. I have only written one fan letter in my life and it was to the nurses who cared for Andreas. I needed them to know how much I appreciated everything they did for us. I will never be able to truly put into words how much I appreciate the work they do for all families, and especially for the comfort and kindness they showed to my family in our desperate time of need.

Once I was finally able to bring Andreas home, I still had to bring him back to the hospital for monthly checkups with Dr. Twist to be certain there were no long-term effects. Not only were there no lingering issues, but Andreas turned out to be a very happy baby and a gifted boy. Today, he stands at a lofty six foot three inches tall. He picks me up in one arm and carries me like I am a small bag of groceries. You would never know that he struggled to make it during those first three weeks of his life, but I am so very glad he didn't give up and I am eternally grateful to God.

Andreas has grown into such an outstanding young man. I light up whenever I hear his name. I remember a navy-blue sweater I gave him when he was about two years old. It had the sun, moon, stars, and a rocket ship on the back. I loved that sweater because it represented how he made and *still* makes me feel. He was such a wonderful baby, with a beautiful disposition. He smiled at people and his laughter was infectious. People often stopped me to say what a nice baby he was. And as gorgeous as my son is on the outside, he is just as gorgeous on the inside. He is so smart and has such a big heart, a great spirit, and a fabulous sense of humor. He is the best son any mother could ever have.

Both of my children spent their summers at our beach house in the Hamptons, where they went to a day-camp program called Junior Sports. I commuted back and forth from Manhattan so they could enjoy their summers even if I had to work. It was always important to me to be there for my children, even if it meant a little less sleep or time for me. (I'm sure many of you can relate to this!)

As parents, Helmut and I both believed it was our job to expose our children to as many wonderful things as we could and then see where their interests lay. We'd do our best to give them lessons or put them in the right place to pursue their curiosities, but we always followed their lead. One summer, Liza went to sleepaway camp near our beach house. Although the camp was only a short distance from our home, she did sleep there instead of coming home so she could enjoy the camaraderie that comes with that experience.

When we were together at the beach, I was just their mother. I would forget that I am also a public personality. The first time we dropped Liza at camp, she asked me to duck down and hide in the car so the other kids or parents wouldn't see me. It's not that she was embarrassed to have me as her mother, but she just didn't want the other kid to know her as "Susan Lucci's daughter." So I immediately agreed to duck down on the floor of the car while my husband took her inside. I totally understood how she felt. She wanted to be met on her own terms and as her own person. I had to respect her decision. She went on to enjoy her summer-camp experience very much. I was proud of her in every way.

Andreas spent the summers in the Hamptons learning to swim, playing golf, and meeting lots of girls. Around the age of nine, he was invited to attend a dance at our beach club. He was dressed in a navy blazer and khaki pants. As I was changing to take him to the dance, he came up to me and said, "But, Mommy, I don't know how to dance!"

"Oh, I am sure you do. You have such good rhythm and you're a great athlete," I said. "I am sure you'll be fine. But just in case, why don't you come over here and we'll give it a try." Then I reached my hand out to grab ahold of his. I taught him the box step in my bedroom that afternoon so he would know that if he asked a girl to dance, he'd be able to do it.

"Andreas, there's one more thing I'd like you to know before you go to your dance tonight. When you ask a girl to dance, go over to her table and politely ask her if she would like to dance with you and then take her hand to lead her out to the dance floor. And, when you're finished, remember to walk her back to her seat at the table. Don't just leave her high and dry. Okay?" I wanted him to know that it is always important to be a gentleman.

When I drove him to the dance that night, there were a dozen or so girls waiting on the front porch of the club. When they saw it was Andreas, they clapped and giggled. They were so cute. I told Andreas to go and have a good time and that I'd be back to pick him up later.

After the dance, Andreas got back into my car.

"How did it go? Did you ask anyone to dance? Did you escort her to and from the dance floor?" I was quizzing him like a typical mother.

"It's not like that anymore, Mom. The girls ask the boys to dance!" That's when I knew that my children were definitely growing up in different times.

Like his father, Andreas is an excellent athlete. Growing up, he loved lacrosse, was thirty hours shy of getting his black belt in karate when he was only twelve years old, and showed immense interest in golf. When Andreas was born, it gave Helmut so much pleasure to tell everyone that he now had a son who could play with him in the father-son golf tournaments.

"In twelve years, I'll have a golf partner. It's only twelve years, but just wait!" Helmut was giddy with excitement. Little did he know that Andreas would grow up to become a fiercely competitive golfer who would eventually beat his dad on the golf course. By the time Andreas was twelve years old, he had already been asked to play on the high school varsity golf team. He had been playing lacrosse with his friends since he was eight years old, but when he began to do so well in golf, he had to make a choice between the two so he could focus on just one and really excel in it.

One day I picked him up from school and we sat in the car for an hour talking through the pros and cons of his decision. His biggest dilemma was that golf is a solo sport and he thought his lacrosse friends might think he was abandoning them. I explained to Andreas that his friends would understand because they're his friends first. He ultimately made the choice to play golf and he did really well. He played in many tournaments, making it to the USGA Junior Amateur quarter-finals when he was seventeen. That particular tournament was televised on ESPN. Helmut was there with him, but I couldn't attend because I was shooting a movie on location in Toronto. I was so grateful to be able to watch him play in between takes. Even though Andreas was frustrated by his performance—he finished in the top eight—it was an extraordinary achievement.

Golf is a sport where you have to compete and succeed every week, especially if you have ambitions to make it to the PGA. You have to have the grace of a dancer, the strength of an athlete, and the mind of a chess player.

Andreas was showing tremendous promise. He and Helmut shared such a passion for the sport. Ultimately, Helmut and I realized we had a child with an outstanding ability who had the desire and drive to pursue it. Because we felt he was too young to travel by himself to tournaments, Helmut became Andreas's personal valet and travel partner.

I tried not to attend the tournaments on a regular basis because I wanted my son to have his privacy. I didn't want the attention focused on his mother's presence. I wanted it aimed at his incredible talent. And, to be fair, Andreas didn't need the extra pressure of having me there and having to hear, "Did you see his mother?"

By the time Andreas attended college, he had been recruited by the very best, including Stanford. When he received that invitation, I didn't think he was going to look any further. I secretly wanted to be one of those mothers who told her son he could go to school anywhere as long as it was east of the Mississippi, but when the time came, I had no parameters. My feeling was that Andreas had to choose the college he attended on his own. My parents told me that choosing a college is the first major life-changing decision that you make for yourself. I thought they were right, so I gave both of my children the same freedom my parents gave to me. When we visited Stanford, for whatever reason, Andreas decided it wasn't home. It wasn't where he wanted to live for the next four years. He finally chose Georgetown, where he could golf and represent his school in collegiate play. As a freshman, he won the Big East Championship and Georgetown Invitational. My son had gone on to become both a scholar and an athlete.

It took Erica Kane years to discover the joys of motherhood, but these were things I felt from the moment I knew I was pregnant, and really understood when they placed my firstborn baby in my arms. Children are not possessions. They are our treasure. They're entrusted to us, and the best thing we can do is to fully help them to become who they want to be and to become the best they can be. After I became a mother, my number one priority was raising my children. And I have to admit that I didn't do it alone. Far from it. There were so many people along the way who helped me be the best parent I could be so my children would come out unscathed while I kept working at my career.

I could never have become the mother I did without sharing parenthood with my husband. Something I came to admire about Helmut, and even about my father over the years, is that they both grew up without a father who was present in their lives, yet they were both such good fathers themselves. This is such a fine trait to find in a husband. To be a good parent means you have to be present in your children's lives. I realized that my children would grow up asking questions about life that I wanted to be around to answer. I didn't want to miss a single moment. When I couldn't be there with them because of work, I made sure a piece of me was with them at all times. I planned their menus so that I could be in charge of their good nutrition and so they would know I was thinking about them. If I couldn't be home to cook for them, I always found a creative way to be their mother and nurture them. Still, there was a lot of doubt and insecurity, especially when my schedule at work changed. By the time Liza was two and half years old, my schedule at the show went from working three days a week to five days a week. I was worried that the extra hours at the studio would negatively impact her, and later, Andreas, too.

I remember breaking down in our pediatrician's office one day because I was worried my children were somehow suffering for my occasional absences. The pediatrician could see how upset I was. He looked me right in the eyes and said, "I've got a daughter about your age in med school. I would *never* tell her not to dream her dreams, and give up on everything she wants to be and can be, simply because she was born female. Your children are wonderful. They are flourishing, and if I ever see those things changing, I will tell you and we will figure out what to do from there."

Those were the perfect words at the perfect time. Hearing the doctor share his story about his own child really took the pressure off of me to go forward with confidence that I was a good mother. I didn't have to give up my dreams and such an important part of who I am in order to answer this *most* important part of who I am. There were ways to negotiate so I could be an actress and be there for my children, too.

So when my contract came up for renewal, I made sure to put some restrictions in my new agreement that guaranteed that I wouldn't miss the big events in my children's lives. I actually negotiated their first day of school off, their birthdays, and the ability to take blocks of time whenever they were going through a major change. I am told I was the first actress to get these clauses added to her contract at the network. The network executives relentlessly teased me about this, but I didn't care. I believe they supported me and thought it was really the right thing to do, but nobody had ever done it before me, so they had some fun teasing me. And, ABC was great to help me. I was and will always be a mother first.

When I was home, I was fully home. I drove in a car pool, was their class mother, attended school plays or sporting events, and remained an integral part of their daily lives. My children always knew I was happy to be there with them. I don't think they ever felt like I would have rather been somewhere else, doing a movie, play, *All My Children*, or any other outside interest. That belief was totally confirmed when Liza came to me one day and said, "Mommy, you are with us more than a lot of mothers are. They're out playing tennis, having lunches, running errands, and doing stuff, while you come home and pick us up from school, make our lunch, and are here when we get home."

Hearing Liza say this to me made every moment I found for my children worthwhile because I knew in the deepest part of my heart and soul that my children knew how much I loved them.

And at the times I wasn't able to be there, Helmut and Frida, our longtime nanny who has been with my family for thirty-two years, picked up where I left off. Frida has been an enormous part of why I could keep doing what I do as an actress and still raise my children.

She never lived in with our family, as she had three boys of her own and went home at night to care for them. When my children were young, Frida was at the house primarily during the days and at times when I was at work. As my career really began to take off, Frida, God bless her, took pity on me and started taking care of all of us. She kind of became my wife—and *everyone* needs a wife. There was nothing she wouldn't do for my children and family. I always knew my children were in loving hands, and at the same time, Frida never tried to be a substitute parent. I was and am so lucky to have her. As Hillary Clinton so wisely put it, "It takes a village!"

CHAPTER 9

———— e⏜⏜⏝ ————

Annie Get Your Gun

A s an actress, I have known many times throughout my career when I've had to take a step back and recognize how blessed my life has been for having the opportunity to play a character such as Erica Kane. Even with that great success, I sometimes wonder what my life would have been like if I had followed Mr. Weyand's advice and auditioned for the John Houseman Theater after graduating college instead of taking the job with *All My Children*. I've never looked back on my decision with even so much as an ounce of regret, but every now and then, an opportunity presents itself that leaves me wondering *what if?*

In the summer of 1999, my then-agent Sylvia Gold of ICM received a call from Barry and Fran Weissler, two of Broadway's biggest and best producers who were the dynamic team behind many hit shows, including *Grease*, *Chicago*, and *Fiddler on the Roof*, just to name a few. The Weisslers were calling to see if I had any interest in playing Annie Oakley in *Annie Get Your Gun* on Broadway. They told me that the star of their play, the fantastic and talented Bernadette Peters, was leaving the show. I was thrilled with the idea of acting on Broadway, especially in one of the greatest roles ever written and in an Irving Berlin musical. It was absolutely a dream come true.

If I agreed to take on the role, however, I wanted to be completely certain of two things. First, I wanted to know that I could play the part. And second, I had to be satisfied that I was worthy of it—not just for myself, but for the company of actors I would be joining. Taking on a role that Bernadette Peters had made uniquely her own was a daunting task. I felt a huge responsibility to make sure that I could fill those very big shoes she was leaving behind for me or anyone else to fill.

I vividly recall the Broadway shows I saw with my mother when I was younger as if those days were yesterday. I remember sitting in the theater dreaming that someday I would be the star up there on the stage—someone all the young girls sitting in the audience would dream about, too. I didn't want to disappoint those children or somehow squash their dreams if somehow the famous television actress they came to see and might have admired wasn't quite up to the part. There have been many times when actors and actresses are cast in roles for their box-office appeal. I give producers a lot of credit for thinking creatively and bringing in someone who the audience may not expect to see or may not readily associate with Broadway. It has boosted theater in every way, from attendance to recognition. But when these actors are not right for the part, sadly the critics can and often do kill the show. There's a lot of power in the pen. If they write negative things about a particular performance, the entire company suffers for it. Worse than that, sometimes critics will write negative things without ever seeing the show because they automatically assume an established film or television actor has been brought in strictly for their marquee value and not for their talent. I didn't want to be a name brought in to merely capture an audience. I wanted to prove to everyone that I *was* Annie Oakley.

I discussed this opportunity with everyone who was guiding my career, from my husband to my agent, Sylvia Gold. I was very lucky to be a client of Sylvia's. She was a legend in the business and very much a part of helping me grow over the years. I loved Sylvia very much. And although she knew I enjoyed acting in the variety of television movies I had done, she and I never really talked about my desire to work on the stage before this opportunity arose. When we did explore the notion together, the fact that I hadn't been trained as a singer (though I had some training as a stage actress and had done a little singing in my high school and college days) naturally came up. Sylvia was candid, saying she had some reservations about my taking the role.

I reminded Sylvia that I had participated in some large, onstage production numbers in recent years. I did *Night of 100 Stars*, the fabulous Alexander Cohen–produced extravaganza that took place at Radio City Music Hall in New York. It was a thrill to have met that challenge head-on and succeeded, though admittedly the bigger thrill at the time was watching from backstage as Ginger Rogers danced with Christopher Walken along with Gregory Hines and a number of other famous dancers from years gone by. It was a large production number that was highly choreographed and grueling. I stood in the wings after my own performance, simply mesmerized by theirs. I was pinching myself in disbelief that I was backstage at Radio City watching the legendary Ginger Rogers strut her stuff.

When they came offstage, Ginger threw herself into a chair and lay back, clearly satisfied with what she had done. Unfortunately, there had been a glitch with the taping and they had to do the whole thing one more time. Ginger let out a great big sigh and then got up to do it all again. I was so inspired by that.

Six weeks later, I was part of another equally phenomenal show at Radio City when ABC was entertaining its affiliates. It was the eighties and the show *Dynasty* was at the height of its popularity on the network. I was part of a fashion number that included many glamorous women, mostly from television. There were a number of film stars participating as well, including Claudia Cardinale, Dyan Cannon, Diahann Carroll, Joan Collins, and Linda Evans. A representative from the famed jeweler to the stars, Harry Winston, was backstage with millions of dollars' worth of necklaces around his wrist and rings on his fingers, doling them out for each of us to wear onstage. We could choose whatever piece we wanted to borrow, as long as we understood that we had to give it back after the show. Claudia Cardinale had her own emeralds and diamonds. It was absolutely breathtaking to see her pull these remarkable pieces out of her purse. She put the earrings and necklace on with her white Yves Saint Laurent suit. She looked absolutely incredible.

I had to make an entrance onto the stage from up right and down the center, where I would be met by the Rockettes and chorus-boy dancers. During rehearsal, I talked with several of the dancers in the number and it turned out that the Rockettes and the boys were big fans, so they took me under their wing. I was grateful for their help because it was my first time on the enormous Radio City stage and I didn't want to make a giant fool of myself. The chorus boys taught me how to walk that big stage walk and how to make an entrance. I was thrilled with their helpful tips. Boy, could they walk the walk!

When the show got started, I was standing stage left with Ruth Warrick and Lana Turner, waiting for Linda Evans to make her appearance. She was going to be raised up onto the stage by a hydraulic lift. Chorus boys were coming down beautiful stairs, where they would meet and then escort Linda down center to the mark she had to hit on the stage. While they sang and danced all around her, she stood motionless, looking like an absolute goddess. When the number was over, the lift lowered her back beneath the stage. The number was very glamorous and spectacular.

Lana Turner was peeking from behind the curtain, watching as Linda's number went off without a hitch. She turned to me and said, "I have to follow that?"

Lana was next up. All she was supposed to do was walk across the stage. No chorus boys, no dancers, no hydraulics. Just Lana Turner walking. Let me tell you, when Lana Turner walked across that stage, she was fantastic. She owned it every step of the way.

As I spoke about these memorable experiences, Sylvia could tell I was passionate about theater and live performance. I suppose that I do light up when I think about life in the theater. After all, it is where all of my dreams began.

A few days later, Helmut recalled a chance meeting we had with Marvin Hamlisch at a benefit for the Bay Street Theatre in Sag Harbor, New York. The Bay Street Theatre is an old clapboard building with a wooden interior. It smells like old greasepaint, in the best sense of the word. It's charming and wonderful in every way.

It was a lovely summer evening benefit made extra special by Marvin Hamlisch performing some of his most memorable hits in this very intimate setting. Just as we were leaving, Marvin's wife, Terre Blair, came over to say hello. She asked if Helmut and I would like to come backstage to meet her husband.

"Marvin would love to meet you," she said.

I had never met Marvin Hamlisch before that night. I had no idea that he would have the smallest interest in meeting me, let alone know who I am.

"He is a big fan of yours, Susan. He watches your show all the time," she said.

I was very touched and delighted to have the chance to meet him. We went backstage, where we were greeted by Marvin, who was so warm and generous with his comments. We spoke about the current season of *All My Children*, and the story line in which Erica became addicted to prescription painkillers. The story had been done in real time. The network had arranged for me to speak with doctors and counselors at the Betty Ford Clinic so I could act the part in the most authentic way possible. It was a very success-ful story line that was also a tremendous challenge for me because it was way outside my comfort zone. I shared this information with Marvin as he and I spoke. I told him it was very important to me to make sure I showed a lot of respect for people who are really struggling with addiction. Marvin must have sensed the sincerity in all I was conveying, as he was very complimentary—going so far as to tell me I should definitely win that first Emmy for my acting throughout that particular story.

"Susan, I just want you to know that winning the Emmy has nothing to do with your talent. You are very talented and so it should happen for you soon," he said.

Unfortunately, I didn't win the Emmy that year, but it was nice to hear that someone thought I should. Here, he had just finished a wonderful performance and he somehow found the time and words to offer encouragement to me. I was very grateful for our meeting and for all of the nice things he had to say.

Not long after we met, Marvin called to ask if I'd like to appear onstage at a benefit he was doing for Carnegie Mellon University in Pittsburgh. He said he'd like to write a song for me to sing. I told him that I had no formal training as a singer. Thankfully, that small detail didn't seem to sway his desire to write a musical number for me. In fact, he jokingly suggested that I could simply dance in the show with a group of handsome boys from the school if I liked. *That*, I said, I'd be happy to do!

A few weeks later, Marvin called to sing me the song he'd written to the tune of "Hello, Dolly!" I held the receiver to my ear and listened as *the* Marvin Hamlisch serenaded me over the phone. This was definitely one of those great life "pinch myself" moments.

Helmut and I went to Pittsburgh to join Marvin, where I did several performances with him onstage at Heinz Hall. I also had a wonderful opportunity to speak to some of the students at Carnegie Mellon, which was really terrific. I loved hearing their comments about the show, my performance, and anything else these kids wanted to ask me about or to share with me.

Marvin and I really bonded during that experience. Before heading back to New York, he turned to me and said, "Susan, if there's anything I can ever do for you, please let me know." I thought that was very generous. I had no plans to ever take him up on that offer—that is, until I began thinking about doing *Annie Get Your Gun.*

Helmut suggested I give Marvin a call to talk about the opportunity. I was too shy to reach out to him myself, so Helmut made the call for me. Although Marvin was in Scotland when we finally connected, he was an absolute doll. He told Helmut he would be back in New York in a few days and could make some time for us when he arrived that Sunday evening. He literally got off the plane and met with us that same night.

"Come to my apartment at seven-thirty. I'll have Susan sing through some of the songs from *Annie Get Your Gun* and I'll give her my honest opinion about whether I think she can do it or not," Marvin told Helmut.

I thought this was a very good plan. I felt that Marvin was now a good enough friend to tell me to go for it or let it go. I was extremely nervous to sing for him, but I figured if I could get past Marvin Hamlisch, maybe I had a real shot at this part.

I was breathless as I rang the bell to Marvin's apartment. I could hardly believe what I was about to do. The whole experience was surreal. We walked into his home, a beautiful prewar gem, where we were met by Marvin; his wife, Terre; and his lyricist. Marvin sat down at his piano and began to play through all of the music. I froze for a moment when I realized that Marvin would be the one accompanying me on the piano. I had been rehearsing but hadn't yet sought out any professional training. I figured I would get more aggressive when and if Marvin gave me his approval.

I picked two songs to sing that I thought the Weisslers would want to hear. I selected "I Got Lost in His Arms," a ballad, and "You Can't Get a Man with a Gun," a song I was certain they'd want to hear. Those two songs epitomized Annie Oakley. Strangely, when we first spoke about the role, Fran and Barry didn't ask me to sing for them. I asked if they would allow me to. I didn't think it was right to hire me for their musical without first hearing my voice. They eventually agreed that yes, it was a good thing for us to do. I wanted them to know what they were getting into if I were to accept the part.

I sang the selected music for Marvin as if I were auditioning for the very first time. It was very reminiscent of A Chorus Line, one of Marvin Hamlisch's all-time greatest shows, except I was not in a theater trying out for a part with a slew of other hopefuls. No, I was all by myself singing in Marvin's apartment.

When I finished, Marvin pulled his hands back and placed them on his lap. He looked up at me and said, "You can do this."

I was thrilled and shocked all at once. I wanted to jump up and click my heels three times.

"And now I am going to go stand in the back of my apartment. I want you to sing to me again, knowing I am all the way back here," he said.

Marvin's lyricist sat down and began to play as I belted out song after song.

When I was done, Marvin slowly walked toward me. He looked me right in the eyes and said, "Oh yeah, you can definitely do this—if you really want to." Marvin began to explain that it would be a heavy load, especially on top of my already overscheduled life and work obligations. He was very reassuring that if I really wanted this, I could most definitely do it.

"You're very brave, Susan. Tall you're not, but brave? Yes!" Marvin made me laugh with that summation. He suggested I work with his lyricist for ten days or so and then come back to see him one last time so we could assess where I was and what I should ultimately do. Marvin explained that his lyricist, Craig Carnelia, was a wonderful musician and a fantastic vocal coach. I agreed with the plan and spent the next ten days working with him at his apartment.

When we were ready, we went back to see Marvin once again. I was more scared this time than I expected to be. I like a big stage where there's a little distance between the audience out there in the darkness and me. I don't like to see faces when I perform. That's one of the things I like best about doing television—I don't have to see the audience. I can just be my character. Theater wasn't going to offer that same luxury. That was definitely something for me to think about.

When I got to Marvin's, he and his wife sat on their sofa directly in front of me. I sang and did my best. When I finished, everyone there was very supportive. They each felt I could really do this. I was ecstatic, which felt amazing. Marvin made one final suggestion to me. He said I ought to get my sheet music printed up so I looked very professional when I sang for Fran and Barry. Note to self: Get that sheet music printed up because you are definitely going to go for this.

Once I had Marvin's stamp of approval, I began working with his lyricist so I would be absolutely ready to sing for Fran and Barry. I knew that if I decided to move forward, I'd have access to the greatest teachers in the world. Several people had suggested that if I took the role, I ought to try to work with Joan Lader, the most spectacular vocal coach in all of New York. She has worked with all of the Broadway greats, including Patti Lupone and Mandy Patinkin, and with Madonna while she prepared for her role in *Evita*, and so many more famous names in the business. I was very motivated. I was loving every minute of this journey.

When I felt absolutely ready, Helmut and I took my beautifully printed sheet music and headed to the Weisslers' apartment. I stood outside their door for a moment, took a very deep breath, and rang the bell. Much to my surprise, John McDaniel answered the door. I had met John a few times over the years—many of you may remember him as the musical director from *The Rosie O'Donnell Show*. It turned out that John was also the Weisslers' musical director.

He was very warm and welcoming and told me that the Wiesslers weren't home at the moment, but would be by later. He suggested we do a couple of run-throughs while we waited. John told me they wanted us to work on two songs—thankfully, the same two I had already picked out. I handed John my sheet music. He commented on how beautiful it was. All I could think was, *Thank you, Marvin!* I told John that Marvin Hamlisch had suggested I get it printed. I wasn't name-dropping. I really wanted to give Marvin the credit.

John played through the songs as I sang along. When we finished, he told me he thought I did very well and then excused himself for a minute. I watched John walk down the hallway toward a back bedroom. When he returned, Fran Weissler was with him. She had been in the bedroom listening the whole time. She and John made a deal that if they didn't think I could do the part, he wasn't going to embarrass me or bother Fran. But if he thought I was capable of playing Annie Oakley, he would excuse himself, get Fran, and have me sing again for her. I have to say, Fran's presence really broke the ice. I actually thought it was a good thing she heard me singing from the back of her apartment first. But then, she and her husband, Barry, who had also joined us, sat on the sofa in front of me just like Marvin and Terre had, and asked me to sing for them once more. I really belted out those songs. I have no idea how many times their neighbors have had to endure these in-home auditions in the past. I certainly hoped they all liked what they heard that night because it was truly this actress's dream. And you can rest assured that this, too, was one of those "pinch me" moments in my life that I will never forget.

Fran and Barry told me on the spot that I got the part. We spent the next several hours talking about all of the possibilities. We mapped out several different scenarios that began when Bernadette was scheduled to leave the following April. By the end of the night, I was completely exhausted. However, when Helmut and I left their apartment, we wanted to have a moment to take in and celebrate what was happening. We stopped into a nearby restaurant to drink a glass of champagne, have dinner, and breathe!

"This is like a scene from a movie for me," I said to Helmut. "I just want to jump up on the table and scream, 'Drinks for everyone!'" That is really how I felt.

"You'll be very sorry in the morning if you do that. You should probably stay in your seat," Helmut said, ever the voice of reason.

I started working on learning the music right away. I went straight to Joan Lader and got started. I wanted to give myself plenty of time to be ready for my debut right before the millennium, in December 1999. Much to my surprise, shortly after I signed on, the producers came to me to say that Bernadette Peters was taking a month off in December for the holidays, so they wanted me to start earlier than expected. Even though it meant I would only have three weeks to prepare, I jumped at the opportunity. My Broadway debut was now slated for December 23, 1999. A date that was important for two reasons—first, it would mark my official Broadway debut, and second, it was my birthday.

My schedule was very full, as I spent every day getting ready while also continuing *All My Children*. I really wanted to do this right, so I learned the part fast—really fast. Helmut and I went to see the show five times to get a feel for whether or not I could do it and to see what it was like to sit in that audience. The Annie Oakley character is in virtually every scene, and I loved it. The first time I saw Annie come flying across the stage on a trapeze, I thought, *Okay, I can do that!* It's funny, because when I was a little girl, the only thing I ever wanted to be other than an actress was a trapeze artist. I would have liked to do the stunts in the show, but only if I had the proper time to train. I had heard there were trapeze classes at Chelsea Piers on the west side of Manhattan. I thought, *I have to do this!* Every time we saw the show, so many thoughts raced through my mind. I didn't have to take the trapeze lessons, but I certainly would have and think I might have really enjoyed them, too.

During the week of Thanksgiving, shortly before I was set to open in *Annie Get Your Gun*, I was asked to ride the lead float in the Macy's Thanksgiving Day Parade. There was a steady, freezing cold rain on that particular Thanksgiving morning. However, being on the lead float that day was a momentous experience for me, so rain or shine, I was going for that ride. There was nothing obstructing my view as we were the very first float in the entire parade. I could see people looking out of their windows from way up high in their apartment buildings or standing on their terraces as we headed down Central Park West toward Broadway. When we made that final turn onto Broadway, my breath was literally taken away knowing that I would soon be making my Broadway theater debut. There were tens of thousands of people cheering for me as the float continued toward its final destination in front of Macy's in Herald Square. All I could think of was, "How lucky am I to soon have my Broadway dream come true!"

I knew there was going to be great pressure to get ready. Talk about baptism by fire! My days were long and my nights even longer. I worked at *All My Children*, did rehearsals, and whenever I had to, went to a fitting with the wonderful iconic costume designer William Ivey Long, who was so charming. One day, William Ivey noticed that I was losing quite a bit of weight. At first, I thought I was battling the flu or had caught a really bad cold. I was feeling run-down, but I chalked it up to burning the candle at both ends. When I went to see my doctor, he prescribed an antibiotic, but it didn't seem to be working. If I had an early call at the studio, I would have some fits of coughing, but that only happened early in the morning. I thought that maybe I had some type of bronchitis. I didn't know what was wrong, and frankly, I didn't have the time to be sick.

Four days before opening night, I went for my final costume fitting. At one point during that fitting, I looked in the mirror and thought, *Wow. I have lost more weight than I thought I had.* Now, I am a woman who has never thought her hips were too small—ever. When William Ivey came back into the room, he had hip pads with him so he could better fit my costume, which was falling off of me. I didn't realize it, but I had lost eight pounds. I know that doesn't sound like a lot of weight, but on me, it was a lot. I had dropped to eighty-four pounds, a very unhealthy weight for me. I left the fitting that day very concerned

I went from the fitting back to *All My Children* and then to a voice lesson with Joan Lader. She is an incredible teacher. She hears everything and lets you get away with nothing. If you're not perfect, she tells you so you can work to get better. At the same time Joan remains your greatest and warmest supporter. When I began to sing, I got no further than a few bars before she stopped me cold.

"I can't let you sing," she said. "You have to go to see a doctor."

"Joan. I am supposed to open in four days. I can't be sick!"

She insisted I go to see Dr. Gwen Korovin, who treats all of the Broadway singers. It was early evening, but Joan was able to get me an appointment. Although I didn't always have a car and driver, I happened to have one this particular night. My driver was a woman named Barbara who was always very kind and considerate. She offered to take me right to the doctor's office. By the time I got there, I couldn't even sit up long enough to fill out the new-patient forms. I was slumped over the chair trying my best to write. The nurses had to assist me as I made my way to an exam room. When Dr. Korovin came into the room, I thought she was lovely, beautiful and as smart as could be. I explained that I was set to open in *Annie Get Your Gun* in four days. Nothing was going to stop me. I told Dr. Korovin, "I know you don't know me, but I usually have a lot of energy. This is not me. I can't sit up. And I know you're going to look at me and say you think I'm too thin, but I eat like a truck driver. I do. I really do." I was pleading with her not to give me orders that I couldn't sing or go onstage.

"Susan, I want you to go right to Lenox Hill Hospital. They will be able to run tests on you that I cannot do here. I will call and get the results right away and will let you know. Come back here right after your tests." The doctor was insistent.

My driver Barbara helped get me back into the car and drove me to Lenox Hill. She wouldn't let me go in by myself. She was being very protective. The truth is, I really wasn't well. She came in and sat with me while I waited to be examined. When we finished, Barbara drove me back to Dr. Korovin's to await the results.

"Susan, you have pneumonia," Dr. Korovin said. Luckily we caught it at the very beginning stages, but she was very clear that I had to go home and stay in bed for the next four or five days. If I didn't go home and beat this thing, I would likely end up going into the hospital and wouldn't be able to go onstage at all. I was crushed by this news. I had worked so hard to prepare for opening night and now it appeared I'd be lying in bed while an understudy went on instead of me. The doctor said she would call Fran and Barry to explain the situation. I was sure they were going to fire me.

Barbara put me in the backseat of the sedan, where I proceeded to lie down and cry all the way home. I was so sick that I threw up in the car. I was terribly embarrassed. Barbara didn't miss a beat. She told me not to worry about the car. I spent the entire ride back to Garden City trying to figure out how I could possibly do the show.

There was so much music in the show that required me to be strong to sing it. The staging was very active. I was always on the move, climbing ladders and running around. There was no way I'd be up to the task if I didn't allow my body to heal. I could do it, but only if I were strong.

When we got to the house, Barbara took me to the front door, where I was met by Helmut and Frida. Frida never left my side. She was very caring and nurturing. Helmut made me mashed potatoes every day to fatten me up. I have to admit, that was the best perk after being so sick.

Here I am at eleven months old . . .

on the day of my First
Communion . . .

and sitting on top of a pony at age three. I used to have so much fun riding with my father!

It was great training for when I rode horseback on *All My Children*.

I always marvel at how the truck in this picture would hint at my future. I love ice cream . . . and years later I would fall in love with a man named Huber, too!

This is my wonderful Nana, exactly how I remember her . . .

my father in uniform (he was so
proud to serve his country) . . .

and here I am dancing
with my dad when I was
seventeen.

This is my very first professional
headshot taken prior to
landing the role of Erica on
All My Children . . .

SUSAN LUCCI
michael hartig agency, inc.

SUSAN LUCCI

HAIR: CHESTNUT   HEIGHT: 5'3"   AGE RANGE: 18-25
EYES: DARK BROWN   WEIGHT: 100 lbs.   VOICE: BELT

TELEVISION: * currently · "ERICA KANE MARTIN" ALL MY CHILDREN
ABC-TV, Mon.- Fri. at 1 pm.

FILM: female lead in DADDY, YOU KILL ME - KDC production

Commercials: on request

Theatre: stock - The Chase Barn - Whitefield, N.H.

"ABIGAIL" — The Crucible
"Iphigenia" — Iphigenia in Aulis
"Maria" — West Side Story
"Tuptim" — The King & I
"Luisa" — The Fantasticks
"Elvira" — Blithe Spirit
"Grandma" — The Sandbox
"Corey" — Barefoot in the Park

Education: - Marymount. Hartman. Studio
- Harold Clurman
- B.A. in Drama - Marymount College
(faculty: Yale, Royal Shakespeare,
Martha Graham Dance)

with my handwritten
resume on the back . . .

my first publicity photograph
for *All My Children*—
it is currently used in
the opening of the show . . .

WHAT A HANDICAP!

Here's a girl
too beautiful
(they said)
to be an actress

By Ross Drake

Larry Masser, Susan Lucci's agent, says he "fell in love with her the minute she walked into my office." No wonder. In a business bristling with explosive starlets, moist-lipped sex bombs, and assorted low-grade weaponry, Susan Lucci—Erica Martin on the ABC serial *All My Children* —is, stripped of hyperbole, a distractingly beautiful girl. She is also, according to reliable testimony, an intelligent actress and a down-to-earth lady with sane values.

Masser spent the better part of a year trying to get Susan a job, discovering, to his dismay, that nobody was looking for a gorgeous, serene, unspoiled actress, fresh out of college and strikingly self-possessed. "The trouble is," Masser says, "she's a chic, fine lady. And they don't want girls in her age range for that sort of role. She's just a little too classy."

Thus encumbered, and hindered by a long blank page of professional inexperience, Susan startled even herself by winning a lead role in a movie, playing a prostitute's suicidal daugh- →

Susan Lucci

TV GUIDE JUNE 5, 1971   27

and my first professional
profile in a publication
(*TV GUIDE*, June 1971).
I had no idea this article was
coming out.

Our days on and off the set were always fun. Here I am dining at Tavern on the Green with Debbie Morgan, Carol Burnett, Darnell Williams, Kim Delaney, and Larry Lau . . .

at Club A in New York with Julio Iglesias . . .

and at the Friar's Testimonial Dinner for Dean Martin with Dean, Shirley MacLaine, and Sammy Davis, Jr.

This is Mona and Erica in the early days of the show.

I loved working with Fra Heflin from our very first scene together!

Here Erica is dressed to the nines. . . .
She *loves* to make a grand entrance.

And, of course, she *loves* getting
men's attention, too. This is
Erica with her many grooms:

Dr. Jeff Martin . . .

Phillip Brent . . .

Tom Cudahy . . .

Adam Chandler . . .

Mike Roy . . .

Dimitri Marick (they were the equivalent of daytime's Taylor and Burton!) . . .

Travis Montgomery . . .

Jack Montgomery (on the day of the wedding that never happened) . . .

and with Jack as they consoled each other after their divorce!

Jack Montgomery again (on the day of the wedding that definitely happened) . . .

Among Erica's many other lovers, there was the soulful Jeremy Hunter . . .

the valiant Chris Stamp (Ryan's stepfather who was shot in the line of action, but not by Erica!) . . .

and heartthrob Ryan Lavery, pictured here in quite a steamy scene.

All of these storylines were great fun, but Dick Shoberg and I really enjoyed the one in St. Croix as it was daytime drama's first shoot on location!

Some of the people joining us there, included Sylvia Lawrence, my first makeup artist, Jack Coffey, Dick Shoberg, Agnes Nixon, head of ABC daytime Josie Emerich, Steve Fenn, two of our producers Bud Kloss and Felicia Menei-Beher, Agnes's husband, Bob Nixon, our wonderful director Jack Wood, and our fabulous crew.

Another fun shoot held outside the studio, but closer to home, involved Erica modeling at New York City's Metropolitan Museum of Art. It was my favorite outdoor shoot of all!

Although *AMC* had many firsts, its pioneering spirit is most apparent in its storylines. This is Bianca's Intervention, the story that won me the Emmy . . .

and a scene from the story line in which Bianca comes out.

Here I am receiving my star on the Hollywood Walk of Fame . . .

and on that same day with some of the cast members of *AMC*.

This, of course, is me holding my long-awaited and treasured Emmy . . .

and hosting the Emmy award show with Regis Philbin at Radio City Music Hall.

I've always had great fun acting with guest stars, such as Rosie O'Donnell who played Adam Chandler's maid . . .

and, of course, acting with all my cast mates. Dear, longtime colleagues such as Jimmy Mitchell . . .

and the beloved Eileen Hurley, who was a great actress and wonderful storyteller, are both sorely missed.

I am forever grateful to *All My Children* creator, Agnes Nixon, for the world she imagined for us to play in.

The Mouse has been very good to me, too.

You never forget the kindness of people when you're sick, but Fran and Barry, God bless them, went beyond the call of duty when they called the next day to tell me they postponed opening night for a week so I could take care of myself and get back on my feet. As hard as it was, I spent the next four days following my doctor's orders. And it was a good thing I did because it paid off. My strength returned and I was back at rehearsals in time to make the new opening night of the show. I have to thank Dr. Korovin for her insistence that I lie low. If it weren't for her supreme care, I would never have fulfilled my lifelong dream to perform on Broadway.

By the time I was up and out of bed, *All My Children* was on hiatus for the holidays, so I was able to put one hundred percent of my focus on final preparations for the big night. I poured my heart and soul into the days I had left. I used to lie in bed at night with an earpiece, listening to the music and practicing my blocking and dancing. Helmut would endure an hour or two of stomping and moving around until he'd finally lean over and say, "Are you done yet?"

The first time I worked with the orchestra for the show was the day we were set to open. Up until then, I had only worked with a piano. Since the show was already up and running, a new actor taking over a role only gets around three weeks' rehearsal time before they are basically put in the mix on their very first night in the cast. My only dress rehearsal was on the day of opening night. And if that isn't enough to make you nervous, there is a whole additional show that happens backstage while the play is going on in the front of the house. Wardrobe people, other cast members, and crew are all scurrying about. *Annie Get Your Gun* required some very quick changes that meant lots of Velcro in the costumes and people helping me do everything from changing my shoes to grabbing my props. I had to literally hit the ground running.

We took a break between rehearsal and my first performance. I was a basket of nerves. I didn't want to eat before going onstage but forced myself to get some chicken soup down me so I wouldn't get light-headed. I had some hot water with lemon and honey to keep my vocal cords well coated and sucked on some delicious glycerin drops Joan had suggested I use.

This particular production introduces Annie on page thirteen of the script. I got ready early so I could watch the show from the wings. I was in such awe of the company I was performing with, especially Tom Wopat who was my costar. The kids from the show came and put their arms around me and we would stand in the wings together and watch until it was my turn to go on.

Annie's entrance required me to climb up a wooden ladder and into the orchestra pit stage left while holding my rifle. Climbing that ladder felt so elementary, as if I were putting on a show in my backyard with my friends. And yet fitting, too, because it was as if I were actually coming onstage through a barn. As I reached the top rung, one of the clarinet players would grab my rifle so I could pull myself over the top of the ladder and duck down until it was time for me to appear. Once I was securely in place, I'd grab my rifle back and wait for my cue. When I heard the line, I'd walk down a flight of stairs on the side of the stage and make my grand entrance, filthy and muddy, as Annie Oakley.

That moment was magic on opening night and every night there-after. My parents were in the audience that first evening, surrounded by my friends and cast mates from *All My Children*. It was very sweet to know that all of those warm and familiar faces were out there, even if I couldn't see them. In fact, I made a point to tell the stage manager that I never wanted to know who was in the audience on any particular night until after the show so I wouldn't get nervous before going on. I remember asking Tom Wopat how he did it. He loved looking into the audience and seeing familiar faces. He was very much at ease doing that, which I respected but could never understand.

"I have been doing musicals since I was twelve years old," he said.

To this day, I would rather not see the faces of the audience or know who is out there. Don't get me wrong. I want you to come, but I don't want to know where you are sitting or that you're even there until after my last curtain call.

Although I am shy, I'm at home onstage. I'd much rather be surprised to learn who came to see the show at the end of the evening. It's a funny combination, but there are a lot of people in the theater who feel this way.

My friends who were in the audience that first night later told me that they saw my father beaming with great pride as he watched his little girl up onstage. Kelly Ripa told me that she was sitting right near him and generously shared her observations with me. "Your dad was so proud of you. *So* proud," she said.

My parents never held back from telling me how proud they were of me over the years, but it is always great to hear, especially since my dad wasn't completely on board with my decision to pursue acting in the beginning. They were always in the audience whenever I performed, but my father in particular had not been so anxious for me to become a professional actress. It was extremely meaningful to me that my Broadway debut was at this particular theater because my father had a hand in building the original steel structure for the Marriott Marquis Hotel, which was the building in which the theater was housed. Talk about a coincidence!

I don't know that there are words to describe what it feels like to be up there on a Broadway stage for the very first time. It took my breath away and it was THRILLING! The expression "There's no business like show business" comes from this very show, and in a way, that just about sums it all up. Being onstage, in a theater on Broadway, is everything I ever wanted as an actress. Opening night was a moment when I can honestly say that all of my dreams from the time I was a little girl had finally come true. I didn't realize just how thrilling it would be, and I certainly did not expect the standing ovation I received at the end of that performance and after all of the other performances that followed.

At the end of that first night, the press came running down the aisles of the theater, snapping photos and waving their recorders with their pens in the air. I'd seen them do this at other openings for other actors, but I never paid as much attention to that kind of excited reaction as I did that night. It was an absolute dream.

After I changed out of my costume, Sallie Schoneboom, my publicist from ABC, and I walked outside through the stage door. We were headed to the after-party to celebrate my wonderful and unforgettable Broadway debut. There were police barricades everywhere holding back mobs of people. It was utter mayhem, as some people even stood on top of their cars, screaming. I turned to Sallie and said, "Did something happen? Is there a fire?"

"No, Susan. They're here for you," she said, beaming with great pride as we took in that incredible moment together. I had no idea such a thing would happen. But then again, I had been one of those fans many times, waiting to meet Sammy Davis Jr., Lena Horne, and Richard Burton. I guess I just never thought there would be those types of fans waiting for me.

I only appeared in *Annie Get Your Gun* for four weeks, with the understanding that I would jump back into the role when Bernadette Peters left the show the following April. I was very pleased with the experience and eager to come back. Unfortunately, that opportunity never came to fruition. Bernadette decided to extend her contract twice, which was well within her prerogative. Fran and Barry assured me that when Bernadette decided to leave, the part was mine. When she actually did leave the show, however, the producers of *All My Children* wouldn't let me commit to the show because they were about to embark on one of the most important story lines in the show's history—a story that would require more of my time than ever and the material would be very intense and demanding. They simply couldn't guarantee that I would be done filming and out of the studio in time to make an eight o'clock curtain every night. Although they wouldn't tell me exactly what that story was

at the time, it ended up being the story of Erica's daughter Bianca
coming out as a lesbian.

*T*he part of Bianca was played with so much intelligence,
compassion, and skill by the outstanding young actress
Eden Riegel, whom I came to love and admire and count as
one of my closest friends in the industry. From the moment
Eden was cast, I knew she was the right choice for the part.
The material was so complex, yet she was undaunted by
the challenge. She brought that special something to the
role that made her character even richer than the words on
the page. The story line was potentially controversial. We
were told to expect a lot of talk in the media around what
we were doing—and there was. In the end, it was worth
it if we could help one teenager and hopefully even more
who might have been struggling with their sexuality feel
better about who they are and find the inner strength to
live as their authentic selves. Ultimately the story line was
widely accepted and greatly praised. This could not have
been achieved without several important elements being in
place, including intelligent, informed, and sensitive writing, directing, and performing.

Although I understood where the producers of *All My Children*
were coming from, I was very disappointed about not being allowed
to reprise my role as Annie Oakley on Broadway. I DO NOT . . .
take "no" easily. In fact, it was *very* hard for me. At the time I didn't
understand the demands that were going to be put on me with this
new story line. I really thought I could do both. The producers were

continually assuring me that in their opinion, it couldn't be done. I didn't know what to make of this, but I finally, after *much* discussion, accepted it. There was a very strong trust bond between myself and the producers that time and experience certainly had built. This was one of those occasions when I had to rely on that trust. I continued studying with Joan Lader anyway, keeping up my voice, you know, just in case and because I loved the idea of returning to Broadway in this role so much. Sadly, the chance to get up on that stage one more time as Annie Oakley never came. I was very sad the day I met with Fran and Barry for lunch and had to give them the news that I'd be unable to continue. I don't know why I thought of this, but I asked the Weisslers if they had ever considered the ebullient Reba McEntire to play Annie Oakley. I thought she was absolutely born to play the role. The Weisslers are the very best at reaching out to an untapped Broadway crowd because they aren't afraid to cast talent that gives their shows a different perspective than traditional Broadway offers. Naturally, they said they had thought of Reba. In fact, she eventually took over the part and she did a wonderful job playing Annie.

CHAPTER 10

Life Is a Cabaret

Shortly after I was featured in a *TV Guide* article in June 1971, I received a call on the set of *All My Children* asking if I'd like to cohost a local New York City morning show with Alan Alda, who was filling in for the regular host. This was my very first appearance on a talk show since being cast as Erica Kane. I wasn't even a guest—I was a cohost! It was thrilling to be asked, but even more thrilling to have the opportunity to work with Alan. He was an absolute dream and an effortless, gracious cohost. He, of course, recognized that I had never done anything like this before and made it very easy for me to relax. Anytime you get a chance to work with a professional like Alan, it is an ideal setup to go on and do more of the same.

I met Regis Philbin for the first time in the early seventies when he was hosting *A.M. Los Angeles.* His producers asked me to come on his show and do something domestic because it was so against Erica's nature. I was newly married and *All My Children* had just made its debut. It is fair to say that my husband was the real cook in our family. Helmut and I always laugh about my attempts in the kitchen during the early days of our marriage, which is a good thing, because if we hadn't laughed at my earnest efforts, we might have gotten into some very dramatic exchanges. Frankly, we are a perfect match because Helmut loves to cook and I love to eat, especially the foods he makes.

When we were first married, I didn't know how to cook anything. I wanted to prepare delicious meals for my husband, but I lacked the skills and knowledge to pull it off. All I knew how to cook was spaghetti sauce, tuna casserole, and frozen chicken potpies. The first time I made dinner for us as a married couple, I was in the kitchen stirring canned mushroom soup into my fabulous tuna casserole, when Helmut came up behind me at the stove, looked over my shoulder into the pot, and said, "I love you, honey, but I can't eat that shit!"

Thinking I had to up the ante, I attempted to make a roast pork dish because I knew it was one of the national dishes of Austria. I mistakenly ordered a smoked pork from the butcher and tried to roast it. I didn't know the difference between these two varieties of pork, so I popped it in the oven and turned it into a completely inedible piece of shoe leather that smelled nearly as bad as it tasted.

I made another effort to surprise Helmut, this time with a beautiful apple strudel, which was a total disaster as well. I had been inspired by watching Helmut's sister-in-law Erna make this dish in Austria. Erna is the quintessential European wife. She works, comes home, irons, cooks, and keeps the most gorgeous home. I admire her very much, and as a young newlywed, I wanted to be just like she was around our house. Erna spread her dough out on her kitchen table, sharing with me that you cannot work it too much or it will get too hard. I watched her every move, carefully taking notes so I could re-create her strudel for Helmut when we got back to New York.

The first time I tried to make the strudel on my own, I was in the kitchen for five hours. I should have known right then and there that something was very wrong. By the time I finished, my eyes were bloodshot and I was unable to really "see" what I had created. I thought it looked pretty good for a first attempt. I was very proud of my finished product.

Helmut took one look at it and said, "Honey, you have a gift for being an actress. I'm a cook. Why don't we stick to the things we know."

And you know what? I think that has been one of the secrets to making our marriage last for more than forty years.

So, when Regis's producers were looking for something for me to do on his show, we ruled out a cooking segment pretty quickly. Thankfully, my mother was very good at flower arranging, especially ikebana, a traditional form of Japanese flower design. With some quick tips from my mother, I figured I could pull something like that off, so I agreed to go on the show to create a floral masterpiece. The segment was terrific.

Just as Alan Alda had done before, Regis made me feel like I belonged on a talk show. I will never forget how warm and encouraging he was. He was fully aware of my work on *All My Children*, even back then, and has remained totally supportive of me throughout the years. He is very funny, always makes me laugh, and is absolutely wonderful.

Many people credit Regis Philbin with coining my nickname, "La Lucci"—and while it is true that he was the first to publicly call me that, long before he and I met, I was often called to the set of *All My Children* as La Lucci by one of the producers or director. Somewhere over the course of time, La Lucci became my moniker at our show. Whenever actors are wanted on the set, someone announces it over a loudspeaker so you know your scenes are coming up next.

"Next up, item twelve, Phoebe, Chuck, Mona, Tara, and Erica— LaLucci to the set, please" was quite common.

It wasn't until Regis began calling me La Lucci outside the set of *All My Children* that the name became so well known. Ever since then, it has just stuck. It feels so natural whenever I hear it. It's become so synonymous with Susan Lucci that there's even a La Lucci panini named for me at Hoffman's deli in my hometown.

Regis Philbin and I became very friendly over the years. Although we don't socialize that much, we do occasionally see each other at functions in New York or meet for dinner. Now that I am in Los Angeles, those opportunities are rare, but I always look forward to spending time with him and his gorgeous wife, Joy, who I think is a great lady. There is a lot of warmth between us.

Much to my surprise and delight, Regis and Joy attended my opening night of *Annie Get Your Gun*. After the show, he came backstage to congratulate me. It was on that same night that he broached the subject of doing a nightclub act with him.

"Are you asking me to open for you?" I replied, thrilled at the prospect, but not sure I was really hearing what I was hearing.

"I don't want you to think of it as opening for me—let's do an act together." He was being very kind and generous.

Unfortunately, I didn't have a nightclub act. I thought it was really great that Regis was proposing that I do one with him, but I had never tried anything like this before. I had just enjoyed my first night performing live on Broadway. I wasn't sure that I wanted to jump right into another commitment. I graciously thanked Regis for the offer, but thought it wasn't the right thing to do at the time.

"C'mon, Susan. Let's do this. Why don't you get an act together and we'll take it on the road!" he coaxed.

It didn't take a lot of cajoling before I said, "Okay." I explained that I needed to get through my commitment to the Weisslers, but when I was done, this would become my next project.

John McDaniel was the first person I thought to call. I knew he would know just how to put together an act. We began working together in his downtown Manhattan loft. John and I shared our thoughts on song selection and style. We picked a wide variety of music that worked for my key and range, including "If I Were a Bell," "You Better Love Me While You May," "I Can Cook Too,"

and Marvin Hamlisch's original composition for me, "Winning Isn't Everything."

John had access to the very best musicians in the city and used his influence to get them to agree to accompany me using his orchestrations. He was absolutely terrific to work with because he helped me get out of my comfort zone and challenged me to create this type of show. This nightclub act was another dream come true.

We decided I'd do my first show at Feinstein's, an intimate venue inside the Regency Hotel in New York City, where I'd perform for two consecutive weeks in late September and early October 2001. I was very excited about the show. However, the closer we got to those dates, the more nervous I became. Once again, I wasn't sure I was totally up to the task at hand. I had been working hard all summer on the material, but as the show dates loomed, so did my nerves.

I went to work on the morning of September 11, 2001, as if it were just another beautiful sunny day in New York City. The skies were the bluest of blue without a single cloud in sight. There was a crisp fall feel in the air as I made my way from the car into the studio on the west side of Manhattan. Shortly after I arrived in the hair and makeup room, I saw on one of the monitors that a plane had just crashed into the World Trade Center. Val Reichenbach, my hairstylist, and I looked at each other, asking, "How could this happen?" It was a picture-perfect day outside. We started formulating various theories. Maybe the pilot was lost or had a heart attack and died. We didn't realize what was really happening. How could we?

Fifteen minutes later, we all understood that this was not an accident. It was shortly after nine o'clock in the morning, when a second plane crashed into the other tower. Something inside me knew right away that this was the handiwork of terrorists.

When that second plane hit, we all felt immediately vulnerable. The largest Red Cross in Manhattan was located just a few blocks away and Con Ed was across the street. We had no idea if that made our neighborhood a target or not. Still, our beloved city was under attack and there was nothing we could do. Word of what had just happened began to spread around the set. There was no protocol for this. We had no idea what we were supposed to do next.

Were we supposed to keep working?

Would it be better to stop and try to get home to our loved ones?

Although we were hearing bits and pieces of what was happening practically outside our stage door, no one in the studio had really clued in to the impact or severity of the situation quite yet. There were still people arguing about where to move a set or when to get a camera in place. It all felt so wrong. I wanted to make some phone calls, to check on my family, but I was told that cell service was out and getting through on a landline was next to impossible. When I tried to use my phone anyway, for whatever reason, it worked. I was able to reach Helmut and then Liza at her apartment on the east side of Manhattan, and then Andreas, who was at school in Georgetown. I was worried that he would wake up and hear what was happening in New York from someone else. I wanted him to know we were all fine. I had no idea that he would soon be dealing with another crash, at the Pentagon, a short distance from where he was living.

I told Andreas to go to the college campus and stay there. I wanted him to be with his friends. I lost our connection right after telling him that. I tried to call him back, but there was no service. There was only silence.

My inclination was to go to the basement of our building, where the production offices were located, so I could check on everyone down there. It didn't take long before we were all gathered in the basement and watching together as the world changed in front of our eyes.

Once both towers came down, we were asked to stay in the building until two o'clock that afternoon. Everyone on the set was very emotional and in pieces. There was so much anxiety about the safety of our loved ones, but we all hung in there together.

When we temporarily lost power in the studio, people began talking about whether or not we should keep working or go home. Canceling a day of shooting can cost a network hundreds of thousands of dollars. It simply isn't done. Once the power was restored, it was decided that we would try to carry on and keep shooting. That decision reminded me of the play I did in high school a few days after the assassination of John F. Kennedy, when we were told that the show must go on. So, as wrong as it felt, the cast and crew at *All My Children* did what we were told to do and tried to get through that very sad day. But despite everyone's best efforts, we just couldn't do it. The cast and crew—everyone was in tears. This was the second and only other time in my career that the show did not go on.

We stayed in the building and waited, trying to reach our families while making our plans to get home. There were a number of us who had gathered in the hair and makeup room that day. Jack Scalia, who played Chris Stamp, was among them. I vividly remember us looking at each other and saying, "The world will never be the same."

New York City was on full lockdown. The airspace had been closed, the bridges and tunnels were blocked, and the subways padlocked shut. There was no possibility of getting back to Garden City that day. Thankfully, our wardrobe department was able to outfit almost everyone with comfortable walking shoes, sneakers, and anything else we needed to make the trek to wherever we could get to after leaving the studio.

"No-No"—our wonderful and warmhearted wardrobe mistress whose real name was Nanette, but everyone called her No-No—had a car in the city and offered to drive as many people home as she could fit. I took her up on her offer to drive through Central Park and drop me off at Liza's apartment.

When we finally all piled into No-No's car and got to the east side, it was as if no one there knew what was happening. It was strange and surreal. Some of the stores were still open, so I stopped and bought a dozen bagels just in case Liza and her friends needed them to hold them over for a few days. I had no idea about the far-reaching impact of the attacks on New York City. No one did.

As the grim situation continued to unfold, like many of my fellow New Yorkers, I wanted to go downtown and offer help, but since I am not a nurse or a medic, I knew there wasn't much I would be able to do, and truth be told, there wasn't much to do. However, the show gathered sweatshirts and other items from the wardrobe department and brought them to the Red Cross to distribute to volunteers.

By six o'clock that night, we heard that the Triborough Bridge had been reopened and we could leave the city to go home. We piled into a borrowed SUV and made our way toward Long Island. When we were crossing the bridge, I looked behind me at my beautiful city. There were two gaping holes in the skyline and billowing smoke that had created the darkest cloud I had ever seen over the lower third of Manhattan—one I never want to see again.

A week or two later, I was asked to participate in a television commercial that would help the country and the rest of the world know that New York City was alive and open for business. Since I had been on Broadway, they asked me to assemble with the "Help Broadway" community to bring audiences back to New York. After the attacks of 9/11, all of the Broadway shows had gone dark, resulting in millions of dollars in losses every single day. Theater is an important tourism draw in New York City. And, for a time, people were afraid to come.

I felt so happy to be involved in this promotion. Joel Gray, Bernadette Peters, and Michele Lee were just a few of the Broadway greats who participated. On the day we were set to shoot the commercial, we were all being held in one of the local theaters until the producers were ready for us to head out to the heart of Times Square, where the piece was to be shot. I sat next to Michele Lee, who is a marvelous performer and someone who I knew had lots of experience doing nightclub acts. I told her I was working on a nightclub act, too.

"Where are you trying it out?" she asked.

It wasn't a strange question, but it threw me for a loop because I didn't expect it. Was I supposed to try my act out? I was so focused on working at *All My Children* during the day and then singing at night with Joan Lader, my voice teacher, that I'd never considered the notion of testing the show outside of Manhattan.

"I haven't done that yet," I said.

"Oh." That was her response.

Uh-oh was the first thing that came to my mind as I felt my stomach sink right down to my toes.

I felt ridiculous. I was scheduled to open at Feinstein's in a couple of weeks and I hadn't tried the show out in a "soft opening" anywhere. Michele was absolutely right. But I momentarily reassured myself by recalling all the challenges I had successfully met before. *I have always given my all to everything I do*, I reasoned. *So I might as well do this big, too, right?* I suppose that type of thinking was really my lack of experience talking. I had no idea how much you learn each night that you perform. I am used to working quickly—even when I did *Annie Get Your Gun*, I essentially learned my part in three weeks. I live in a world where I am handed a new script every day. I am expected to learn that script, rehearse it, shoot the scenes, and move on. It never dawned on me that people actually take their time and work through the kinks before they open at one of the top venues in New York City. Besides, with everything that was happening in the world, maybe the question wasn't "Should I have tested the show somewhere else?" Maybe the question was "Is this the right time to do the show at all?" But then I remembered why we were all sitting in the theater that day. We were promoting tourism and bringing visitors back to New York City. If I didn't go on with the show as planned, I'd be giving in to the terrorists. I wasn't going to let that happen. No, I would find the strength and courage to do something that would make people feel good again. So once more, the show would go on.

Understandably, Feinstein's delayed the opening of their season by two weeks. Shirley Bassey was scheduled to appear only a couple of days after the attacks, but of course that didn't happen. This meant that my show would be the first to open there after 9/11. I wanted to do something to honor those we lost and all of the brave men and women of New York City by putting a table aside for the firefighters, police officers, and rescue workers who were out there laboring so hard to piece our city back together. I felt it wouldn't be right to open and not pay homage to these people for saving our lives, so I went to Mr. Tisch, the owner of the hotel, and asked if he would reserve a table each night for these brave workers. It was a very easy sell. Mr. Tisch was very much on board with my idea. The public relations team at the Regency reached out to several local heroes and invited them to come down and enjoy the show each night I was there. I opened the show by introducing the fine men and women so everyone else in the room was aware of their presence and contributions. That table was full every night as the audience showed their immense appreciation for those very special guests.

Doing a nightclub act is interesting. Much like my experience on Broadway, I didn't do a dress rehearsal until the day of my first show. I worked with my band a couple of days prior to opening, but the first time I did a full run-through with them in the venue was a few short hours before going onstage. This is fairly common wherever you perform. John McDaniel was accompanying me, so he knew the music as well as I did. He spoke to the lighting designer before the show to give him an idea of our needs.

The most interesting thing about performing at Feinstein's is that they serve lunch in the room where you will later perform. So during our dress rehearsal, waiters were breaking down tables and setting up for dinner. I had to laugh because I thought to myself, *It can't be any noisier than this at night,* which was a good thing and maybe the best preparation I could have had.

I always get butterflies before going onstage, but on this particular opening night, I had big butterflies. Feinstein's is a small room. Thank goodness I had been through the experience of having to sing for Marvin Hamlisch and the Weisslers in their living rooms because this felt eerily the same. Performing at Feinstein's, you are very close to the audience. You can see every face in the room. It's a small stage that's placed a couple of feet in front of the first few tables. This was a very different experience from Broadway, far more intimate and very personal.

I sang a plethora of songs by artists ranging from Peggy Lee and Quincy Jones to Marvin Hamlisch. I especially liked doing a song called "New York City Blues," a song John McDaniel and I both knew, yet hardly anyone ever performs. John was blown away that I was even aware of the song. I told him I remembered Peggy Lee singing it on *The Ed Sullivan Show* when I was a young girl. I don't know why I remembered it, but I did. I thought it was a great New York song, and under the circumstances, appropriate to include in my act.

I also sang "Winning Isn't Everything," a signature song Marvin Hamlisch had written just for me. I was so excited to introduce this song. I closed with "Alright, Okay, You Win," which seemed like a good choice, as the audience appeared to like it.

I was astounded that so many people came out on opening night to support my show. Liza Minnelli, Michael Feinstein, and Regis Philbin were all there to cheer me on. In a way, I think we were all there to cheer our great city on. Barbara Walters and Judge Judy Sheindlin came to see me during my two-week run, too. I didn't know Barbara well. She had interviewed me as one of her Most Fascinating People in 1999, the year I won my Emmy and did *Annie Get Your Gun*. I didn't feel all that fascinating, but it was a real honor to be included and thrilling for *All My Children* and Agnes Nixon because it crossed the show over from daytime into prime time. I often saw Barbara around the studio, in the hallways, on the elevator, and near the stage doors, as *The View* shared space with *All My Children* in New York. I had been a guest and even cohost on *The View* many times and loved that experience. I surely admire Barbara, as the rest of the world does. As busy as my schedule gets, Barbara Walters is someone who makes me wonder how many hours there are in a day for *her*. She does it all with such grace, dignity, and finesse. She interviews world leaders, hosts her talk show, and still finds the time to come out and support my nightclub act.

After seeing the show, Regis was more convinced than ever that we should take an act on the road together. And after this brief experience, I agreed. I asked John McDaniel to be my musical director, but he had other commitments, which didn't allow him the freedom to travel. Much to my delight, however, he introduced me to another wonderful and talented musical director named Shawn Gough. Shawn looks like a picture-perfect, blond Ralph Lauren model. He is very handsome and a pleasure to work with. He appears too young to be doing what he does and yet he is so very talented and good at it. He conducts the Christmas show at Radio City Music Hall and has worked on many Broadway productions, including *Billy Elliot, Sunday in the Park with George,* and *Emerald Man.*

Shawn is a perfectionist and a lot like Joan Lader—he doesn't miss a thing. He can listen to an entire orchestra and hear one violin miss a single note. Although he is an unbelievable musician who has the respect of so many people, Shawn doesn't bring his ego to the stage—a trait I find is common among the very best and most talented artists.

Regis Philbin and I ended up taking our nightclub act on the road for five glorious years. We had a fabulous time performing with each other. There has always been great chemistry between us. We toured and toured and performed in casinos, nightclubs, and concert halls all over the country. We even appeared with the very funny Don Rickles in Mississippi. We usually played to crowds ranging from two to five thousand people and you never knew who was going to be in the audience.

Occasionally, I did shows without Regis. During one particular performance while I was headlining at the Kravis Center in Palm Beach, Vic Damone was present. It just so happened that I sang "Old Black Magic" that night—a song he is known for. If you've ever been to a cabaret show, you may have noticed that the performers often keep water somewhere nearby. The reason for this is that sometimes your mouth gets dry and it's hard for you to sing unless you drink something. As luck would have it, I had just gotten off a plane—flying is notoriously dehydrating—and I was trying to belt out "Old Black Magic." After the show, Vic came backstage to say hello. He asked if he could offer me some helpful tips for future shows. I'm sure he noticed how much water I drank onstage. He shared his experience and few tricks of the trade with me, which were very useful and greatly appreciated. Vic Damone! Believe me, I've used those tips ever since.

One of my favorite parts of my show is the overture. Shawn had done a great arrangement of "Too Darn Hot" for me to come on-stage. When I appeared, I would sing and tell anecdotes for about forty minutes. I loved that connection with the audience because it was the first time I allowed myself to share a little bit more about me than I generally do. When I was done, Regis would come on and sing, then he'd ask me to come back out to do a few more numbers with him. Regis always brought me back onstage as "La Lucci" while singing "You Ought to Be in Pictures." Hearing him sing that song to me is so charming. Regis and I always closed our show singing a wonderful arrangement of the great Louis Armstrong's "What a Wonderful World." The audiences really enjoy that song as a duet. What fun we had, and the audiences did, too.

*H*ere's a typical set list for the songs I sang while touring with Regis:

SUSAN LUCCI
RUNNING ORDER

1. Too Darn Hot
2. Alright, Okay, You Win
3. Do You Wanna Dance?
4. They Say That Falling in Love Is Wonderful
5. New York City Blues
6. Fever
7. It's All Right with Me
8. Winning Isn't Everything—Segue
9. Too Darn Hot Playoff (Watch for Cut)
10. It Don't Mean a Thing—Segue
11. It Don't Mean a Thing Bows

Segue to Regis Act

As much as I enjoyed doing these shows with Regis over the course of more than five years, I had to step away from doing them after I agreed to do a little television show called *Dancing with the Stars*. This time it was pretty clear that there was no way I could keep doing *All My Children*, tour with Regis, *and* learn to dance all at the same time and on two different coasts. Something had to give. Even I had to concede that sometimes, unfortunately, there really are limits.

CHAPTER 11

The Cycle of Life

In early 1999, Helmut was set to have shoulder surgery as a result of an injury he had suffered while playing soccer in Europe as a young man. Golf is a passion for my husband and his shoulder pain was interfering with his game. His doctors assured him that the procedure was routine and that he had nothing to worry about. If all went well, he'd be back on the golf course swinging his club in no time.

When Helmut went in for the standard presurgical exam, the doctor discovered that he had a condition called atrial fibrillation, (also known as "A-fib"), which is an irregular heartbeat. I had heard of an irregular heartbeat, but I always thought that there were telltale signs, including dizziness, shortness of breath, or even the sensation of an irregular heartbeat. Helmut had none of these symptoms. Had he not gone in for his examination, we would never have known about his condition.

When he left the doctor's office, we both felt like we had more questions than answers, so we began making phone calls to friends and other physicians we knew so we could talk about the diagnosis.

I called a very good friend who is also a top cardiologist at a hospital not far from our home. We listened to everything he had to say before seeking out a second, third, and fourth opinion from other top doctors in Manhattan.

We found out that people who have A-fib are five times more likely to have a stroke, even if they don't have any obvious symptoms. What's more, if you have a stroke with A-fib, you double your chances of suffering a debilitating, or worse, a fatal one. These were not statistics I was willing to gamble my husband's life on. Thankfully, we caught it early enough to get Helmut on a program that involves medication, diet, and exercise. He has to go to the doctor every six weeks for blood work so the doctor can monitor his condition and make sure there are no changes that could increase the likelihood of having a stroke. As long as he stays on top of this, he will be fine.

Helmut and I have a very close relationship. For the most part, he is the caretaker. But whenever he has faced an unexpected medical condition, those roles are quickly reversed. I want to be by his side *every* . . . step . . . of the way. If he has a doctor's appointment, I like to go with him. I believe it's important to always have an extra set of eyes and ears—especially caring ones—seeing and hearing what the doctor has to say. Sometimes the person with the injury or condition is dealing with their emotions instead of listening to the explanation or various treatment options being discussed. Their wheels are spinning, so they may not hear everything someone else might hear. Also, in the case of my husband, English is not his first language, so I always want to make sure he doesn't miss something or misinterpret what is being said. I want to be there with him through the good times and the challenging times. He has always been there for me, too.

Shortly after that diagnosis, Helmut went to the doctor for some other tests because his PSA levels had gone up to alarming levels. The doctor recommended that he perform a biopsy. We were waiting for the results, but the doctor never called. We figured that no news was good news, so we decided to head out for dinner at a restaurant near our beach home. We had a visitor from Austria with us who was nineteen years old and who spoke almost no English. We wanted to have a casual dinner with this young woman so we could speak to her in German and help her feel welcome and comfortable in her new surroundings. When we got to the restaurant, it was surprisingly crowded for a Wednesday night. It turned out there were quite a few people we knew seated all around us.

Shortly after we arrived, Helmut's cell phone rang. It was the doctor calling to say that my husband had prostate cancer. Just like that. He was direct and to the point. Helmut hung up and placed his phone on the edge of the table. I could see that he was shaken up.

"Do you want to leave?" I asked. It was obvious he had been given some disturbing news.

"No. Let's stay and enjoy dinner." Of course, I think Helmut worried it would call more attention to the situation if we abruptly got up and left, so I tried to follow his lead and acted as if nothing was wrong.

When we went home that night, Helmut broke down, as well he should have. *Cancer* is a word you never want to hear in relation to yourself. It was really smart that he had made a point of going for regular checkups because his cancer was caught early enough to be operable. We called the children right away to let them know what was going on.

I spoke to Liza, who was at her home in California. She had been in Los Angeles working on *Passions*. I told her that I was planning to go to the local library and would stay there until I found out who was the very best doctor for Helmut to see. Before I could finish my thought, Liza said she had already pulled that information up on the Internet. She and I sat on the phone for an hour going through every bit of information she could find. Helmut sat next to me on our bed listening in on another phone.

We found out right away who the leaders in the field were, who the number one physician in New York was, and what our next step should be. We learned what all of our options were and we all came to the same conclusion. If it was operable, get it *out* of there. I hadn't had a lot of exposure to the wonders of the World Wide Web before that night, but afterward, I was a complete convert.

We wound up going to see Dr. Lapore in New York City, who'd studied with the leading physician in this field, Dr. Patrick Walsh, at Johns Hopkins. He was spectacular. He assured us that Helmut's cancer was operable. We didn't want Helmut left wondering if his cancer had spread, grown, or come back—he wanted it gone for good. We agreed and scheduled Helmut to have surgery as soon as possible. Thank God, there was no collateral damage from the procedure. Helmut was a great patient, and although it was quite a process, he recovered spectacularly.

Right after the surgery, he spent a couple of days in a room with four other men before transferring into a private room. Once he was there, I just wanted to do everything I could to make him feel better and to make him smile. I knew hospital food was never going to cut it with Helmut, so as a surprise, I arranged to have Café Boulud, one of our favorite restaurants in New York, cater dinner for him during the rest of his stay. I had to go to work during the day, but I was back at the hospital with him every single night. He had no idea I was doing this until a waitress from the restaurant showed up in his hospital room with a warming container and a complete, beautiful dinner for two. That excellent French food put a smile on his face from ear to ear.

Just two weeks after Helmut's diagnosis, I received some bad news about my father's health as well. My father was a lot like Helmut. He was an extremely athletic man. After he retired, my dad played golf three days a week and worked out three days a week in the gym; because he worked in construction for so many years, he had a really great physique. His big vice, however, was that he had been a longtime smoker. Worse yet, he smoked unfiltered cigarettes most of his life. This habit had plagued him before and it seemed as if it was causing some issues now, too. Years ago, when he was only fifty-one, he suffered a mild heart attack. My husband and I were only recently married at the time. We rushed to be at his side. When we arrived, I overheard one of the doctors telling my mother that "Mr. Lucci has done something very bad. He ripped out his IVs, ordered pizza for the staff, got dressed, and went outside for a smoke." As amusing as that sounded, the doctor was making it very clear that he didn't approve of my father's actions.

Thankfully, my father gave up smoking shortly after being released from the hospital, although there were a few occasions when I'd catch him bumming a cigarette from a perfect stranger, thinking no one was looking. "Hey Johnny, ya got a cigarette?" he'd ask. I think that was a World War II expression. My mother was upset whenever she'd find out he was sneaking a smoke here and there. The doctor assured her that bumming a couple of cigarettes a week was a lot better than his previous habit of smoking a couple of packs a day. "Don't give him too much stress over it," he'd say, knowing my mother wouldn't give up anyway.

Sadly, in 2002, at the same time as Helmut was ill, my father was diagnosed with a worsened heart condition. By this time, he was in his early eighties. His doctors were doing routine tests when they found a tumor in his lungs the size of a grapefruit. It could have been all of those years of smoking, or maybe the many years of working in construction, that caused the tumor. I don't suppose I will ever know the true cause or why it wasn't diagnosed earlier. Whatever the reason, the prognosis wasn't good.

My father's doctor wanted to take care of his weakened heart before addressing the issue of the tumor. That seemed like a wise course of action. Although I wanted to bring my father to New York City to see the very best doctors we could find, he seemed very content with the physicians he was seeing in West Palm Beach, Florida, where my parents were now living. When I met his surgeon, he seemed very confident and experienced. I knew why my dad was happy being in his care. The doctor inspired confidence in my father as well as in me.

The first leg of the surgery went very well. My father came out of the OR and the minute he could open his eyes and speak, he looked at my mother, who never left his side, and said, "Are *you* okay. How are *you* doing?" That was my dad. He was more concerned with how my mother was doing than with his own condition. He was selfless in so many ways.

My father recovered very well from this surgery. It was a good thing that he had been so active, as he was extremely physically fit for a man of his age. Even in his eighties, he was built like a much younger man.

The doctors sent him home with a lot of different medications. My father went from taking nothing before his surgery to taking lots of pills every day. Very late one night, he awoke and was completely disoriented. He got up out of bed and fell. He was taken back to the hospital, where they intubated him. That was not a pleasant experience. My mother spoke to the physician on duty to see if they could figure out what had happened. They soon realized that there were specific instructions on my father's medical records to avoid giving him a certain medication. Somehow, those directions slipped through the cracks and he had been given that medication.

During that same night, my father had another adverse reaction to the medication he was on. This time when they intubated him, something happened to his vocal cords and he was no longer able to speak. We were told he might not be able to talk again. I think my father was terribly demoralized after that. I could see him losing his spirit. When I spoke to his doctor about his prognosis, he said they might be able to repair the damage if my father could get stronger. It was a catch-22 for my dad because he was on oxygen and just couldn't eat well enough to fortify himself. He didn't have the wherewithal to get stronger.

Throughout this time, Helmut and I had been involved in a massive remodeling job on our home in Garden City. We were essentially doubling its size. Helmut and I were living in our apartment in New York City while he recovered from his cancer and while our house remained in shambles for almost two years. It seemed as if everything around me was falling apart. The two most important men in my life were struggling and I didn't know what else I could do to help them. I prayed to God to let my husband be well and to help my father to heal.

I wanted my house back the way it was because I thought that everything else would go back to being the same, too. My home became a metaphor for the great big mess that was happening all around me. I did my best to take each day one at a time, but it was very difficult.

After my dad's surgery, he was taken to a nursing home to recover and gain his strength so he could ultimately go in for the reparative surgery he needed. Unfortunately, he wasn't eating well, so his condition continued to deteriorate. I was touched to see my mother take such good care of my dad. She brushed his teeth, washed his hair, and kept him shaved and clean. My father was a proud man. We all knew how much he hated not being able to care for himself. My mother tended to my father like she was a teenager. She moved with such grace and never-ending stamina as she constantly checked his oxygen tank, monitors, and charts between visits from the doctors and nurses on staff. It was wonderfully comforting to see my mother being so attentive and nurturing when my father absolutely needed it the most—especially because I had never really seen her in that role. My father had been her rock, and now she *had* to be his.

She did everything she could to keep my dad comfortable, despite the obvious fact that he was miserable. My father was the kind of man who would have given you the shirt off his back. He was always so protective. He always held my arm when we crossed a street together. Always, even as an adult. It was really hard to see him so vulnerable. I flew down to Florida as many weekends as I possibly could to be with him and to make sure my mother was taking care of herself, too. Although my father wasn't able to articulate what it meant to him, I could see in his eyes and in his face that he was so happy to have my mother and me there together. I wished so much that I could help him more. The main reason my father could no longer eat well was that his teeth began to bother him to the point where he was in a lot of pain and discomfort. I hadn't been told until my father got sick that he had suffered some type of infection while serving in the South Pacific during the war. The solution the doctors came up with at the time was to pull out all of his teeth and put in dentures. When my father began losing weight from his illness, the dentures became loose and terribly uncomfortable. He couldn't speak, and now he couldn't eat. One weekend, while I was visiting my dad, I asked one of the nurses if she could let me speak to the hospital chef. Since I had experience making my children's baby food, I had the idea that the chef might be able to blend some tasty and nutritious meals for my father so he could better manage his eating. I explained the problem to the chef, who was extremely open to my idea, but the facility manager said she couldn't commit to helping my dad until she could file the proper paperwork with the hospital administrators. She thought this procedural formality might take a couple of days. Well, I didn't think my father would last that long if he couldn't eat. So I did the next best thing. I had a tray of his favorite cannoli and an assortment of other Italian pastries hand-delivered from Carmine's in nearby West Palm Beach. I figured the creamy filling inside the pastries would be easy for him to eat—and I knew he'd enjoy it—and I thought the staff would, too.

At the time I don't believe any of us realized how quickly he would deteriorate. I was working in New York, but was monitoring the situation every single day. Liza was busy working at a new job in

Los Angeles. It never occurred to me to tell her to come be by her grandfather's side. I honestly believed he would recover and come home. Andreas was very close to his grandfather, so he wanted to fly to Florida to be with him. My father had spent a lot of wonderful time with Andreas over the years. They both shared a love of golf. There were many times when my father went to the driving range with Andreas, watched him practice, and played in the many tournaments he competed in. My father was an early riser, so he frequently picked Andreas up in the mornings to take him to a diner for breakfast before heading out to the golf course together. I know it meant so much to him to have Andreas by his side during his illness, even if he couldn't tell him so.

My father passed away at five-thirty in the evening on November 22, 2002. My mother had gone home to get some things done and was on her way back to the hospital. It was devastating for all of us that no one was with him when he died. In a way, it was very much like my father to go when no one was around so he could protect us from having to suffer through his dying.

I saw my father be so good to my mother for my entire life, and now my mother was in that role for him. She was so hands-on good to him during his last days. Any insignificant differences we had with each other melted away. There was no meaning in petty grudges or family squabbles. None of that seemed important anymore. My father could sense this. I know he could and I am certain he had tremendous joy in his heart because he regained that twinkle in his eyes that I recognized from when I was a little girl. He had watched our family coming together during those last weeks. Knowing he felt that way before he died filled my heart with happiness, even if my heart was slowly breaking each day as he slipped away.

After receiving word that my father had passed, Andreas and I flew to Florida on the very first flight the next morning.

When we arrived in Palm Beach, we helped my mother make the proper arrangements. My mother asked me if I would give the eulogy. I wasn't prepared to speak at the funeral. Although I was very glad to have the opportunity to tell everybody how wonderful my dad was, it was also very difficult for me, as I was extremely distraught and very emotional. I was having a hard time comprehending that my father was really gone. I couldn't believe that it happened so fast. Three months had passed from diagnosis to his death. As I look back, maybe this was a blessing in disguise, but at the time it all felt unreal and like there hadn't been enough time to prepare, to heal, to fix, or to say good-bye.

After my father passed away, I worried about my mother being all alone. My mother and father had each other for so many years. She didn't know any other way of life except being with my dad. There is never enough time on this earth with your loved ones and never a good time to watch them go. My natural progression was to begin thinking about what my life would be like if I ever lost Helmut. I found myself going into an imagined mourning for when he's not there anymore. I started playing a terrible game of "what if?" and "when?" that took me several years to stop doing. Imagining my life without Helmut was the worst feeling I have ever had. The hardest thing about loving someone is how vulnerable it makes you.

I miss my father so much.

I could see that my mother was really lost without my father. There have been many times when I've called out to ask him to look after her, and while he's at it, to put in a few good words for my children and grandchildren, too, because he was such a good man that I am sure my father has God's ear. My mother has been such a trouper. Somehow, she managed to pick herself up by the bootstraps and continue on with her life. I have no idea how she does that, but I have seen it happen over and over again.

I don't think I ever realized just how capable and able my mother could be. Although it has been several years since my father passed away, I am sure there isn't a single day that goes by when my mother doesn't miss him. I know I do. After a decent period of time had passed, I began encouraging my mother to start accepting invitations from her friends to go out and do things. She has terrific friends in her life in Palm Beach. Although I offered to bring her up to New York to be closer to us, she wouldn't hear of it. She likes her life in Florida. She likes living so independently. I totally understood what she meant and why that was so important to her. She hasn't let her loss break her spirit.

CHAPTER 12

Celebrations

Thirteen has always been my lucky number. Helmut and I were married on September 13; my mother and father were married on October 13; my daughter, Liza, was born thirteen days late; and Andreas thirteen days early. All of these life-altering events made it hard to ignore the significance of the number thirteen in my life.

As our twenty-fifth wedding anniversary was fast approaching in September of 1994, Helmut and I wanted to do something very special to celebrate. But, as we discovered after we married, September is a challenging time of year to get away. Our kids were going back to school, I was busy at work, and there were lots of demands that found us postponing a celebration for this milestone anniversary.

In an effort to make some time to spend with the family, I decided to take a week off around Thanksgiving. Helmut and I thought it might be a good time to take the kids to Austria and visit his family. I couldn't think of a better way to celebrate our anniversary than a family vacation.

We arrived in Vienna on a Saturday night. The next morning, Helmut arranged through a friend of his for us to go to the Hofburg

Kapelle, the emperor's private chapel, to hear the Vienna Boys Choir perform. I hadn't realized the Vienna Boys Choir was a five-hundred-year-old institution. They sing at high mass on Sunday in the chapel. It was breathtaking. The boys sounded like angels. Literally every note I heard gave me goose bumps.

It had been a very rainy and dreary day. When we left the chapel, we dashed across the street and stopped into a café for some coffee. Liza, Andreas, Helmut's brother Gunther and sister-in-law Erna were with us, too. About twenty minutes after we all sat down, Gunther turned to Helmut and asked if he had seen the package he had been carrying. He was speaking in German, so I was doing my best to understand. Helmut told him he didn't notice a package. Gunther asked Erna, who also said she didn't know anything about it.

"I must have left it in the chapel," Gunther said.

We finished our coffee and walked back across the street to see if we could locate the missing article. By the time we got to the chapel, however, everything was closed up tight. There was a big Gothic-looking door and beside it was a tiny bell. Helmut pushed the button, hoping someone would come to answer, but no one did.

Helmut then turned to Andreas, who was carrying two oversize umbrellas, and said, "Use those to knock on the door." Hearing that loud pounding, the altar woman we had seen arranging flowers earlier opened the door, but only a tiny little crack.

Gunther explained the situation, again speaking in German. The woman nodded her head and motioned for us to come in and look around for the missing package. She opened the door just wide enough for us to walk through. Once we were all inside, she slammed it shut behind us. From that particular entrance, the only way to get into the chapel was to walk down the long center aisle. As we started to make our way, I noticed that all of the lights were turned on. I looked up and saw the most beautiful arrangements of flowers on the altar. I didn't think anything of it because we were, after all, inside the emperor's private chapel, in Vienna. This was obviously how they always keep the church—beautiful and spectacular!

Helmut took me by the arm and began walking me down the aisle. That's when I noticed that he had the biggest smile painted on his face. And, as I looked to my right, so did Liza and Andreas. And then I saw Gunther and Erna smiling, too, and suddenly I heard a soloist singing "Ave Maria" from the balcony. As we continued walking down the aisle, I looked up and saw the archbishop of Vienna walking toward us.

He very pleasantly took Helmut and me by the hands, looked right into my eyes, and began to speak *very* slowly in German so I could understand him.

"Do you want to marry this man again?" he asked.

By this time tears of joy were streaming down my cheeks. Helmut had arranged all of this through his great friend Klaus Zyla, who is a former Austrian diplomat. Klaus was able to help Helmut arrange it so we could renew our vows in his home country and in front of our children, who were with us to witness this very intimate and romantic moment. Everyone was in on it except for me—even the altar woman who answered the door! She deserved an Academy Award for that performance . . . or at the very least an Emmy!

After the ceremony, the woman collected all of the flowers on the altar and placed them in my arms. I was told it was an Austrian tradition to have the bride walk through the streets with her wedding flowers, so that was exactly what we did. Helmut and Gunther had arranged for us to have a beautiful Sunday dinner at a very special restaurant, which we had all to ourselves. It was spectacular.

I have always believed in celebrating as much as you can, because let's face it, life can sometimes be hard and unexpected things can happen. That's why celebrations are very big in our family. We don't take a single moment together for granted. The demands of my professional life have been enormous, which means I often end up spending many more hours of my day with my colleagues than with the people in my personal life, including my family. If I ever let myself get caught up in that whirlwind, I feared I would lose my focus on what really matters most in life because every moment of every day could easily be filled with phone calls, meetings, and work, and under those circumstances I might wake up one day and realize I had no life.

As I mentioned earlier, when *All My Children* was extended to its one-hour format, my work obligations grew exponentially. It wasn't so much the added thirty minutes of showtime that took me away from home more often and for longer periods each day as it was the extra hours of preparation and our new shooting schedule. Around the time that Liza was three years old, I was sometimes working for twelve to eighteen hours a day, five days a week. Being away from her that much made me very sad. There were too many days when I wasn't there as she woke up in the morning or I wasn't home by the time she went to bed at night. That was killing me. No matter what time I came home, though, I always made it my first priority to go into her room to see her, stroke her hair, and listen to her breathe.

Before I was able to negotiate a clause in my contract that allowed me to take my children's birthdays off, I would have to be on set if my schedule called for me to be there, whether it was Liza's birthday or not. Because I was determined to mark those special days in special ways even if I did have to work, I came up with something that has become a favorite tradition in our home—the birthday breakfast. At the very least, I made sure I would be in the house in the morning so I could make her a special morning meal. There would always be a large bouquet of streaming balloons tied to the birthday girl's chair and some wrapped presents waiting for her on the table. The most important thing was to spend some special time with Liza so she knew I wasn't abandoning her or placing greater value on work than on her.

Those birthday breakfasts must have had a lasting impact, because to this day, Liza still celebrates all of the wonderful occasions in her life by starting the morning off with a special family breakfast. So even though I couldn't always be there exactly as I wished in the early years, something good came out of making the time to be with my daughter.

Many years later, Liza wrote a poem for her honors English class that spoke about all of the times I came home and snuck into her room while she was sleeping. I was stunned to read her incredible words because I never knew that she was aware I was there. Her poem spoke to all of those nights I didn't take a hotel room or stay in New York City when it might have been easier for me to do so. We never had an apartment in the city while the children were young because we didn't want to be tempted not to come home. I wanted to see my children, even if they didn't see me. I would always be there when they woke up in the morning or had a nightmare in the middle of the night. Knowing this made me feel good, but it also meant that my children grew up with a sense of security that they were always my number one priority.

*M*y Mother

> She rises like an early bird
> And flutters down the stairs like a ballerina
> To catch just a glimpse of the morning sun
> Rising like a budding flower
> As she inaudibly flies back up the stairs
> The radiant light of the budding sun
> Bursts through the windows and illuminates
> The domain like a temple
> She then proceeds to put on her clothing
> Her chestnut hair shines in the light, like a star
> After dressing, she glides down the hallway
> As if she were an ice-skater, so as not to wake us

I sense her presence as she enters my
Room full of dreams and kisses me on my
Forehead. And I know it is my mother about
To descend upon her daily journey to her studio
In the city.
Liza Victoria Huber
Christmas 1990

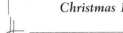

Although Helmut planned the most romantic and wonderful surprise for me in Vienna, I have to take credit for doing what most people would consider pulling off the impossible: I was able to successfully organize and execute a surprise seventieth birthday celebration for my husband without him ever having a clue about it!

Helmut is the type of man who sees everything and misses nothing. He is always acutely aware of what's happening around him, so to fool him was going to take a precise and well-thought-out plan— and a village. I enlisted our personal assistant, Helene, and my good friend Mike Cohen, the head of ABC daytime publicity for *All My Children*, as my partners in crime. I needed Mike to help me because I wanted the party to be portrayed as an official ABC affiliate event. This was the only way I could think of to keep Helmut out of the loop while requiring him to accompany me.

Mike had only one invitation printed up, but he made it look like any number of ABC invitations I'd received over the years. My picture was featured because I was listed as the mistress of ceremonies. The plan was to have Mike phone me at home and break the news that the network had planned a special affiliate event for a weekend in October, "coincidentally" the same weekend as Helmut's birthday. Of course, when Mike called, we had planned that I would tell him there was no way I could attend the event. I kindly explained that it was my husband's birthday and we had an agreement to always be together for happy occasions and holidays. I pretended to be very upset and emphatic in saying there was no way I would consider doing the event.

When the invitation arrived in the mail, Helmut could see that I was the featured person. He also understood that this was an official black-tie event for the network to meet the affiliates at the Rainbow Room, a gorgeous space high above midtown Manhattan at the very top of Rockefeller Center. I could tell Helmut was rethinking my "decision," maybe giving in just this once and making an exception about mixing my personal and professional commitments. Still, I refused. I told Helmut that I wouldn't work on his birthday. It was a very big birthday and I simply couldn't see myself giving it up for anything.

"You have to go," he said.

And, of course, had this been a real event, he would have been absolutely right. Still, I called Mike one more time to tell him "I was out."

A few days later, Mike called Helmut to apologize about the timing. He explained that he and I had spoken six months earlier without realizing there would be a conflict.

"If you and Susan could just come, give us a few minutes to make some opening remarks, and say a quick hello to everyone, I am sure we can get you out of there within half an hour so you and your family and friends can get on with your night and private celebration." Mike was pleading with Helmut.

When they hung up, my husband gallantly came to me and pitched the idea. I remained very reluctant.

"I will only do it if you are absolutely sure we can be out of there in half an hour because there is no way I am spending your birthday at that event," I said. If I hadn't already won that Emmy, I sure deserved it for this performance.

Meanwhile, Mike, Helene, and I were like little elves pulling every string and dealing with every last detail. I went to the

Rainbow Room to meet with the executive chef, who just happened to be from Austria! When I explained that my husband is Austrian, too, he and I planned the perfect menu, consisting of all of Helmut's favorite foods and wines. I snuck out of the house one day in the guise of getting a manicure and met with the Hank Lane Orchestra, my very favorite in New York. Some of my most fun times in Manhattan have been dancing to the wonderful music of this orchestra. I handpicked what they were to play that night, making sure each and every song was meaningful to my husband without being "cheesy." My children have rolled their eyes at me on more than one occasion, and so I had a very vivid picture of their faces if they were to catch me being cheesy on this special night. I remembered Steven Spielberg once saying in an interview that his kids rolled their eyes at him. If his kids could feel that way, I guess I'm in good company.

I had thought of every last detail, just in case Helmut managed to get someone else to slip up. Helene was mission control, keeping track of all of the RSVPs. I even had everyone at *All My Children* in on the secret. One day, I told Helmut I was going to a costume fitting at the studio before work but was really going to the Rainbow Room to check on last-minute details. I had put the entire studio on red alert, just in case Helmut called. Sure enough, out of the blue, he phoned the wardrobe department looking for me. This was a little unusual, and thankfully, the crew there knew how to handle the situation in my absence. Mark Klein, who took over as head of wardrobe after No-No left, immediately took Helmut's call and lied through his teeth.

"Susan's just finishing up her fitting. I will have her call you as soon as she comes out," he very convincingly said.

Michael Woll, the amazing assistant to the head of wardrobe, picked up his cell and immediately called to alert me that Helmut was on the loose and looking for me.

I calmly found a quiet spot where there would be no telltale taxi horns honking in the background and called my husband. He was none the wiser and the plan was still fully in motion.

Mike and I made sure to invite some very noticeable faces from the network and included friends like Regis and Joy Philbin and Cameron Mathison, who would each act as great decoys on the faux "red carpet" we had planned to have. Mike and I arranged for actual photographers from the press corps to stand outside taking pictures as we walked in so it would look and feel extremely real. To give an even more authentic touch to the event, Cameron Mathison, who was doing *Dancing with the Stars* at the time, got right off a plane and showed up so he could meet us curbside to walk into the "event" together. That was above and beyond the call of duty and I will never forget him for doing that!

In addition to these familiar faces, I invited people from every walk of Helmut's life, including his son Danny and grandson, Christian, who flew in from Switzerland, and some business associates who have known him for many years. All in all, there were around 250 people inside enjoying the music that the Hank Lane Orchestra played for the crowd while they waited for our arrival. I had large screens set up all over the room so people could see themselves and other guests arriving, including us as we made our way down the red carpet. In reality, I needed a way for the guests to see that Helmut was about to make his entrance so they could welcome him with a hearty and loud "Surprise!"

Regis Philbin was set to be the master of ceremonies at another event across town at the Waldorf that night, so he was on a tight time schedule. The van that Mike; Helmut; Liza; her husband, Alex; Andreas; and I were in was held up in some very heavy midtown traffic, so we ended up getting out and hightailing it on foot to make sure we made it to the party before Regis had to leave. Thankfully, Cameron was waiting for us on the street. He escorted us toward the express elevator to the Top of the Rock. When we got off as planned, Mike had hung ABC posters all around. We were met by the photographers, who snapped lots of photos as we walked the faux red carpet. There was even a roped-off area where we were supposed to stop and pose. Cameron and I danced a little, and then I did a brief interview before we headed into the reception. It was perfect.

The doors flung open, and as we walked into the room, everyone inside yelled, "SURPRISE!"

Helmut was dumbfounded, but when he saw his son and grandson, he realized the party was for him and he got very choked up. He was completely surprised and thrilled as everybody joined in singing a robust "Happy Birthday" to him.

Helmut is a born nurturer. He's very capable and is one of those people on this great earth who gets joy out of making things happen and taking care of others. It was very touching to Helmut to have that party be for him.

Nobody could believe that we were able to pull off this remarkable feat. People told me that if the acting thing didn't work out, I could get a job working on covert missions for the FBI or the CIA.

Helmut and I have always had a great love of adventure. We especially enjoy traveling together, which is one of our secrets to keeping the fun factor alive in our relationship. We have been invited to attend parties and events at which I sometimes have to pinch myself and ask, *How did I get here?*

In 1986, Martha Layne Collins, the first woman governor of Kentucky, invited us to be her guests at the Kentucky Derby. We immediately accepted her invitation, as we had never attended the Derby before and I have always loved horses. Although I never competed, I rode horses as a little girl. My interest in riding started as a hobby that my father and I shared. Whenever my dad and his friends went riding at the local public stable in Bethpage, they'd take me with them. I'd hop on a horse and ride along the path. Although I was only seven years old, I didn't like how slow those stable horses moved. I instinctively gave them a swift kick with my heels to make them go faster, but for whatever reason, the horse I was on one day still refused to go. So I got off to lead him back to the barn. My father turned around and saw me walking away.

"Where are you going?" he asked.

"This horse doesn't go fast enough!" I replied.

My father broke a twig off a nearby tree and gave it to me to use as a crop. He told me to hold it right behind the horse's eye, just close enough for him to see it. I got back on the horse, thinking, *This will never work!* We walked from the stable, back to the path, and toward an open field that surrounded the famous Bethpage golf course. My father and his friends liked to go there so they could let the horses really run. When it came time for me to hold the twig, I placed it where my father told me, and sure enough, that horse took off. He kept up with the pack of fast-moving horses. I loved every minute of that ride. When I finished—in one piece, I might add—my father said I could take lessons so I would know what I was doing.

I was able to put my horseback-riding skills to good use while shooting a scene for *All My Children* on the beach in St. Croix. In 1978, Erica had married her third husband, Tom Cudahy, played by the very handsome and sexy Dick Shoberg. Dick and John James were the only Swedish men I ever worked with on *All My Children,* something I liked because of my own Swedish background.

Dick's character, Tom, was an ex–football star who owned the Goalpost, a new restaurant in Pine Valley where Erica went to work after leaving Nick Davis and the Chateau. Erica had a long-term affair with Nick, who was not only many years older than she, but was also one of Mona's dearest friends. Tom fell for Erica after she confessed that Nick had actually broken off their engagement and dumped her. Tom and Erica went away together for a weekend in the country that was filled with endless hours of passionate lovemaking. Erica believed she was in love with Tom and it was clear that he had fallen for her. Tom proposed and Erica accepted.

Erica's mother knew that she didn't love Tom. She accused her daughter of using him to get back at Nick Davis. Erica threatened never to speak to Mona again if she tried to stop the wedding, so Mona sat in silence as the two exchanged their vows. The following day, Tom and Erica went on their honeymoon in St. Croix.

Dick Shoberg, who was newly married at the time, joked that he spent his honeymoon with me rather than with his actual wife. Thank goodness his wife was a very understanding woman.

Agnes Nixon loved St. Croix. She had a home there for many years. She often went to her Caribbean hideaway to write her scripts, so I imagine this was a very special and magical location for her and for our show.

My very favorite "on location" dressing room was on the beach in St Croix. The crew strung sheets together and nailed them into four palm trees. Inside, they hung a little mirror, barely big enough for me to see my face, let alone check what I was wearing. I was supposed to change into proper equestrian clothes to shoot a horseback-riding scene on the beach in a jungle. There was no time to go back to the hotel for the various wardrobe changes, from bathing suits to riding clothes and back again.

I had a chance to ride a beautiful black horse on the white sand in the Caribbean—as part of my job! Does work get any better than that? I was in heaven.

The following day, I was told I'd be snorkeling off the back of a boat. Although I had never been diving or snorkeling before, I didn't think it would be a challenging task. That is, of course, until I discovered exactly what I was being asked to do. At nine o'clock the night before we shot the water scene, our hotel agreed to turn on the lights in their pool, as the producers had arranged an impromptu snorkeling lesson for me. We had been shooting all day at the beach. I was tired from riding the horse, but still game. It turned out that snorkeling in the pool was a piece of cake. I thought, *I can definitely do this!*

The next day, we boarded a boat and headed toward an area where there were lots of coral reefs. I was told that the fish were exceptionally spectacular in this area. There were several extras who came with us and jumped into the water before I did. Suddenly the boat felt very high up above the water. I went to the edge of the boat and looked over the side and then up to the deck I was supposed to dive off of. I was doing everything I could to psych myself up and take that initial plunge.

I slipped on my mask and snorkel and prepared to go for it. As I was springing off the boat, Bobby Behr, our head cameraman, came up behind me and loudly hummed the theme song from Jaws. *Ba, Bum, Ba, Bum, Ba Bum.* When I came up from the water, I looked back at him and thought, *I'm going to kill you, Bobby!*

You never know what to expect or whom you will meet when you go to new places. It's one of the things I truly love about traveling, and attending the Kentucky Derby as the guests of Governor Collins was no exception. She was so very gracious as she invited us to stay at the governor's mansion, which was really lovely and quite comfortable. As you might expect, the governor was invited to all of the festivities surrounding the Derby that weekend, including the best parties. Let me tell you, those Kentuckians sure do know how to have a good time. They do everything on a great big scale, in a glamorous and wonderful style. The homes are large and the parties are, too. Everything is spectacular in the grandest way.

The first party we attended was held at the home of a woman who tented her private polo field for the event. The party's theme was Egyptian and revolved around some very handsome bare-chested men rowing in large canoes suspended from the ceiling. All of the waiters were dressed—or undressed—in the same attire. I had never seen anything like it, but it was very theatrical and extremely effective.

The next party we attended was at the home of the fabulous Marylou Whitney, whom I feel so lucky to know. I remember seeing two very large urns atop the pillars at the front gate. The urns were filled with flowers. They weren't plants. They were freshly cut flora that had been placed there by hand—and beautifully arranged.

When we approached the front door, I was expecting to be greeted by a butler or some other member of her household staff. Much to my surprise, Marylou answered the door herself. She is the most gracious hostess ever. She greets every single one of her guests. She had on a beautiful white gown and was wearing a crown of white flowers in her hair. She made a point of telling us that she had just put this particular gown on because someone had accidentally spilled red wine on her original dress. She looked exquisite and very welcoming. Her husband, C. V. "Sonny" Whitney, joined her at the door. Although we had never met, I could see that his health was failing. Still, he was every bit as gracious as his wife. When we walked through the door, I was surprised to discover that we were not in their main house, but in their pool pavilion. Later, after cocktails, we proceeded into the main house for dinner. A great time was had by all.

As we left Kentucky, the warmth and grace shown by both Governor Collins and Marylou Whitney made us feel that we had come to know firsthand the true meaning of southern hospitality.

Marylou and I hit it off from the very start and forged a lovely connection that night at her party. A few months later, I was being honored by the Red Cross in Palm Beach. Marylou had a home there and asked if I would attend a party she was hosting the afternoon before the event. Of course I said I would be delighted. I was seated directly next to her at the party, which I thought was very charming. Marylou excused herself from the table so she could mingle with her other guests. When she left, two gentlemen who were also seated at our table moved closer so they could sit on either side of me.

"Welcome to Erica Kane County," one of the men said with a big twinkle in his eyes.

After that night, Marylou and I developed a very special friendship. She is one of the most delightful and strongest women I know. Several years after her husband, Sonny, died, Marylou met John Hendrickson, another wonderful man, whom she married in 1997. John was a former aide to Governor Walter Joseph Hickel of Alaska. John has become one of our favorite people. I just love it when I am seated next to him at events, as he is such a good guy and very funny.

Helmut and I have maintained a friendship with Marylou and John, attending their annual gala during the height of the horse-racing season at Saratoga Springs, in upstate New York. I love Saratoga and the Adirondacks, so I am always happy to spend time in the region and with them. Marylou has demonstrated her love in so many ways, and the townspeople just love her in return.

In addition to being one of the greatest beauties and legendary hostesses of all time, Marylou is a champion horse breeder and one of the greatest adventure seekers I have ever met. We were absolutely thrilled when she asked if we would be interested in taking a trip with her and her husband to Alaska to experience the Iditarod. The first Iditarod race was held on March 3, 1873, with thirty-four teams. The dogsled teams pass through twenty-six checkpoints on the route. Three of those checkpoints are in such harsh country that the only time people are there is during the race. The rest of the year they are uninhabited. This is no race for the fainthearted.

The race crosses two mountain ranges, follows the Yukon River, and leads the sleds over the frozen waters of Norton Sound. This was definitely one of those once-in-a-lifetime trips you have to pinch yourself to believe you are actually going to be a part of. Marylou always put together a great guest list and we were excited when we were told that Joan Rivers would be joining us.

We flew to Anchorage, Alaska, on Marylou and John's private plane, stopping in North Dakota to refuel. Joan told us about her hilarious adventures trying to get outfitted for this trip in Manhattan. It turns out Chanel doesn't make gear for the conditions we were headed to. Still, she brought along enough luggage with her, leading us to believe that she was carrying everything with her but the kitchen sink. We had so much fun on the flight and even more when we got to Alaska. I will never forget our approach into Anchorage. It was the most gorgeous and sunny day. The sky was the clearest blue without a single cloud in sight. It looked like all of the Alps I had seen in Europe had been carefully placed in one spectacular location. The landscape was so vast and the mountains were incredibly majestic. They seemed to go on forever. The natural beauty was nothing short of breathtaking.

Thankfully, John and Marylou know Alaska very well, so they were able to point us in the right direction of the best sights. I love to travel and see things through the eyes of someone who knows a place well. The only problem we had was that Joan was having a hard time walking on the icy streets of Anchorage in the boots she had brought. She was slipping and sliding all around. Afraid she might fall and really hurt herself, she immediately went shopping for a new pair. Helmut and I happened upon Joan while she was shopping. Having grown up in the Austrian Alps, Helmut sat down and helped her get some new boots that he knew wouldn't slip. After that, she was good to go!

Although Marylou has never been the musher of a dogsled team, she has been an avid sponsor and she has followed along the trail of the Iditarod several times before this trip. Believe me, to "follow along" is no easy feat! She is full of salty and fantastic stories about her experiences, which she shared as we enjoyed a wonderful dinner together the night we arrived. Fortunately, she is friends with Martin Buser, one of the most experienced and winning dogsled team leaders in the history of the race. We got to go to Martin's home, where he raises his dogs and trains his teams. We had the opportunity to spend quite a bit of time with him and his wife, Kathy, as well as experience what life is like for his dogs. We saw where each dog lives in its own separate little house. Those dogs who have some type of relationship are kept facing each other so they can see each other. I expected the dogs to look like the big fluffy husky dogs I used to watch on *Sergeant Preston of the Yukon* when I was a little girl. But Martin asked, "Have you ever seen a marathon runner? These dogs are built like them." They're great athletes, and though they are leaner than I thought they'd be, they eat—a lot! When you're in their company, you can easily see that these dogs love to run. They live to race. They get excited, jump, and are ready to go, go, go.

The musher must dress in special clothes that are designed for the environment he will live in over the course of the nine- to twelve-day race. Mushers wear a very thin underlayer and a specially designed suit that is not bulky, but very aerodynamic and warm. The best mushers have a great rapport with their dogs and will often sleep with them during their breaks. There are mandated breaks along the race, which range from twelve to twenty-four hours. The dogs have a special chip inside of them so they can be tracked. If one of the dogs dies during the race, the team is automatically disqualified.

The night before the start of the race, we attended the Musher's Ball. It was so much fun. I was surprised to learn that there were several female mushers participating in the race. One of them came up to me at the party and said, "Wait until you get on the sled and pull out of the city limits. All you will hear is the sound of the dogs' paws on the snow." I thought that sounded fantastic. I could hardly wait.

The next morning, the sun was shining and the sky was a brilliant blue. It was very cold—bone-chilling cold. You couldn't recognize any of us that day because we were so bundled up. However, Marylou somehow managed to look glamorous even in those freezing cold conditions. I was all set to ride along with one of the mushers for the first leg of the race, which was eleven miles long. The musher I traveled with gave me a comfortable pillow to sit on because these are very bare-bones sleds. They want to keep things as aerodynamic as they can. He also gave me a stuffed animal husky to hold on to for good luck. The musher stands on the back of the sled and the team of dogs pulls everyone from the front. The strongest dogs are the two kept closest to the sled because they will bear the brunt of the initial pull. The smartest dogs are the lead dogs. The middle dogs are the workers. All the dogs wear tiny little felt booties on their paws not only to protect their feet, but to also help them grip the ice. Volunteers from the area make thousands of pairs of booties for the dogs each year for this incredibly demanding race.

My Iditarod experience lasted a total of forty-five minutes. Sadly, it went by in a flash. I would have stayed on the sled much longer because it was so exciting and fun that I actually forgot about how cold it was. There were people all along the route cheering us on as we passed. It's a local tradition to bake muffins and throw them at your favorite musher. The mushers grab at the flying muffins and place them on their sled to eat later. I got off the sled when we finished that first leg. The teams restart the race the following day. My musher continued on to the finish line, coming in a very respectable fourth place. Having the opportunity to participate in the Iditarod, even just a little, was an experience I loved and will never forget. I hope to return to Alaska someday to explore the beautiful terrain and breathtaking landscape.

I certainly have had some extraordinary opportunities to travel as a result of my career. When I was asked to play Hillary Taylor, a villainess in the last season of the television show *Dallas*, I had no idea we'd be filming my scenes outside of Los Angeles. My character was somebody who came from an oil family in Texas. I was delighted to be working with Patrick Duffy—unfortunately, I was the character who was going to shoot his wife.

When the producers of *Dallas* said they wanted to set part of the last season of the show in Paris, I said a *very* quick yes. We went to Paris at the end of July and stayed into early August. For the most part, the city was empty, as most Parisians go away during August. It was very hot, but because we were shooting for the new season, which started in September, the script called for us to be wearing heavy fall clothes. As a woman, that meant a black cocktail dress, but poor Patrick's costume was a tweed jacket and cowboy boots. What little air-conditioning we had was turned off because it was making too much noise during filming.

I was given a half day off, so I did what any self-respecting American girl would do—I went shopping at Chanel. This was the first time I was ever in a Chanel boutique. When I got to the store, the staff told me it was a good time to be there, as the Parisian women were gone and they had just received their fall shipment. I had the pick of the best in the store. I tried on many different dresses and suits and finally settled on a perfect rich dark red tweed skirt and jacket that I still have to this very day.

At one point, a salesgirl was showing me a charmeuse blouse to go under the suit. I was agonizing over whether or not to buy it because I had never spent so much money on one suit before, especially without my husband being there to see it first. I asked the girl if she could hold my items until my husband could come back with me later that day. She understood and put everything aside. As she was moving away from the hold rack, I saw that Sophia Loren was sitting in a chair right behind her. It was so hot that I almost didn't even go to Chanel that day—now, *that's* really hot! When I saw this screen legend, my idol and a goddess of a woman, sitting right there in front of me, I almost fainted—not from the heat, but from her presence.

I still remember that she was wearing a sky-blue silk dress, with elbow-length sleeves and a low neck. Her legs were crossed and seemed to go on for days. She had the creamiest olive skin. She was more beautiful in person than I could have ever imagined. Sometimes when you see a celebrity in person, they can be disappointing. She was not. She was so much more than I ever expected. She was with a gentleman I didn't recognize. I don't know who they were to each other, but certainly Sophia Loren was not walking around Paris by herself. I looked at her and I could not help myself, I just stared until she felt my gaze. When she looked up, I simply smiled. She smiled back. I don't think she recognized me. I merely think she was being warm and gracious. I didn't say a word to her. I would not invade her privacy. I was just thrilled to see her. For a moment, time stood still. When I told Helmut that I saw Sophia Loren at Chanel, he quickly agreed to go back to the store with me. Of course, she was already gone. Nonetheless, he loved the outfit and bought me my first Chanel suit. *That* was a very good day.

Although Helmut and I have had incredible opportunities to travel to places like Alaska and Paris at times when our children didn't come along, they have also had some wonderful experiences traveling with us. I always thought it was very important for them to know their father's family and history, so they've been all over Europe, especially Austria. We also spent a lot of time in Vermont and skiing out west in Colorado together. I looked forward to our family vacations because they were always filled with great adventure and, occasionally, a few surprises. Still, no matter how many locations the kids have been to over the years, they've never lost that sense of wonder or desire to explore and experience new places, people, and things.

When the children were very young, Robin Leach asked me to do the first episode of his new show, *Lifestyles of the Rich and Famous*. We really didn't know what the show was all about, but I agreed to do it anyway. When it came time to watch that episode, the kids, Helmut, and I all gathered in our bedroom and turned on the television. Kenny Rogers was the first celebrity being featured. At the time he lived in a very large home with many, many acres of land and kept cattle and horses. The next celebrity profiled was equally rich and fabulous. Then along came my profile. I do not live on a million acres with horses and cattle. I knew the kids were wondering why I was even on the show, so I quickly turned to them and said, "They're Rich and we're Famous."

The next time I did the show, Robin invited me to go to Europe and he said we could bring the kids along. We went to Lyon, in the south of France, which is a culinary paradise. It's so good that people helicopter in from Paris as well as Switzerland and Scandinavia just to eat lunch. We got to go to some really fabulous restaurants, such as Paul Bocuse, during that trip courtesy of Robin and his show. Even though the kids had to be seated at a separate table while we filmed, I could hear the waiters being very deferential, charming, and jolly with them.

Thankfully, our children grew up really liking to eat. Since they had traveled a lot and maybe because I made their food for them when they were babies, they developed a taste for fresh ingredients and unprocessed food. Plus, it didn't hurt that their father is a master chef, so they ate well, have always been adventurous eaters, and learned to enjoy the experiences that surround a great meal. When we finished in Lyon, we took the bullet train from Lyon to Paris. The train had a fine dining car with white-clothed tables and full waiter service. Zooming to Paris with first-class dining all the way was an experience none of us has ever forgotten.

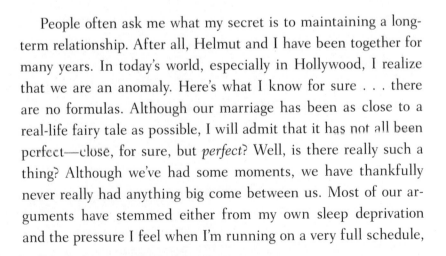

*H*elmut and I were visiting friends on their boat in Porto Cervo, Sardinia, when we all decided to take a swim in the emerald waters of the Mediterranean. We thought we'd swim the short distance to the shore so we could have lunch at a great little restaurant high up on the rocks that was only accessible by boat. When I dove into the water, I was surprised by how chilly it was. Helmut came up behind me and threw me into the air. When I landed in the water, my engagement ring slipped off my finger and slowly sank to the bottom of the sea. I saw it fall off, but the sand beneath us was so soft, it got lost as soon as it hit bottom. I dove underwater several times to see if I could somehow find it, but I kept coming up empty-handed. It was gone. I felt so bad about it that the captain of the boat continued to search for an additional hour and a half. Unfortunately, he didn't find it either. I can only hope that a young Italian boy in love will walk down the beach one day and come upon my ring and give it to the girl he wants to marry.

People often ask me what my secret is to maintaining a long-term relationship. After all, Helmut and I have been together for many years. In today's world, especially in Hollywood, I realize that we are an anomaly. Here's what I know for sure . . . there are no formulas. Although our marriage has been as close to a real-life fairy tale as possible, I will admit that it has not all been perfect—close, for sure, but *perfect*? Well, is there really such a thing? Although we've had some moments, we have thankfully never really had anything big come between us. Most of our arguments have stemmed either from my own sleep deprivation and the pressure I feel when I'm running on a very full schedule, or from miscommunication. (I would hate to have to argue in German! I'd never win.)

I've learned to put things in their proper place over the years, which has helped me not take my own frustrations out on my husband, who has always been my biggest ally in life. When you deal with a highly scheduled, highly demanding life by choice, you invite a lot of stress into your life. I am one of the lucky few in this world who gets to do the work I love. I know how blessed I am. As an actress, I am also aware that someday this will all go away, so when opportunity knocks I feel as if I have to answer with a resounding yes while the acting world still wants me. Sometimes all of those yesses come at once. Until you get the hang of doing that great balancing act in life, it can be really daunting, especially when you have young children. That was when I felt I was being split into too many pieces. I still feel that way from time to time, but I've gotten better at putting limits on how much I will take on and I have also learned to stop and breathe. Even though my children are grown, I still want to be accessible to them if they need me. I want to be in their lives. And I want my husband to know that he is a priority, too.

As my father used to tell me, "Don't forget to stop and smell the roses, Susan." For Helmut and me, it's important to maintain romance and intimacy. There are plenty of days when we've got the house to ourselves and no place to be, and we'll make the best use of that time. We'll turn off the phones and enjoy each other's company. An absolute perfect day with my husband depends on what time of year it is and where we are. We love to be on a cable car heading to ski the mountains in Europe. We will have lunch somewhere at the top of the mountain, where we will enjoy a great meal while feeling the warm sun on our faces. The most important thing is that we are together.

I also love to drive with Helmut. He is a great driver—fast but safe. I really adore taking long drives with him. I've spent a lot of my life looking at my husband's profile from the passenger seat of our car. He has the best dimples, the sexiest slant to his eyes, and so much charm in his face. We can talk for hours, with no interruptions, in complete privacy, which is a total luxury. It's a rare but wonderful occurrence to find several hours when we're completely alone. One of our favorite spots is the Lake Placid Lodge in the Adirondacks. It's so important to take some time together in your relationship. Helmut once told me early in our marriage that someday we'd have kids and then someday we'd be alone together again. I didn't understand what he meant until our kids left home and it was just the two of us once more. We make a point of carving out time together so we can stay connected as a couple and let go of all the things that encumber our lives.

One true sign of a good marriage is if your husband willingly chooses to save your life—not once, but twice.

The first time Helmut saved my life was during a ski trip in France. We were skiing in Lac Tignes, near Val d'Isère, in the Haute-Savoie region of France. It was just the two of us. We ventured out onto the slopes on the first day we were there. Helmut said he was going to check out the mountain to determine where he thought I could ski because he and I definitely do not ski at the same level. Helmut grew up skiing in Austria. His mother's house was at the top of a mountain in Innsbruck. He skied down that mountain every day to go to school. Needless to say, Helmut is a spectacular skier, shushing the terrain like it's second nature. My husband skis like he drives—fast and smooth. I, on the other hand, grew up on the flats of Long Island, so I don't have that second-nature thing. I am an okay skier, but nowhere near Helmut's level of expertise.

For whatever reason, I told Helmut I wanted to go with him that morning. He was reluctant at first, but I can be very persuasive. He finally gave in and said I could come along. That's when we got into trouble. I should have listened to him. I should have let him check out the mountain first, but I didn't.

Tignes is a very large mountain. The area it's in is vast and very challenging. Most of the ski terrain is above the tree line. We took a lift to the top of the mountain, where I suddenly found myself in the thick of all "expert only" runs. I was slightly panicked until Helmut suggested we take a short ride on the poma lift to go even higher because he thought there might be an easier way down.

A poma lift is essentially a disk that you slip between your legs and then lean on as it carries you up what is usually very steep terrain in Europe. These particular poma lifts were on such a tight spring that you had to be a linebacker in the NFL to pull down fast enough to get it through your legs. And if that wasn't challenging enough, you then had to pull hard and with just the right amount of pressure to make sure the disk didn't give in and cause you to fall. It took me about six tries before I got the hang of it. As I slowly made my way up the mountain, my skis kept getting caught in ruts that were carved by other people who had gone before me. The path was very uneven, which meant I felt as if I had no control over my skis or the ride up. I was afraid I would fall off at any given moment. And if you're scared, your body gets stiff, and of course, you will fall. When we were almost to the very top, I lost my footing and my poma lift. I was in the middle of no-man's-land at ten thousand feet above sea level. Thankfully, Helmut was right behind me. He let go of his poma lift in order to stay with me. Note: If you should ever find yourself in this situation and your husband keeps on going up the mountain, you may want to rethink your relationship!

Helmut began to figure out our best path down the mountain. The only reasonable course of action was to sidestep even farther up the mountain and then try to find the service road that is usually at the top. We sidestepped up for what felt like another mile. It took quite a bit of time, maybe an hour or more, because it was a very rough climb. We finally reached the very, very top. There were no markings to tell us how difficult the terrain below was supposed to be, and frankly, I didn't need any. I knew right away I was in way over my head. I stood there, looking down and wondering how I was going to get to the bottom. I couldn't see two feet beyond where I was standing because the drop was so steep.

Two skiers came by who looked like real experts. You could just tell! And . . . they were about eighteen years old, too! Yes, those are the only people who should have been where I found myself that day. Helmut flagged them down to ask if they could direct us to the easiest route. They pointed to the way they were going. They kept saying, *"Facile, facile"* ("easy" in French). All I could think was, *Easy for you!*

I had no choice but to point my skis downhill and just go. A short way along I found myself in the middle of a traverse, the narrow path that sits between and connects two mountains. It was only about eight to ten feet wide. I was following Helmut and I am not sure how it happened, but I suddenly slipped on the side of the traverse and over the edge. I screamed, "Helm-u-u-u-t!" as loud as I could.

Let me be very clear. I never call my husband by his first name unless it's an emergency. I call him "honey," "darling," "sweetheart," and any of several other terms of endearment. The only time I say "Helmut" is when I am in trouble, and boy oh boy, was I in trouble!

"Grab on to something," Helmut yelled to me as I continued to slide down the mountainside. Unfortunately, there was nothing to grab hold of or to stop my fall. Thank God Helmut is such a great skier. He skied down and miraculously managed to get himself below me to stop my rapid descent to the bottom of the mountain thousands of feet beneath me.

Thankfully, I was fine. My ego was a bit bruised, but other than that and a few nightmares that followed—there was no damage done. I told Helmut I had had enough skiing for the day. I have never begged to accompany Helmut on the first day again. Whenever he wants to check out a mountain, I say, "Go, honey. Go. Check it out." Lesson learned!

The second time my husband saved my life was during dinner at a restaurant in New York City with Andreas and two of his friends from college. We were eating in one of our favorite Italian restaurants. I had ordered chicken cacciatore. I had eaten this dish dozens of times at that particular restaurant. I knew there were no bones, but sometimes things just happen.

We were speaking and laughing, having a good time, when I took my second bite of my delicious dinner. I realized that a piece of chicken had lodged in my throat. Not wanting to make a scene, I turned my head to the side and tried to clear my throat by coughing, but nothing happened. So I stood up, walked a few steps away from the table, and tried to dislodge the chicken again. Still, nothing happened.

I remembered seeing a news story on TV that you can give yourself the Heimlich by throwing your body over a chair. Just as I was about to do that, Helmut came up behind me. I had closed my eyes, hoping I wasn't going to choke and die and make a terrible scene that would end up on "Page Six." I could hear people shouting across the dining room in very heavy New York accents, "Give her the Heimlich! Give her the Heimlich!" Fortunately, Helmut was already taking action. He gave me two thrusts under my ribs and the chicken finally dislodged.

When I sat back down, Andreas was staring at me. I felt awful. I didn't want to embarrass him in front of his friends, so I did the first thing that came to my mind—I made a joke.

"Well, honey. The good news is that your father *did* give me the Heimlich. It's a good sign when your husband saves your life." We all had a good laugh and went on with our night and I looked at Helmut with a lot of gratitude.

CHAPTER 13

∞

That Elusive Emmy

I was nominated for my first Emmy in 1974, the inaugural year of the Daytime Emmy Awards. To put things into perspective, I started working on *All My Children* before there were Daytime Emmys being handed out. I heard about my nomination in a roundabout manner. Judith Barcroft, the actress who played Ann Tyler on our show, came to me one day and very casually said, "The Academy is thinking of having a Daytime Emmy Award show, and if they do, you are nominated for best actress."

Although I was flattered, it didn't mean that much to me to hear the news because, at the time, I thought it was pure speculation. And besides, there had never been an award handed out for daytime television, so there wasn't a lot of hype surrounding it. When I got the official word that I was, in fact, nominated, admittedly, I was thrilled.

Back in those days, the Daytime Emmys were held . . . well, during the daytime. They weren't televised for the first few years. They were simply a way for our industry to acknowledge the work of our peers in the company of our peers.

In the beginning, the awards show took place in random locations around Manhattan, including Lincoln Center, a boat, and other venues around the city. As the event grew in size and popularity, it was set up more like the Golden Globes are today, being held in ballrooms at various hotels such as the Waldorf-Astoria and the Plaza. There were tables of actors from all of the different shows, eating lunch and having a good time. Backstage, there was a designated waiting area. If you were presenting an award, there was also a common space where you could change outfits. There was always a lot of action going on backstage in those days, especially with several of us doing our best to get in or out of our gowns all at the same time.

One year, the makeshift dressing room was set up near an elevator bank where fans could somehow walk right off the elevator and into wardrobe. And they did! With cameras! Show business certainly can be very glamorous, but these early awards shows made it a challenge.

The fact that I was nominated for an Emmy so many times, or that anyone cared outside of my husband, my parents, my children, or me, was shocking. The attention I received surprised me in the most wonderful ways. The fans cared and so did the press. So many people over the course of time told me they were rooting for me all of those years. *All My Children* and Erica Kane had gotten a lot of attention from the public. It was unexpected, but that recognition was nothing short of amazing, lovely, and very, very touching to me.

The process of being nominated for an Emmy has evolved over the years. I don't really remember how the initial voting took place, but I do recall that it was always based on your body of work rather than on one particular scene. Some reels were submitted with one episode to reflect the whole season, while others contained two. When it came time to submitting my reel for nomination, I made a point of seeking the input of our producers, associate producers, and editors. They were enormously helpful because these people knew my scenes better than I did. They had seen the finished product, whereas I shoot scene by scene and rarely get a chance to watch an actual show.

I typically have eight to ten scenes an episode, so you can only imagine how challenging it became to try to whittle down my reel selections to one or two scenes per season. I never thought that submitting one or two episodes was the best way to display one's work for the year, especially if you play a character that has a lot of depth, breadth, and range. To make things even more difficult, there were conflicting thoughts about whether you should submit what you consider to be your best work or scenes that show off your range, for instance one comedy scene and one drama scene. Of course, everyone in my category was in the same boat because there were always such talented women nominated for—and *winning*—best leading actress.

For many years, there was a "blue ribbon panel" consisting of actors who volunteered their weekends to watch submissions and judge a particular category that was not their own. So, for example, I couldn't judge the best leading actress category, but I could judge any of the other categories. If you agreed to participate, you would be given several VHS cassettes (and later, when the technology progressed, DVDs) to watch. For many years, the viewing of these scenes was held at a designated hotel, but more recently judges have been permitted to watch them in the privacy of their homes. I judged the best actor category one year when I was not nominated in my own category. The process of viewing each of these reels took several hours. I made a decision to view the best actor nominees in an office in the New York City studio so I could watch each nominee's work all at one time without any distractions. I thought viewing their material in the same environment was the fairest way to give each actor the same level of attention.

Judging the best lead actor category was a really interesting experience. For the first time in my career, I had the opportunity to watch other daytime actors whom I had never worked with do their thing. They were all extremely talented men. I realized that so much of what we do as actors depends on the writing we are given, the directing, the production values, and the other actors who work around us. From what I could tell, there was a lot of talent outside of *All My Children*. Many daytime actors have floated between shows over the years, so they have experienced different writing and different working environments. I have never done this, so it was rather eye-opening to peek inside other shows, if only through the scenes of those actors.

This experience made me even more aware of how important it is to be the best we can be each day, because our colleagues are depending on us to deliver so that they can work to their fullest potential, too. Doing this brings more richness to the scenes we're in, which ultimately makes the viewing experience so much better for our loyal viewers.

Long before I won, I was asked to cohost the Emmys with Regis Philbin at the fabulous Radio City Music Hall. Dick Clark was producing. He assembled a spectacular group of people who put together a fantastic experience I will never forget. My entrance was very dramatic. The Rockettes danced to an elaborate musical number as I was raised onto the stage in a limousine by a hydraulic lift. The driver of that limousine was, of course, Regis, who gallantly opened the door for me as we were both introduced to the cheering audience

It was magical waiting beneath the stage of Radio City, hearing the music while the Rockettes danced above my head. I grew up in New York, where the Rockettes are an institution. Radio City Music Hall is full of glorious entertainment history. But to me, there was the added personal significance of having once been a little girl in the audience with her parents watching the Easter and Christmas spectaculars in awe and now being the cohost of a celebrated and dazzling event on that very same stage. It was overwhelming and breathtaking, so much so that by the time I was lifted onto the stage, I had to stop myself from getting teary and remind myself to breathe so I could get on with the show. Hosting with Regis was a lot of fun. The perspective of being on that stage rather than in the audience was exhilarating. And although I didn't win that year, I had been nominated, and that made the experience even more poignant.

To be honest, winning the Emmy was not something I thought about from one year to the next. The set of *All My Children* is an atmosphere in which people don't talk about the Emmy or any other award per se. I don't believe winning an award was ever anyone's goal. In my mind, we are all there to play our scenes and do the best work we can. It is a daily occurrence to see veteran actors and newbies alike running lines in the hallways and corridors of the studio, trying to squeeze in that last rehearsal before doing their scene. Personally, my main goal as an actress is to leave the studio each day feeling good about my contributions. I suppose it is also true that I want to have the respect and admiration of the people I work with—and the admiration of those I work for, too. If the producers and directors love my work, or the fabulous crew members applaud, cry, or laugh after one of my scenes, then I feel very good knowing I did what I was there to do—especially if they're still affected after twelve- or eighteen-hour days! An Emmy award is the extra icing on the cake. It's delicious, but it isn't necessary in order for one to still enjoy the cake.

Every year at nomination time, I would begin to feel butterflies, especially as the swell of speculation began about my prospects of winning. I never wanted to know when the nominations were supposed to be announced. I really tried to stay away from all of the hoopla. Besides, I am usually on the set working most mornings the Emmys are announced. When I did get the word that I was nominated again, it was always thrilling because that is a terrific confirmation that the work I love so dearly is being recognized by my peers.

After I heard the good news, I would almost immediately get worked up into a frenzy of hope, excitement, and anticipation all over again. My angst was only magnified as the press, other media, and the fans began to get worked up, too. They were all so hopeful for me. Knowing this was so very moving and it certainly cushioned my fall each of the times I didn't win.

During the many years when I did not bring home an Emmy, my happiness for my peers who won instead of me was genuine. There was never a disingenuous moment. Don't get me wrong. I wanted to win, but in that moment, I felt they had to be really good at their craft to be named "The Best."

Yes, there were many times when I—and so many fans from *all* walks of life—asked, "What would Erica do in a moment like this?" The answer, of course, is she would have run up onto that stage, grabbed the statue out of the other actress's hands, and said, "Are you kidding me? I've earned this award. It's mine, damn it!" And she would have done it long before receiving nineteen nominations. In the end, though, we all know how well that tactic worked for Kanye West, right? Still, it was fun at least to momentarily fantasize about pulling an Erica Kane even if I never had any intention of following through.

In the years that someone else took home the Emmy for outstanding lead actress, the outpouring of fan appreciation was overwhelming. I received cards, letters, e-mails, flowers, and all sorts of gifts as consolation, all of which were so lovely and thoughtful. There were two little girls in Pennsylvania who sent me their ballet trophy. They thought having their award would make me feel better. Thankfully, they enclosed a card with their phone number on it. I called their mother to let her know that I had her daughters' trophy, because I wasn't sure even she knew it was missing. I told her how touched I was by their gesture, but that I was going to send it back. The girls protested, saying they didn't want it. They wanted me to keep it so I didn't feel sad. I thought their generosity was beyond gracious, so I invited the family to come to New York and meet me. They came to the set of *All My Children* to watch a taping, and I am so glad they did. Those girls were adorable. I told them I would agree to keep their trophy until I finally won an Emmy. When I did, I promised I would send their trophy back. They agreed, and that's exactly what I did.

And not to be outdone, another fan, Randy Stone, sent me his Oscar! He won the Academy Award for Best Documentary in 1994. When his Oscar arrived at my doorstep, the note simply read, *Keep this until you win the Emmy.* Helmut and I knew there was no possible way we could keep his precious award. When we called to thank him, he simply insisted that I keep it until I had an Emmy of my own. I told him I could be using a walker by the time that happened, but if he felt that strongly, I'd hold on to it, under the same conditions as the ballet trophy. When I won the Emmy, I returned the Oscar. Randy came to New York after my win and joined Helmut and me for dinner at Jean-Georges. It was the first time I actually met him. We had a lovely evening and I gratefully returned his Oscar.

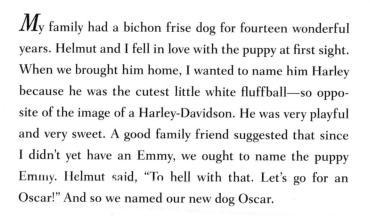

*M*y family had a bichon frise dog for fourteen wonderful years. Helmut and I fell in love with the puppy at first sight. When we brought him home, I wanted to name him Harley because he was the cutest little white fluffball—so opposite of the image of a Harley-Davidson. He was very playful and very sweet. A good family friend suggested that since I didn't yet have an Emmy, we ought to name the puppy Emmy. Helmut said, "To hell with that. Let's go for an Oscar!" And so we named our new dog Oscar.

And then, there was one very memorable summer day when Shelley Winters appeared in the hair and makeup room at *All My Children* to hand-deliver a note to me written and signed from a number of actors from the Actors Studio. Shelley told me that she came to see me personally because she believed, along with the others, that I deserved the Emmy. She talked about Erica as a crossover character—someone people had come to understand better over time. They identified with her and tuned in to watch because of her. She said playing Erica gave me the ultimate boundless career. Shelley was very vocal in her opinion about why I hadn't been given the award. She told me that even though she'd won an Oscar, she felt these types of awards were all political. She was extremely adamant. I didn't know how to respond except to tell her how appreciative I was that she came to see me as a representative of the Actors Studio. It meant a great deal to me for them to recognize my work, because so often, critics underrate the work we do on daytime television, so it was especially gratifying to know my work was being appreciated, especially by such an exceptional group of actors.

It was constantly amazing and heartwarming to find out how many people really wanted me to win. A year before I did, Helmut and I attended a state dinner for the president of Italy at the White House with President Bill Clinton. Although I had been invited to numerous events at the White House in the past, I was never able to accept those invitations because of other obligations. I certainly would have gone if I could, but work kept me from being able to say yes. So when this invitation arrived, I was delighted that it fell on a date when I could attend, especially in light of my Italian heritage, which I am so proud of. I can only say *this* was definitely a Cinderella moment.

It was thrilling to drive up to the entrance. I sat in the back of the limousine and had to control myself from getting too overwhelmed because it was such an unexpected emotional experience. My father was a first-generation Italian American who was such a loyal patriot. He instilled the same love of our country in me from the earliest age. As an American, I couldn't help but feel all of the history and relevance that place holds as we made our way up the driveway to the front door!

It was early May, a picture-perfect spring evening, and when we walked into the foyer, I was struck by all the fresh flowers that were everywhere. We were immediately brought to the receiving line, where we met the president and first lady. They were very cordial as we exchanged a few words. Then we were taken into the East Room, where we collected our table number to be seated. Helmut and I were seated at different tables, which I was certain must have been a mistake. He was at table number one and I was at table ten. Helmut said, "Sorry, honey. There must be a mistake." Of course, we weren't about to say anything. I turned to Helmut and said, "That's okay. There can't be such a thing as a bad seat in the East Room of the White House."

When we walked into the room, some members of President Clinton's cabinet were already inside. One gentlemen came over to me and said, "So . . . Susan, if you win the Emmy this year, you'll become a Democrat, right?"

"It's a deal!" I said.

Helmut escorted me to my table. We found table ten right away—in the middle of the room. The first place card we saw read *President Bill Clinton*. I was seated at the president's table! President Clinton sat directly across from me; Andrea Mitchell was on my left. The first lady, Hillary Clinton, Alan Greenspan, and Sophia Loren were at the next table.

I spent the night listening to President Clinton tell fascinating stories, wishing my father could have been there to hear them. He would have appreciated all of the personal anecdotes about historical events that happened during that administration. My father would have known and adored hearing all of what the president was talking about.

In an effort to involve me in the conversation, the president asked me what my typical day was like at *All My Children*. I kept my answer brief, assuming he was merely being a gracious host by asking. He then asked what my personal interests were. I told the president that I enjoyed listening and dancing to Latin music. He said he liked Latin music as well. I don't know why I didn't expect him to say that, but it was a pleasant surprise.

There were 110 people at that dinner. I was finally able to meet my idol, Sophia Loren, that night. I didn't share the story of seeing her in Chanel because it would have taken too long, but I did have the chance to tell Sophia how much I admired her. She listened, nodded, and smiled.

When I finally did win the Emmy, President Clinton sent me a lovely and thoughtful congratulatory note. It was very touching to receive it. At the bottom, below where he signed his name, he wrote a big HOORAY with an exclamation point. I thought that was terrific.

I will never fully understand why people felt as impassioned as they did about my Emmy journey, but they are obviously incredibly generous. A lot of people expressed the thought that I deserved the Emmy long before I actually won it. Many people said I had been overlooked, robbed, etc. . . . . Their comments meant the world to me because these were all people who had their own lives, their own work, and I am sure lots of other things going on. The fact that anyone would care enough, let alone think to make such a generous gesture like that, was incredible to me.

After my ninth or tenth year of not hearing my name called for Best Actress, I pretty much stopped hearing the name that was called when the envelope was opened. For a split second, my hearing went numb. I listened, but I just didn't hear. It's not that I wasn't excited for my peers; I was. I think it was really more of a self-protective reaction so I wouldn't feel bad or get my hopes up too much. And despite rumors to the contrary, there were never any behind-the-scenes meltdowns after the show or moments of breaking things because I hadn't been awarded the Emmy. How could there be when I knew my children were waiting for me at home with lots of hugs and kisses, precious homemade signs, balloons, handwritten notes, poems, and freshly baked chocolate cake!

The year that I finally did win, however, I will admit, I had a feeling the night before that maybe—just maybe—this was going to be my year. As with every nomination, I agreed to do some press and always hoped for the best, but this particular year, I felt really good about my chances because the story line in the scenes we chose to submit showed some of my best work ever.

The episode that I finally won the Emmy for had to do with an intervention with my television daughter, a then-eleven-year-old Bianca, who had an eating disorder. It was a very rich story line that was wonderfully written. Everyone in those scenes played their characters with such powerful richness. There were many scenes I remember doing that evoked an incredible response from our crew—a true sign we got it right. I feel very lucky to get that type of feedback long before an episode ever hits the air because I know we've done our job well and the viewer at home will react in the same way.

In the days that followed my win, there was an outpouring of love, support, and good wishes. I received congratulatory notes from friends, colleagues, families, neighbors, the president of the United States, schoolchildren, and lots of people I'd never even met. Diane Sawyer told me she was at home watching the show. When my name was called out, she actually jumped up and down on her bed with excitement.

Still basking in the victory, my daughter and I did something we love to do—we had decadent and very yummy hot fudge sundaes together at Serendipity in New York. When our sundaes were put In front of us, all of the waiters came to our table and serenaded us, singing, "Congratulations to you!" to the tune of "Happy Birthday."

The local florists in Garden City later told me that his entire flower inventory was sold out the day after I won. In fact, the buzz around town was that there were no flowers anywhere in Garden City! ABC sent me nineteen dozen long-stemmed pink roses to celebrate my win. I felt so lucky and blessed that I took those roses and placed them before the statue of the Blessed Mother at our church, the same church I attended growing up. Somehow, that felt so right.

There were countless bouquets and arrangements sent to my home and also to the *All My Children* studio. Although I kept some, I donated many to various local hospitals, where I knew they'd brighten up so many people's day. The studio was inundated with mail and a deluge of gifts, too. There wasn't enough space in my dressing room or the hallways to hold all of the items that kept coming, so the producers set up banquet tables in the rehearsal hall that overwhelmed me when I saw it.

When I arrived at work the following day, I was met with incredible cheering and applause from the cast and crew. There were streamers and banners congratulating me everywhere. When I appeared the next day on *Good Morning America*, they, too, gave me nineteen dozen long-stemmed pink roses, except theirs were in all different shades of pink. They were gorgeous.

A couple of days later, I was invited to city hall to accept the key to New York City from Mayor Giuliani. That was a very exciting surprise. I'm told that with this key, I have unlimited access to anyplace in Manhattan. It sits among some of my most treasured keepsakes in my den at my home in Garden City. It's nice to know it's there, just in case I'm ever feeling locked out!

After I received the key at the ceremony, Helmut; my ABC publicist, Sallie Schoneboom; a couple of colleagues; and I planned a celebration lunch at the famed restaurant "21" in midtown Manhattan to indulge in their wonderfully delicious hamburgers before returning to the studio to work. On the way from city hall to "21," a big delivery truck pulled up next to our car. On the side of the truck was the number "19."

Sallie said, "Susan, Look! It's the number nineteen. It's your new lucky number!" What was so amazing was that this truck had no other markings on it. It only had the number nineteen on the back.

We didn't call ahead to the restaurant to let them know we were coming, so the maître d' didn't know to expect us. We thought we'd take our chances of just dropping by, and hopefully, they'd be able to seat us. When we walked through the door, the people in the restaurant stood up and started clapping for me. I was astounded by their warm and very unexpected response. Several people graciously sent over bottles of champagne to our table.

Since my win, people all over have continued to come up to me and say they were glad I finally got that Emmy. A fire truck full of New York City fireman spotted me at a red light while I was sitting in the back of my car studying a script. They looked down from high atop their truck and each of the guys flashed me two big thumbs-up. I was completely blown away by their reaction. This was a sight I will never forget.

I am eternally grateful to all of the people who have expressed so many kind words and good wishes to me—before I ever won—and since I've won, too. There are simply no words to describe that kind of outpouring of love and support. And given my now twenty-one nominations over the course of my career, I will readily admit that although it really is an honor just to be nominated, *winning* is definitely better!

Sallie Schoneboom, my longtime publicist from ABC and someone I think of as a dear friend, had the responsibility of being the courier for my Emmy when we attended a Super Soap Weekend event in Florida later that year. The award would be on display for fans to see throughout the weekend. ABC Super Soap Weekend was organized in conjunction with Disney and ABC to bring soap opera actors from the various ABC shows to visit and mingle with their fans. Those weekends were always a lot of fun because they gave me the chance to meet face-to-face the many people who watch our show.

There was one fan who attended the first Super Soap Weekend who I will say is likely the biggest Susan Lucci fan I have ever met. Carlos is a radio DJ who lives in Miami. He came to the first Super Soap weekend in 1996. He isn't a typical-looking soap fan. In fact, at first glance, he looked a little intimidating. His hair was always a different color each time we saw him and he always had some type of hardware or jewelry through his nose. The first time we spotted him in the crowd, security was alerted because he was so imposing. However, it turned out that Carlos was not only an extremely nice man, but he has really exquisite taste in clothing and jewelry. He never once showed up to an event without bringing me a gorgeous blouse, dress, or a beautiful pair of earrings. Carlos became a Super Soap tradition for the entire thirteen years I attended those events. And, Carlos was also front and center at my opening night on Broadway.

Super Soap Weekends were special because fans could connect with their favorite ABC daytime stars on a very personal level. Upward of twenty-five thousand fans attended. I often did three or four autograph sessions a day, trying to make sure I never left anyone standing on that line without a hello, handshake, photo, or autograph. That extra time often made me late for my next commitment, but I didn't care because it is such an honor to be invited into people's living rooms five days a week, and if they could stand in line to meet me, surely I could stay to meet them, too. I met generations of viewers, including many who said they had grown up watching All My Children because their mothers and grandmothers watched it.

All throughout the 1999 Super Soap event, Sallie kept the Emmy very close to her. Knowing it would be a terrible situation if she were to somehow lose my brand-new award, she carefully wrapped the statue in a towel, placed it in a bag, and then put that bag inside another bag, which she slung over her shoulder like a school bag.

When it came time to transport the award back to New York, the people at security decided it was a dangerous object with sharp edges that could possibly injure someone. They told her they were going to confiscate it for security purposes.

Now, this was pre-9/11, so security was much more lax than it is today. Still, the security guards on duty felt the Emmy was a potential threat or danger to other passengers. Sallie pleaded with them not to take it away.

"You don't understand. This is Susan Lucci's Emmy. You can't take it away." She was literally begging.

"Oh yeah? How did you get Susan Lucci's Emmy?" one of the guards suspiciously asked.

Needless to say, Sallie was then detained for questioning. She was genuinely fearful she was going to be arrested for stealing my Emmy. Luckily, the security team at the Orlando airport believed her story and eventually gave her back my Emmy and allowed her to board the plane to New York, where she immediately delivered the statue to me, I none the wiser. I actually had no idea this event ever took place until I spoke to Sallie while writing this book. When I asked her why she never told me, she said she was afraid to admit how close she came to losing the Emmy it took me twenty-nine years and nineteen nominations to win!

The year after my celebrated win, I was asked to host the Emmys. The 2000 show was set to take place at Radio City Music Hall once again. In an ironic twist of fate, I was not nominated for an award that year. Still, I always enjoyed being a part of the show, whether I was a presenter, host, or nominee.

There was only one time throughout the years that my heart stopped cold, for a reason that is every actor's worst nightmare at an awards show. It happened at the twenty-ninth annual Daytime Emmy Awards in 2002. I was backstage, having just presented the award for Best Actor. The nominees for Best Actress were being announced next, so the producer told me to stand offstage instead of trying to make it back to my seat in time, just in case my name was announced as the winner.

The winner was Susan Flannery from *Bold and the Beautiful*. Rosie O'Donnell was standing backstage with me when the nominees were read. There was so much excitement when everyone heard "Susan" that we never heard the last name that was called out. Someone backstage turned to me and said, "You won! They called your name!" Rosie was pushing me to go out on the stage. "Are you sure?" I asked. She said, "Yes!"

The orchestra was playing the theme from *All My Children*, so I figured it must have been me after all. It was all very confusing because I wasn't sure what was happening. Just as I started to walk onto the stage, I saw Susan Flannery making her way up the steps and her cast mates standing and applauding. That's when I knew I wasn't the winner. Thank God I stopped before I got too far onstage. I literally froze in my tracks and all but moonwalked back behind the curtain, hoping and praying that no one saw my mistake. I felt terrible for Susan because the show had cued the wrong music for her as she made her walk from her seat to the stage. Still, I know the joy she must have felt to accept that award and I was very happy for her win.

No conversation about the Emmys would be complete without talking about all of the spoofs over the years regarding my many nominations and losses. A girl must keep a sense of humor about these things, right?

When Sweet One sugar substitute offered me the opportunity to do a commercial for their product in 1989, their concept was intended to portray me as the opposite of my usual self, while throwing a typical "Erica" tantrum. Even though we actually shot the commercial after my tenth Emmy nomination and loss, the producer presented an idea to me while we were filming that I thought was funny. It was suggested that I act as if I had lost an eleventh or twelfth time, too. Caught up in the humor of it all, I ad-libbed the line "Eleven years without an Emmy! What does a person have to do around here to get an Emmy?" It turned out the Sweet One people and the producer liked it and wanted to keep it in the final cut. Of course, I had no idea my stab at comedy would actually be a premonition of what was to come. As you know by now, I didn't win that Emmy for several more years. But when I did . . . yes, it was a slice of heaven to finally take home that gorgeous trophy.

On October 6, 1990, I embarked upon one of the scariest and funniest experiences of my life; I hosted *Saturday Night Live*. Even then, I was aware I was working with one of the best casts in the history of the show. Here's my opening monologue:

Susan Lucci's Monologue

In the Scene:
Susan Lucci
Victoria Jackson
Kevin Nealon
Jan Hooks
David Spade
Mike Myers

SUSAN LUCCI

Ah, Saturday Night Live—*here I am hosting* Saturday Night Live, *I cannot think of a bigger thrill in my life . . . except, maybe, that Emmy? Most of you may know me from the character I play on* All My Children—*Erica Kane. I have to tell you, though, I'm really nothing like that character, like that scheming, self-centered Erica Kane. For one thing, Erica's been married eight times; I've only been married once, to the same sweet, wonderful man, for sixteen years now—I have had countless affairs . . . but I always come back to the same sweet, wonderful man! He's the father of . . . one of my two children.*
I just said all that for a laugh. That's why I wanted to do this

show. I wanted to work in front of a live audience, and hear you laugh. We once tried a live audience at All My Children, *but they just didn't laugh. Oh, you'd hear an occasional cough. Mainly people would just yell out things, like, "Don't marry her! You're just a pawn in her game!" "Uh-oh! He's coming to walk in on you now, put your clothes back on!" So we got rid of the audience.*

But, anyway, here I am doing this show! Everybody has been so terrific to work with this week, it's been a great week. Except for one minor incident.

[CAMERA BREAKS INTO A FLASHBACK SEQUENCE]

SUSAN LUCCI V/O: *It really was not worth flashing back to . . .*

[FLASHBACK SHOWS SUSAN'S POINT OF VIEW AS SHE'S PREPPED FOR THE LIVE SHOW]

HAIRSTYLIST: *Okay, Susan, this wig looks great. We'll just brush your hair out for the monologue now, okay? [brushes hair] There. That looks good. You had a really good dress rehearsal. Here. What do you think, Sylvia?*

SECOND HAIRSYLIST: *It's nice. Nice.*

VICTORIA JACKSON: *Susan? Susan, are you almost ready?*

SUSAN LUCCI: *Yeah, just about. Thanks, Gloria, you have been so helpful! Really.*

HAIRSTYLIST: *Oh, no problem. I was just doing my job.*

[SUSAN'S VIEWPOINT FALLS UPON AN EMMY STANDING ON THE COUNTER]

SUSAN LUCCI V/O: *Wow . . . is . . . is that your Emmy?*

VICTORIA JACKSON: *That's* one *of her Emmys! She's got* three!

HAIRSTYLIST: *Well, you know, I've been in the business about five years, so . . .*

VICTORIA JACKSON: *Susan, they want you to go over to wardrobe, and get in a costume thing. Come on.*

[SUSAN'S VIEWPOINT STROLLS OVER TO WARDROBE]

WARDROBE PERSONNEL: *There you are, Susan! I want to try this tiara for the next sketch. [places tiara over Susan's head] You know, it's nice. But I have a couple more that I want to try. [Susan's gaze falls upon three Emmys on the table] No, honey, these are Emmys. Back here.*

VICTORIA JACKSON: *[holding up two Emmys] Steven, are these the two Emmys you won for that very special* Benson?

WARDROBE PERSONNEL: *Oh, I don't know, Victoria . . . check the inscriptions.*

[KEVIN NEALON ENTERS, AN EMMY MEDALLION AROUND HIS NECK]

KEVIN NEALON: *Susan? Susan? Hi, Susan. I think they need you over in makeup over there. [Susan's gaze falls upon*

Kevin's Emmy] Oh? You like this? I gave my other two to my parents! Come on!

JAN HOOKS: *Hey! Hey, Susan! Hey, you were great in dress— you excited? You excited? Good! [shakes wobbly makeup table] Look at this, my makeup table is broken, can you believe that? [looks around] Hey, can somebody help me here, please? Makeup table's broken. [union employee Howard enters] Hi, Howard. [Howard places an Emmy under the short leg of the makeup table] Oh . . . Howard. You're a lifesaver.*

HOWARD: *It's only an Emmy, Miss Hooks.*

KEVIN NEALON: *This way, Susan. Susan? Come on.*

VICTORIA JACKSON: *I didn't know Howard had an Emmy!*

KEVIN NEALON: *He's union—he shows up, he does his job, right?*

[SUSAN'S GAZE FALLS UPON A CARPENTER USING AN EMMY TO HAMMER A NAIL INTO THE WALL]

VICTORIA JACKSON: *Susan? Are you all right? Are you okay?*

KEVIN NEALON: *Maybe we should get you a soda, Susan. Come on, follow me.*

VICTORIA JACKSON: *I guess she's a little down because she's never won an Emmy.*

KEVIN NEALON: *Oh, Susan . . . you're gonna win one. Besides, it's just a statue. You know—a symbol of excellence. [they enter the dining area] Okay, here we are!*

[SUSAN'S GAZE FALLS UPON DAVID SPADE AND OTHER CAST MEMBERS EATING CORN ON THE COB, USING EMMYS AS CORN HOLDERS]

KEVIN NEALON: *Susan? Susan, did you eat dinner? There's plenty of corn over here.*

MIKE MYERS: *Hey, everybody! Hey, everybody! Emmy Fight!*

[MYERS AND EVERYONE ELSE IN THE ROOM BEGIN THROW-ING RUBBER EMMYS AT ONE ANOTHER AS SUSAN QUICKLY MAKES HER EXIT TO SALVATION]

[FLASHBACK DISSOLVES BACK TO SUSAN AT CENTER STAGE]

SUSAN LUCCI: *Fortunately, they caught me at the elevator. I was hysterical, but they whacked me over the head with an Emmy, and now I'm fine. Anyway . . . we've got a great show, with Hothouse Flowers, so stick around, we'll be right back!*

Doing *Saturday Night Live* was absolutely fantastic. The cast and crew were great to work with. Everyone there was very funny and superkind. I didn't mind poking fun at myself or at Erica. Let's face it, there were a lot of people in addition to the folks at *SNL* who were having fun at both my character's and my expense over the whole Emmy thing, so why shouldn't I? All of the late-night comedians were having a field day telling "Susan Lucci" jokes that pertained to my not winning. The expression *pulling a Susan Lucci* actually became part of our nation's vernacular for a while. There have even been a number of songs inspired by Erica Kane. The alternative rock band Urge Overkill wrote one called "Erica Kane" which talks about another Emmy passing her by. The late singer Aaliyah recorded a song called "Erica Kane" which was released after her tragic and unexpected death on her album *I Care 4 U.* And the band B5 also recorded a song about Erica Kane entitled "Erika Cain." The song talks about how the singer is in a relationship with a beautiful girl, but she is crazy. B5 contacted *All My Children*'s producers about doing a cameo on the show and ultimately appeared in the April 25, 2008, episode as activists rallying for Erica's release from prison.

What's a girl to do when something like this continues to grow? As the age-old saying goes, "If you can't beat 'em, join 'em," right?

CHAPTER 14

The Inner Sanctum

Everywhere I go, people want to know what a typical day on the set of *All My Children* is really like. How long does it take me to get ready? What time do I have to go to work? What color lipstick do I wear? How long does it take to do a scene or tape an entire show? Who picks out my wardrobe? These types of questions are so common from fans that I thought it might be interesting to take you on a backstage tour of what it's like to go from Susan to Erica.

When we first started shooting *All My Children*, the show was actually shot in sequence. We would do a table read, a run-through and dress rehearsal, and then we would tape. I have no idea how we got our hair and makeup done at the time because we were running around the studio like crazy people. If you had a minute and a half, you might be able to duck into the hair and makeup room, but there were no guarantees, which meant we'd tape looking "as is."

If I had only half a blowout done by the time they called me to the studio floor for rehearsal, that was how I went to the set. We'd usually have to wet it down and start all over again before taping, with the hope there might be enough time to get it done right.

The hair and makeup room is really the inner sanctum of any show. It is a place of privacy and safety for people. It's where we can share secrets, bad jokes, and funny stories, and tackle every possible topic under the sun, from politics to relationships. People say the funniest things, which I don't feel right actually repeating, but there have been lots of times I wished I had a tape recorder to capture some of these humorous conversations. Every time an announcement is made over the PA, there is a quick witty response from someone in the room. Hands down, the funniest person I ever shared the hair and makeup room with was Kelly Ripa. She is a natural-born stand-up comedienne. I loved the years she spent on our show. She is such a talented woman, who has found her calling in life by entertaining people daily.

My typical day starts early. I am up at four-thirty in the morning. Glamour, glamour, glamour! Believe me, I am not looking so glamorous at this hour.

I get up that early so I can exercise before I have to be at the studio, usually by six or seven. I make the time to do Pilates each day so I can stay fit and feel good about myself. I remember reading a front-page article in the *New York Times* many years ago that talked about how important exercise is for women's health. I took that information to heart and that was when my commitment to keeping fit really started. I wasn't even sure how I was going to work exercise into my schedule between raising my children, working, and juggling other projects, but I knew there had to be a way.

I wanted to exercise, but I didn't want to bulk up. I worked near Lincoln Center for so many years and saw all of the ballerinas and dancers, not to mention Victoria's Secret–looking models who strolled along Columbus Avenue and Broadway on a regular basis. I loved how their bodies looked so long and lean. I knew what I wanted to accomplish, but I didn't know how to get there, so I found Christine Fee, a knowledgeable and experienced personal trainer and someone who has become one of my closest friends. I asked her to help me define a workout that was right for my bone structure and needs.

I knew about Pilates from friends who were dancers, but I had never done it. I knew that it was a way to tone and strengthen your core. That was what I was after. Chris and I started a workout regime that incorporated the Pilates method, which I loved. I suddenly felt so much better. As an added benefit, the exercise was releasing any kind of stress my body was carrying. My only regret was not finding out about it sooner.

Years later, I worked with a team of experts at Guthy-Renker, the top infomercial company in the business, to become the spokes-woman for a fitness system called Malibu Pilates, which adds cardio training to a Pilates workout. With Malibu Pilates, you're off the floor, off a mat, and onto a cushioned bench. You still do traditional Pilates moves that will stretch, tone, and sculpt your body while burning more calories by involving cardiovascular aspects through the pedals and springs that can be adjusted on the Malibu Pilates chair. You can get your heart rate up and burn more fat at the same time by doing a cardio blast.

I do twenty to thirty minutes of Malibu Pilates in the morning before I move on with the rest of my day. Once I've worked out, I eat breakfast, have a second cup of coffee, and I'm off to the studio. I usually spend somewhere in the neighborhood of ninety minutes to two hours getting prepped before my actual call time. Men have it so much easier than the women at *All My Children*. They are in and out of their chairs in about fifteen minutes—tops. They can roll into the studio twenty minutes before a scene, get prepped, dressed, and make their scene happen all within an hour. I cannot even fathom what that would be like. Erica is such a glamour girl, there's no get-ting around the time it takes to transform me into the woman you all see on-screen.

Over the years, my makeup artists have always commented on how youthful my skin looks. Although I've never been shy about divulging my age, people don't seem to ask all that often, so I haven't made it a point to shout it out to the world. If someone wanted to know my age and I were to answer quickly, I'd say thirty-seven or thirty-eight because that is how I feel. The truth is, I am older than Oprah and younger than Cher—barely—and, incidentally, I adore both of these women.

*N*ever just throw up your hands and say, "Oh well. Now I'm just this or that!"

I turned sixty and became a grandmother on the same day. Each one of those labels separately can be shocking as you go along through life, but when they arrive on your doorstep as a two-for-one special, it can take your breath away. I love *being* a grandmother; it's the label I am not crazy about. I've never been one who has embraced labels—and, as you now know, I almost forfeited graduating from college as a result of that principle. When I turned sixty, I worried there would be all types of labels placed on me because I had gotten to a stage of life when many people slow down. I was never that kind of woman.

I'm all for never throwing up your hands and saying, "Oh well, I'm of a certain age now, so it's okay if I gain weight, can't take care of my skin, can't remember anything anymore, and so on." I don't believe in that type of thinking. Never have—never will. We're all given a certain genetic makeup. All we can do is try to live our lives and do the best we can.

Whenever the ladies of *All My Children* are gathered in the makeup room, we usually get to talking about our health, skin, and the latest and greatest happenings in dermatology. Sometimes I listen to the other women talk and wonder, *Where have I been? Why don't*

I know about some of this? I was fascinated to discover that the twentysomethings in the cast are just as interested in talking about these subjects as the older women on the show. There's no better place to swap information than the makeup room at *All My Children*!

I was twenty-eight years old when I had my first makeup-and-skin moment. I looked in the mirror one day and thought to myself, *My skin looks good today. If I take care of it, I won't look old by tomorrow.* You have to take care of your skin every day, just as you have to take care of your body, mind, and spirit. Tomorrow is another today. Knowing that, I wear sunblock every day, and make sure I wash my makeup off every single night. One of my main rules for good skin care is to remember that no matter how good that party was, take off your makeup before you go to sleep! You will do your skin the greatest favor and, in the end, will find yourself looking healthier and fresher for it.

I went to a luncheon several years ago with about twenty women to celebrate the holiday season. The ages at the table ranged from early twenties to late seventies, with several of my contemporaries thrown in for good measure. The conversation turned toward a procedure called microdermabrasion. Microdermabrasion is a noninvasive mechanical exfoliation treatment that removes the outermost layer of dead skin cells on the face, chest, neck, or anywhere on the body. At the time it was a procedure done only by trained skincare professionals using a mechanical medium for exfoliation, such as crystals, diamond tips, or bristle tips along with a vacuum to sweep away the dead skin. It is also known to help with circulation. I was intrigued listening to the other women talk about this procedure, as it was something I had never heard about, but thought sounded wonderful.

Shortly after that luncheon, I met a woman in California who was a little bit older than I am who told me that she goes to the dermatologist who invented the procedure. She looked fabulous, but after doing some due diligence, I discovered that for microdermabrasion to be fully effective, it requires seven or eight consecutive monthly visits. I didn't have that luxury of time with my schedule. Plus, I worried that the machine might be too abrasive for my sensitive skin. I don't know for sure if this was the case because I had never tried it, but it certainly was my perception.

Not long after the word *microdermabrasion* entered my life, I was approached by Guthy-Renker to partner with them on a new at-home microdermabrasion product called Youthful Essence. I was aware of the company's great reputation, so I knew I would certainly be in good hands and that I'd be working with people who have integrity. Having done so much research on my own, I was very excited about this opportunity. Before I could commit, though, I wanted to do my own testing by using the product at home. I had too good of a relationship with my audience to tell them that something works if it doesn't. I had been approached to do other skincare lines in the past, but the samples people sent me didn't meet my expectations, so I declined those opportunities.

*P*eople have written to me for many years asking questions about my personal style, my grooming regimen, and the products I wear and use on-screen and off. Prior to electronic media, my husband came up with the idea of launching a phone-in number that fans could call for answers to many of the most frequently asked questions. For example, if you wanted to know what fragrance I wear, you'd press 1. What hair products I use, you'd press 2, and so on.

It was around this same time that someone came to us with an opportunity to become involved with a line of shampoo, conditioner, and other products. I was on a movie set shooting *The Bride in Black,* in Pittsburgh, when the care package of products arrived. In the first part of the movie, I played a girl working in a deli. It was not a glamour-girl part. My hair was going to be au naturel during these scenes, so I thought it seemed like a great time to give those products a try. If they could make my hair look good for those scenes, I'd be sold. It's very important to me that I use all of the products that I sell. Many other products have been brought to me over the years that I turned down because something about them didn't work for me. Again, I have too good of a relationship with my audience to deceive them in any way. I will not get involved with anything I do not fully believe in. If I like the products and think they work, I can be secure in telling my audience the same.

When the product trial arrived at our house, I suddenly had some reservations. It wasn't that I didn't like what I had heard, I was simply nervous about trying something new on my skin. I had to be on camera and didn't want to risk an adverse reaction or some noticeable side effect. The package sat in the kitchen for three weeks. Helmut kept cajoling me to give it a try, but I was too afraid.

One afternoon, Helmut appeared in the kitchen looking more radiant than I had ever seen him. His skin looked really great. The improvement was immediately noticeable. He told me he had given Youthful Essence a try. I liked the results I saw with my husband, so I finally agreed to try it, too. I had no adverse reaction at all, and after one use, my skin was really glowing. When Helmut saw me he couldn't believe how smooth my skin looked. That told me everything I needed to know. I informed the people at Guthy-Renker that I would happily be a part of this journey to help women have brighter, smoother, healthier-looking skin. After having sold close to eight million units worldwide, I'd say we're on to something!

Sitting in the makeup chair is an intimate experience. Anyone who has ever gotten that close to my face can see every line, discoloration, change in texture, and even the scar above my eye that is a reminder of going through the windshield of my former boyfriend's car. When I had surgery after that accident, I was told there might be some long-term effects from the impact and subsequently from the healing. As I got older, the cartilage on the inside of my nose grew thicker, making the outside of my nose look constantly swelled. My nose had never been perfect before I went through the windshield and it wasn't perfect after either. As time went on, I began developing some difficulty breathing through my nose. The doctors told me they could thin out the thickening areas, which would allow me to breathe easier. Although I didn't do anything drastic, I decided to have a minor reshaping to alleviate the discomfort I was having and as a precaution for problems down the road. Although the procedure changed the appearance of my nose, the difference was only slight, which I was so grateful for. I didn't want to take away from the gifts that God had given me, and best of all, I could actually breathe again!

By now you know my hair has been the subject of several moments throughout my life. As my career has spanned over four decades, my hair and I have survived every fad, look, cut, color, and style from the seventies, eighties, nineties, and the two-thousands. You can look back on my career and tell what decade we were in simply by noting the style of my hair. I was definitely never afraid to try new looks. As much as I don't want to admit this, I actually liked my big eighties hair . . . a lot. I was so sad when I woke up one day and was told that big hair was over! However, when I see photos from those days, I can honestly say that my hair could not possibly have been any bigger. It was borderline ridiculous! What was I thinking?

Looking back now, I do regret my decision to get a perm. I already had naturally curly hair. After my perm, my hair was so big that I was giving Don King a run for his money. I remember my mother looking at me and saying, "Oh, Susan. Why did you do that?"—using a tone that only a mother can use to make one feel like they are a teenager all over again. Thankfully, the stylists at the show were able to save me from myself by blowing out my hair. And when I did let my hair go curly, they were there to reel it in.

There was only one time I sat in a stylist's chair and told her to "cut it." They say that people make drastic changes to their hair when there is something major going on in their lives, such as a divorce, a death, or a new job. None of these things was remotely on my radar screen—I just wanted a change. So, I went to work in the morning with long luscious hair and came home that night with a new, very short cut I had seen on a model in Italian *Vogue* magazine. I did a lot of minor experimenting over the years, but that was my most radical change. Much to my surprise, both Helmut and I ended up liking the way short hair looked on me. I eventually grew my hair long again because I missed that style. As it turned out, I went through a lot of different looks as I slowly made the transition back to long hair, and I enjoyed that part of the change, too.

When it comes to my character, I personally like Erica's hair to be moving. I don't enjoy the up-dos as much as I like a good sexy, messy cut. I often ask the stylist to put her hands in my hair and really shake it up. Whenever I do that, the control room usually sends word to the set to have someone tame it a bit once I get there. Ever since we started shooting the show with high-definition cameras, there has been a tendency to coif my hair a little neater because it looks better when taping. Still, I like the messy look better. There are no mirrors on the set, so I rarely have the ability to "check" myself before doing a scene. I have to trust the experts to make sure everything is in its proper place. Thank goodness I have been lucky enough to work with some of the best hair and makeup people in television. They have made the process enjoyable and worthwhile day in and day out.

It is so much fun to go to work and get paid to play dress up. I sometimes think I am the luckiest girl in the world because not only do I get to have my hair and makeup done each day, I get to play in someone else's closet, choosing between this gorgeous dress and that fabulous gown.

My wardrobe decisions for Erica are part of a collaborative process. Our costume designer, David Zyla, and I usually have the first discussion. But I also rely on the expertise of our wardrobe department and the amazing alterations they do. And when it comes to Erica's wardrobe, David and I are always on the same page. He really understands Erica and knows what works for her. David's job isn't just to dress each actor in a way that makes them feel good and look good. He's also concerned with storytelling. I sometimes think we should all get dressed in the morning asking ourselves, *What story am I trying to tell?* and *What am I* expressing? Ask yourself what image you are trying to present to the world. How do you want to be perceived by your boss, colleagues, that cute guy, and by the world at large? Doing this before you get dressed just might influence your decisions in a very positive and fun way. Try it.

I have never worked with a stylist outside of *All My Children*. My dress decisions are usually made in conjunction with David, my mother, and my husband. They all have exquisite judgment and each knows what looks good on me. Ever since I was a little girl, my mother has had a great eye and has enjoyed picking out clothes for me. She has wonderful taste and had a hand in choosing my last four Emmy dresses. She's great to shop with and I still find it so endearing that she is so thoughtful and patient with me. David likes her taste so much he once told me that if my mother ever wanted a job, she could go to work at *All My Children*.

But there was one time that was an absolute fashion disaster. It was in the late eighties and I was on location in Toronto doing a film when I realized I needed to find a dress for the Emmy Awards. At that time most designers simply couldn't put enough stuff on a garment at the same time. The dress I chose was a strappy number that had every extra a dress could possibly have—and shouldn't have. It was black and silver, had lace, and was beaded, too. It was so busy, it was blinding—and in the end, it was a definite learning experience.

Once I've got my hair and makeup done, life can move pretty fast on the set. We shoot ninety pages of dialogue a day. To put that into perspective for you, a major feature film might shoot, on average, two pages a day. An independent film, maybe four or five pages a day. In fact, it took five weeks to shoot the chariot scene in *Ben-Hur*. Since I am generally in so many scenes, I am constantly playing a game of "Beat the Clock." Our studio in New York was about a city block long. If you had to run across it, it would be the equivalent of running the length of a football field. One day, I was running to the hair and makeup room as fast as I could when the heel of my shoe got caught on some cables and I tripped. I fell on the hard cement stage floor, landing on my knees. Cables are usually on the floor, and sometimes taped down. For whatever reason, these cables were raised a couple of inches off the floor. I knew they were there, as I had been jumping cables all day making my way back and forth from the stage to the makeup room. I got up and thought I was okay to walk back to my dressing room. I didn't feel great, but I was able to make my way back. By the time I got to my room, I was in so much pain I really could not take another step. I had heard that if you break your kneecap, you cannot walk. I could walk, so I thought I must be all right.

One of the producers came into my dressing room to see how I was doing. He offered to send me to the emergency room, but I declined. I thought I could shake off the pain. The producer was worried about me, but he seemed more worried about the four-hour delay an impromptu visit to the hospital would create in his shooting schedule, so I decided to tough it out.

As the day went on, I had a scene where I was supposed to walk down a flight of stairs to get to my table at a local nightclub. By this time, my legs had become Jell-O. Although the scene had not been staged this way, I asked the actor I was working with if I could hold on to his arm. I somehow made it down the steps, played the scene, and was finally able to call it quits, as that was my last scene for the day.

By the time I got home that night, I was in terrible pain. My mother was at our house for dinner. I was sitting opposite her at the table. When I tried to cross my leg, she could see that something was wrong.

"What are you doing, Susan?" she asked.

"Trying to cross my leg," I said.

"If one of your children was sitting here hurt, you would be right to the doctor's office with them. You are my child. You need to see a doctor now." And she was right.

Fortunately, Helmut had a golfing buddy who was an orthopedic surgeon. Even though it was ten o'clock at night, we called Woody Greiner, who graciously agreed to meet us at a nearby hospital so we could have some X-rays taken. Woody looked at the films and immediately told me that I had fractured my kneecap. It hadn't gone all of the way through, but I was going to have to stay off my feet for two weeks. There was no way that was going to happen. I was fully committed at the show. Woody agreed to give me a Velcro cast that I promised to wear whenever I wasn't shooting a scene. The wardrobe department found the cutest silver metallic flats for me to wear. Those two weeks of healing are the only time in the history of *All My Children* that Erica Kane wore flat shoes.

My working days can last anywhere from eight to eighteen hours a day. If we shoot late, there is no pushing back the next day's start time. It's "see you in the morning" for everyone. The schedule is grueling and hectic, but the fast pace is part of what I love most about working in daytime. I never get the chance to become bored because things are always changing. I have a new script to learn every day because tomorrow we get to do it all over again. I wouldn't have it any other way.

So many times art and life imitate each other—this is me with Regis on the set of his talk show . . .

and Erica spotting a billboard on the street for her *own* talk show.

I've had many moments of great fortune throughout my life and career, including performing on Broadway in *Annie Get Your Gun* . . .

taking my cabaret act on the road with Regis Philbin . . .

doing the tango with Tony Dovolani on *Dancing with the Stars* . . .

seeing myself as a very lifelike figure in Madame Tussaude wax museum . . .

having a doll made in my likeness . . .

and launching many beauty products, including my fragrance, Invitation.

Among the highest honors
were meeting former president
Bill Clinton . . .

THE WHITE HOUSE
WASHINGTON

June 4, 1999

Susan Lucci
c/o Sheryl Fuchs
77 West 66th Street
New York, New York 10023-6298

Dear Susan:

Congratulations on finally winning that Daytime
Emmy Award you deserve! I was so pleased to
hear that you were recognized for your talents
after all these years.

Keep up the great work.

Sincerely,

Bill Clinton

Hooray!

receiving a congratulatory letter from
him upon winning the Emmy . . .

and being named by
Barbara Walters as
one of the ten most
fascinating people in
1999.

I also got to work with the legendary Marvin Hamlisch (pictured here with his lovely wife, Terre Blair). Marvin kindly helped me prepare for my first Broadway audition!

And I got to make films with extraordinary actors including the late great Tony Curtis who signed and gave me his character's fedora after we wrapped the movie, *Maffia Princess*. What a thrill!

I've also had opportunities to help those less fortunate. Here I am in Africa working with Feed the Children alongside Tony Geary, Kelly Monaco, Erik Estrada, Larry Jones, Kyle Massey, Chris Massey, and Devon Werkheiser.

This is one of the beautiful children I met at a school we visited.

I was treated like a rock star for bringing them such simple things as lollipops and rubber balls.

Of course, my greatest blessings
have been family and friends.
This is my real-life leading man
and husband, Helmut Huber,
on our wedding day . . .

enjoying a quiet walk
along the beach . . .

and renewing our vows in
Vienna at the Hofburg
Kapelle, the Emperor's
private chapel, in 1994.

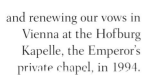

Helmut and I love to dance.
This is us taking a whirl at our
summer home . . .

and again at Helmut's surprise
seventieth birthday party.

This is the one-of-a-kind invitation
I sent to him to be sure he wouldn't
suspect a thing about the party!
Of course there was no affiliate event
that night.

Here we are in Alaska on our dogsled at the Iditarod.

We were there as guests of our good friends philanthropists and racing aficionados Marylou Whitney and John Hendrickson.

And this is us high above Lac Tignes in France, moments before Helmut saved my life . . . for the *first* time!

Here are my wonderful children Liza and Andreas. They accompanied me to the Ellis Island Medal of Honor Award ceremony.

This is adorable Liza, one year old, all bundled up in the snow. (I'm bundled up, too, in a cozy hand-knitted hat and sweater from the Norwegian mom who hosted me during my studies abroad.)

I love this photo representing three generations of women in my family— Liza, my mother, and me.

Here my beautiful mother and I are headed to a charity luncheon in Palm Beach.

And this is a picture of Liza and me on the evening she appeared as Miss Golden Globe. Doesn't she look stunning?!

I tried to hide my real-life pregnancy with Andreas while opening a disco as Erica . . .

but Andreas and I are happy to pose for the camera in this photo—one of my all-time favorites of the two of us together.

I adore being a grandmother. This is me with my first born grandson, Royce.

This is the pure white doe and her fawn spotted outside our window the day our youngest grandson, Brendan, was born. What magic the day held!

Here are my very handsome grandsons together . . .

and having fun with my wonderful son-in law, Alex!

These are my best friends from college—Cathy, Patty, Linda, and Pat—who have been there for me throughout it all.

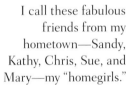

I call these fabulous friends from my hometown—Sandy, Kathy, Chris, Sue, and Mary—my "homegirls."

This is my friend Mary whom I adore as well. Here we are celebrating our Christmas birthdays together.

Finally, my family would not be complete without Frida, pictured here with our dog, Oscar. She has cared for us all since Liza was a toddler.

This is the inside of my dressing room in L.A. I'll just read my script now while you finish reading my book!

CHAPTER 15

———— ᥫ᭡ ᥫ᭡ ————

Dancing with the Stars

The summer of 2005 marked the debut of a new ABC television show called *Dancing with the Stars*. Producers had approached me several times to participate in the first season of the show, but I didn't feel as if I could take on the overwhelming task of shooting *All My Children* in New York while learning to dance and flying back and forth to Los Angeles twice a week. I watched the first season with great curiosity because I love to dance and I have a deep appreciation for those who can really move. I became an instant fan and continued to tune in every week. Despite my personal interest, I turned down the opportunity to participate for several more seasons.

I never even considered the possibility of doing *Dancing with the Stars* until the fall of 2007 when my costar Cameron Mathison joined the cast for its fifth season. Honestly, until I saw Cameron on the show, I didn't even think it was doable for me. But once he was brave enough to try it, I knew I could do it, too.

I debuted as one of the contestants for season seven. I was paired with the wonderful, sexy, talented, and *very* patient Tony Davolani.

Thankfully, the show sends your partner wherever you live, so Tony and I were able to spend five weeks preparing for our first appearance. For season seven, the producers had decided that in the first week they would add a second dance for each couple. The show had become very popular, so introducing new elements and shaking things up kept it interesting for the viewers. The producers are wonderful and very clever that way. There was one challenge, though—not only was I learning to ballroom-dance, I was now charged with having to learn two dances for my first week—the cha-cha and the quickstep!

Tony had to teach me those two dances complete with ballroom posture and technique. One of the reasons I was finally able to commit to the show was that the producers promised me that my dance partner would go wherever I needed him to be in order to rehearse—whether it was Manhattan, Garden City, or the Hamptons, where I spend my weekends in the summer. Tony went where I went. If I had to be in St. Petersburg, Florida, for a Home Shopping appearance, Tony came with me so we could dance. If I was doing an appearance in Altoona, Pennsylvania, Tony came with me so we could dance. Luckily, my schedule that summer wasn't too bad, so we did most of our rehearsals out at the beach at the Westhampton Performing Arts Center. They offered us a gorgeous dance hall to use as our rehearsal space. That room was clean as a whistle. I swear that you could eat off the floor. The facility was perfect and everyone there was very accommodating.

Tony and I got to know each other rather well over the course of those many weeks we spent practicing as I learned proper postures, moves, holds, and style. It was a good thing that I do a lot of Pilates because at least I had excellent core strength to do the moves he was teaching me. They were all very foreign and surprising to me. I had no formal training as a dancer, but I had taken some modern dance back in college. Latin dancing is completely different from the smooth style of ballroom. I had no idea what an art form ballroom dancing is. I knew I loved to watch it and I always loved to dance, but I didn't know that in addition to learning the steps, I would actually have to learn the language of movement. I was taught things I had absolutely no idea I was going to have to learn. I am that girl who loves to move when music is playing, especially Brazilian music. I'm out on that dance floor having a good time, dancing without a care, as if no one is watching. I was never thinking about pattern or choreography. I was just moving. Those days were over! I would dance, thinking I was doing a great job, and Tony would say, "NO!" Up until this experience, I knew I had rhythm and I thought that was the main thing you needed to dance. But according to Tony, you need so much more. And he was right. Once again, I was completely out of my comfort zone. Although I definitely wanted to grow, this time I might have been in over my head. Boy, was I in for a rude awakening.

All I wanted to do was dance! Who knew you're not supposed to bend your leg in Latin dancing—Tony told me the judges consider that an "ugly" leg in routines. Apparently, you're supposed to move from the hips—not the knees. As a two-time International Latin Ballroom Dancing champion, not only does Tony know what he's talking about, he can swivel his hips unlike any man I have ever met—on-screen or off! He is an amazing dancer and a remarkable teacher and choreographer.

The show airs the dancing competition live on Monday nights and the results live on Tuesday nights. Cameron explained that it could be done as long as you plan out your time just right. He told me he'd gotten it down to a science. I really wanted to do the show, so I was willing to do whatever it took. I'd take the first flight out of JFK on Saturday morning, which would get me to the West Coast by nine-thirty, allowing enough time to make my first stop at the CBS Studio where the show is shot, go to my costume fittings, and then on to a dance studio to rehearse and dance—for hours. By Saturday afternoon, we had to perform our routine perfectly to record on camera so the shots could be set for Monday's live show. I'd go to the CBS studio for my final costume fitting early Sunday morning, then head upstairs for the tanning process, then back to the dance studio for several more hours of rehearsal before ending up at the CBS studio again for our first opportunity to practice our routine on the stage.

Monday is showtime, which meant I was back at the CBS studio early in the morning to rehearse onstage and, for the first time, with the orchestra. By late morning, I was in hair and makeup so I could be ready for dress rehearsal at one o'clock in the afternoon. When we finished, I was back in hair and makeup for some final touches, and any free moments after that were spent dancing with Tony, preparing for the live show, which started at five o'clock Pacific time for the live broadcast on the East Coast.

As we stood backstage before the show, there was always a flurry of body makeup and sparkly powder that got sprinkled like fairy dust on us. The powder always matched my costumes. There were final tweaks to hair and makeup as the stage manager wrangled us up the long staircase so we could take our places before going on. The atmosphere was electrifying. The presence of the live studio audience and orchestra was exhilarating. When it was our turn, I stood poised with my dance partner, Tony Davolani, ready to enter, as the British announcer said, "Now, dahncing the chahhhh-chahhhh, Susan Looocci and her dahnce partner, Townee Davohhhlahhhni!" Every time I heard those words, sheer terror would take over my body. It took every fiber of my being to not let it take over! I had to go out there and just dance. At the end of the day, it was so much fun.

Once I finished with the Monday and Tuesday shows, I'd have to hop on a red-eye back to New York Tuesday night. After Tony and I left the studio, we stopped for a late dinner, usually at Maggiano's for pasta, as it was on our way to Los Angeles International. We'd go through security, and then Tony would whip out his laptop in the terminal to play next week's music while showing me a little bit of the choreography he was thinking of using. Occasionally, we'd continue working on the choreography after the plane took off, but only for a short while, as we both needed that flight to get some much-needed rest. We landed at five-thirty in the morning, headed home to get some sleep and take a shower, and then met at a dance studio in New York to start the process all over again and learn a new dance for the following week . . .

I ended up loving the quickstep but didn't enjoy doing the cha-cha as much as I thought I would. I didn't feel free enough during that first dance. The ballroom aspect was very easy for me, but the technique was surprisingly constraining. Although I love dancing to Latin music, I couldn't seem to put it all together for the cha-cha—ballroom style. I memorize things for a living and I thought that would be a help, but in ballroom dancing, not so much. Tony reminded me often that I needed to let my body learn the movements. I didn't understand what that meant at first. He tried to explain it like this. He said it was like driving. When you go to a new place for the first time, you look at all of the road signs, markers, and landmarks to make sure you're headed in the right direction. Once you know where you're going, you just drive, and suddenly you're there. I thought that was a very helpful analogy because it helped me better understand what he wanted me to do going forward.

Even though I was able to get over my shyness while performing as myself onstage when I worked with Regis, I was somehow unable to do it as much as I'd hoped on *Dancing with the Stars*. I had a tremendous amount of apprehension going into the show. I knew I was physically up to the challenge, but I worried that I wouldn't be able to put aside my fear of failure and the judges' criticism to dance well. I didn't want to make a fool of myself in front of millions of viewers. I am sure I was overthinking things throughout the process, and to be certain, I was burning the candle at both ends.

Helmut, Tony, and I were like the Three Musketeers as we traveled back and forth across the country twice a week. The only time we ever hit a snag in our flights was on our first trip back to New York. About an hour into our flight, we were told the plane would be making an emergency landing in Denver. The flight attendant explained that they were having trouble with one of the ovens in the forward cabin. I could see smoke coming from the galley area, which was alarming to say the least. Your mind begins to conjure up all sorts of terrible thoughts, like fire, or worse, an explosion. I was all too happy to get those wheels safely down on the ground. We landed sometime after midnight and were told it could take several hours before we'd be able to reboard another plane and take off for New York. Tony and Helmut quickly scoped out the situation and we all grabbed whatever pillows and blankets we could find before exiting the plane. We figured we could find a cozy corner on the floor somewhere and at least get a little sleep. We were three peas in a pod on the floor of the Denver airport until we were able to take off the next morning.

Each week before we left the studio to fly back to New York, Tony was given our music and dance selection for the following week. I would meet with Randall Christensen, the unbelievably fantastic costume designer for the show, who creates an original handmade outfit for every person each week! Think about what I am saying here. You can't even get a pair of pants hemmed at the dry cleaner in a week, let alone a custom-designed handmade beaded dress. Randall is nothing short of amazing. Working with him is much like what I imagine it was like working with the great Edith Head. He has an entire encyclopedia of costumes from his many years of dance experience. He'll pull stuff up for certain dances that he just knows will move with grace, elegance, sexiness, and flair. Tony and I had some input along the way, too, but I was in very capable hands with Randall and knew that I could step back and let these guys do what they do. There is no doubt that we were always on the same page when it came to designing my costumes. We would discuss options, talk about what would look good on my body type, what would work best for our particular dances, and come up with something we both agreed upon. Randall got me on every level. He's brilliant and comes in each week with no ego, only his unparalleled talent. Once we nailed the design, twenty-four seamstresses tirelessly worked to bring Randall's genius ideas to life.

Although I had no serious wardrobe malfunctions during the season, I did worry that one could happen every time I hit the dance floor. All of my dresses were very low-cut. The producers put a battery pack under my right breast (and I guess all of the ladies' right breasts!) so I could be miked. They would have to pad the left breast to make everything match. Although all the dresses are made of a very giving material that is especially designed for dancing, the addition of that unit made it a scary proposition every time I began to dance. The good news was that I am extremely comfortable wearing high heels, so my dancing-shoe selection was not a problem. One thing Tony taught me about standing in heels that I didn't know is that I should never stand on my toes while dancing. I'm five feet two inches tall on a good day, so I always stand on my toes when I dance with a man. My husband is six foot two, so it seemed natural. Tony had to frequently remind me to get off my toes. I can't say I know how he could feel me doing it, but he did! He warned me that the judges were looking for mistakes like this and that not keeping my feet down would cost us points. That was a hard habit to break.

Luckily, the producers of *All My Children* were very accommodating and were able to work out a shooting schedule that only required me to be at the studio on Thursdays and Fridays. However, the show was in the middle of "sweeps"—an important time for ratings—so those two days were very intense and extremely long because the material is always more complicated at that time of year.

I personally felt I needed more time to learn my dances each week than I had anticipated. Tony and I would meet in dance studios all over Manhattan at various hours of the day and night just so I could squeeze in more rehearsals before heading back to Los

Angeles to do the show. It wasn't unusual for Tony and me to meet as late as nine or ten at night. Sometimes that meant we only got an hour or two of rehearsal in, which wasn't enough but was better than nothing. Feeling like I still needed more time to learn the routines, I asked Tony to come to the set of *All My Children* and dance with me between takes, sometimes with rollers in my hair, just to get in the extra time. We danced in the hallways and corridors, and used the adjacent studio at *The View* and anywhere else we could find so I could learn the dance routine for that week.

If you've ever watched *Dancing with the Stars*, you know that their cameras follow the dance teams to document their week. We were no exception, as cameras tailed our every move. This was my least favorite aspect of doing that show. I never wanted cameras filming my real life. Rest assured, there is no reality television show in my future because I don't like having cameras around me outside of a studio setting. I will admit that the only exception to this was when Tony took me to an underground mambo club in New York City. We were preparing to do the mambo in week six of the show. The producers thought it might be fun to have Tony take me there to experience the real thing. As I've said, I have always loved Latin dancing, so even if I hadn't been doing *Dancing with the Stars*, I would have immediately said "Yes!"

I had no idea these types of underground clubs even existed. The one we went to was across the street from the theater where the fantastic Broadway show *In the Heights* was running, so a lot of the musical's dancers frequently stopped into this club after performances. I asked some of my friends from *All My Children* to join us so we could go with a really fun group. The club looked like the finished basements I'd seen in friends' houses growing up. They played the best and hottest Latin music and served the coolest, most refreshing drinks.

I had the best time dancing at this club. I was free and happy, and I learned to dance Latin style from Tony. Unfortunately, I was

never able to take that freedom with me to any of my actual performances on the show. And that bothered me—a lot.

Having a camera follow me around during the learning process,
even that night at the club, was terribly foreign and absolutely not
my cup of tea. At the time I was especially uncomfortable with how
the producer tried to stir things up on camera or attempted to get me
to say something in the heat of a moment. In retrospect, if I had to
do it again, I wouldn't be so sensitive. Still, there was one particular
day when the camera caught something that I really felt bad about.
The buildup to that moment began with an injury.

The week before, doing an early-morning rehearsal for our next
dance, the jive, I somehow caught my ankle under Tony's leg. Although I was in pain, we made it through the dance that morning.
I didn't think it would be a real setback, as I was able to stand and
put a little pressure on my foot. I dashed off to hair and makeup to
get ready for our dress rehearsal later that afternoon. Tony and I attempted to do the dance, which is full of kicks and jumps. I wasn't
sure that my left ankle could support my jumping on it. I stumbled a
bit and tried to get through it without Tony noticing that something
was wrong.

"Can we do this again?" I asked.

We made a second attempt.

Tony took one look at me and said, "What is the matter? Something is wrong. I can see it in your face. You're in pain."

So I told him what had happened. Tony gallantly picked me up
and carried me back to my trailer, called the doctor, and waited
with me until he came. The doctor told me he thought I had broken
a bone in my ankle. I was so distraught, but I wanted to go on that
night and do our dance! We had worked too hard to stop now. The
doctor wrapped my ankle and gave me a lot of Advil to get through
the show that night.

The following day, I went to Cedars-Sinai hospital and saw a
wonderful doctor who treats many dancers and athletes. After

looking at the X-rays, he told me that I had actually broken two bones and torn a ligament in my left ankle. The doctor had seen my "type" many times in the past—fiercely competitive and unafraid to continue despite the pain. He surely had me figured out without my saying a word.

"I know you're going to keep dancing, Susan. If you can take the pain, I don't think you will do any further damage to your ankle. But remember to keep it wrapped and to ice it after you dance, and I think you'll be fine."

This was music to my ears. I didn't want to be a wimp, so I pushed through the pain and kept on dancing. Advil and good wrapping kept me very much in the competition. Much to my surprise, I ended up not being in as much pain as I had expected. I don't know if my adrenaline had kicked in or if I just have a high pain threshold. Either way, I was happy it wasn't worse.

In spite of my injury, Tony and I received straight sevens. Under the circumstances, I was pretty happy with that score. As an actress, I was used to getting notes from the director to help me prepare for my scenes, so I tried not to take the judges' comments on my dancing to heart. I wanted to do well, but I also knew I wasn't a professional dancer and tried to cut myself a little slack.

I had little to no contact with Len Goodman, Bruno Tonioli, and Carrie Ann Inaba, the judges from the show, other than when I listened to their comments each night after we danced. There's a lot of merit to their knowledge and expertise when they offer their criticism. I respect each of them very much. Carrie Ann was by far the toughest on me, actually saying that I was too thin, fragile, and delicate to dance. Her comment about my weight really threw me because Tony had told me from the first day we met that I was built like a dancer. Although I am physically very strong, I might have accepted *thin*, but *fragile* or *delicate*, never. Telling anyone they are too thin to dance, or too "anything" personal, felt inappropriate. It had no place in a critique of my dancing. I always want to give people the benefit of the doubt, so maybe Carrie Ann simply chose the wrong words or wasn't able to communicate what she was thinking in a more constructive way, and for that, of course, I can forgive her.

Look, I knew I wasn't doing my best work and wasn't completely happy with my performances. I was so terrified every time we went out on the dance floor and sometimes allowed that anxiety to get the best of me. Still, we were safe and moving on to the next round. If I could get through the jive with broken bones, I could do anything. Sure enough, something interesting happened after we got through this round. Up to this point, I had been resisting Tony's advice about letting go of my urge to memorize the dances and overthink each step. I finally said, "Let me try it your way." That was a seminal moment for me—one which I hoped would get us through our next dance, the tango. I was more fully committed than ever to preparing for the following week—pain or no pain

Tony and I flew back to New York and began rehearsing the very next day. We were mostly practicing very late at night and, again, on the set of *All My Children*. I was nursing my injury and may have been a little tired from all of the back-and-forth wear and tear. I had grown frustrated by my lack of ability to really step it up. Tony thought I was frustrated with him and I thought he was frustrated with me. In truth, we were both probably frustrated with me. When I finally hit my threshold, I unexpectedly had a mini-meltdown and broke into tears. The cameras were there to catch this moment of weakness in all its glory. I am sure I was exhausted and in pain, but I certainly didn't need Tony or anyone else to see how I was feeling. We had a lot of work to do. There was no time for crying, yet I couldn't seem to stop. We needed to get on with rehearsal or we'd never be ready for next week's show.

What Tony didn't know was that there was something else very emotional happening behind the scenes. I never shared this story with him because I didn't want my personal life to interfere with my professional obligations or worry him.

When I agreed to do *Dancing with the Stars*, my daughter, Liza, was pregnant with her second child. She was due in October 2008. Helmut and I were ecstatic, and were looking forward to welcoming our second grandchild into the world. Given the timing, though, Liza and I talked about the possibility of me not being in New York when she went into labor. That was something that would have been very challenging for both of us because we are extremely close. I already had one grandchild and knew what a special and important time it was for a mother and daughter to share.

I was reluctant to do something by choice that would knowingly take me away from Liza. There were lots of family discussions, but after talking it over, we all agreed that if Liza went into labor while I was doing *Dancing with the Stars*, I would get there as soon as I could. What we never anticipated, however, was that Liza might go into labor early. But that is exactly what happened.

I was enjoying a wonderful August weekend with my best girlfriends from college at our summer home. We make a point of getting together every year, something we all look forward to. We had just gone down to the beach club for dinner when I received a call from Liza. She told me she was feeling a lot of pain. My daughter is not a complainer, but she said again during that conversation that she was in excruciating pain. She thought she might be in labor and wanted to go to the hospital. Her husband, Alex, was in London for business. Of course, none of us thought that being away from her in August, two months before her due date, would be of any concern. Liza wanted to be absolutely certain she was in labor before Helmut and I drove back to Garden City to be with her. Thankfully, Alex's uncle Gregory, who lives very near to Liza, was able to pick her up and take her to the hospital. Twenty minutes later, Liza called and said she was definitely in labor.

Helmut and I excused ourselves from dinner, leaving my college friends to fend for themselves. We drove from the Hamptons back to Garden City in record time. My husband grew up driving on the autobahn, so he welcomed this excuse to drive fast. If a police officer pulled us over, he had already planned to tell him that our daughter was in labor. When we got in the car, it was a very stormy night, but as we got closer to Garden City, the rain had started to clear. Through one side of the windshield, I could see the full moon, while through the other side, I could see big lightning bolts in the sky. This was an amazing sight—Mother Nature at her most dramatic.

By the time we got to Winthrop Hospital, Liza's mother-in-law, Valerie, whom I adore, was already there. Unfortunately, Liza's doctor was not. He was also away. Liza was going to have her baby with whatever physician was on call that night. I thought she was being very brave. I would have been sobbing if I was having a baby and my husband and regular doctor weren't there for the birth. Alex and Liza kept trying to speak to each on their cell phones, but they were continually disconnected.

Royce was at our house in Garden City with Alex's aunt Claire. Helmut decided to go home so Royce would have a familiar face to wake up to, while Alex's dad, Alex Sr., who had just returned from a business trip himself, was pretty fatigued and decided to also go home. That left Valerie and me to be with Liza in the delivery room. We both kept thinking the nurses were going to ask these two yentas to leave the room, but they never did.

I rubbed Liza's head like I used to do when she was a little girl while Valerie held her hand. We tried to do whatever we could to soothe and comfort her. That's when Dr. McKenzie, the most handsome young doctor with the biggest dimples, wearing jeans and a baseball hat, walked through the door.

"Yes, ladies. I really am a doctor," he charmingly said as he got into his scrubs. He had a great sense of humor and, as it turns out, lots of experience. He just exuded calm and confidence.

When we all heard the baby let out a big healthy cry, tears of joy flowed from our eyes. What an unforgettable experience and a gift from God it was to be with Liza when our grandson Brendan was born on August 16, 2008.

Since Brendan was two months premature, the nurses took him to be checked out right away. He was going to need to be in an incubator in the NICU until he was strong enough to go home. I knew Brendan was in good and capable hands because I had had a long and wonderful experience with this hospital's care for Andreas. It was very emotional for me to be back in the neonatal intensive care unit because it was, in fact, the same unit at the same hospital where Andreas had been treated after he was born. I was so pleasantly surprised to see that a few of the same nurses were still working there. I wanted to help Liza in any way I could because I knew exactly how she was feeling. After all, I had been there myself. I wanted to believe that my presence was a comfort to her. I also hoped it was good for Liza to know that her brother had struggled when he was born and was now a very healthy and strong young man.

Helmut and I stayed by Liza's side until her husband was able to make it back from London. Late in the afternoon after Brendan was born, Andreas came to the hospital to join us. The three of us went to get a sandwich in the hospital coffee shop when we spotted Alex race by the window holding a big bouquet of roses. Once we knew Liza was reunited with her husband, we wanted to give them some much-needed time alone to enjoy their newborn baby. Helmut and I decided to return to the Hamptons to be with our visiting friends.

When we walked through the door, there was a cold bottle of my favorite champagne on ice waiting for us so we could all celebrate the birth of our second grandson. We toasted the new baby at sunset over the bay outside our home. It was such an extraordinary night, with a big apricot full moon rising as the sun set into the horizon. The sky was full of hot-pink and deep purple hues. Helmut left the room for a moment. All of a sudden I heard him call us to the ocean side of the house, which is flanked by sandy dunes and pines.

"Girls, come quick," he said in almost a whisper. "Bring your cameras!"

When we went over to see what Helmut was so excited about, he pointed to a pure white deer and her baby on a nearby dune. They are so rare, especially at the beach. I turned to one of my girlfriends and asked her to please take a picture to capture this most spectacular and memorable moment. It was magic.

Brendan remained in the hospital for six weeks. I told Liza I would forfeit starting *Dancing with the Stars* if she felt it would be better for her to have me around. God bless my daughter. She is so strong and secure. She told me to keep my commitment to the show and not let all of my hard work and rehearsals go to waste. She encouraged me to do the show, voting for me week after week as many times as she could get through on the phone lines. After each show, she called to offer her critique, and she continued rooting for me all the way.

Right around the time I had my mini-meltdown with Tony, I could tell that Liza was really feeling like she needed me to be with her. I had been torn about being away from her from the very beginning. Call it mother's intuition, but I just felt that Liza was done with my coast-to-coast commute and wanted me home. I didn't have the heart to share this with Tony at the time. I didn't want it to seem as if I had given up or that I was somehow quitting. In fact, on those Wednesdays when Tony and I were back in New York and we would meet to rehearse, I'd make sure that he and I got in whatever time we needed, but then I'd leave to join Liza at the hospital to spend time with her and the baby in the NICU. Sometimes we didn't get to the hospital until the baby's late feeding at eleven at night. We'd stay for an hour and a half, until the baby fell asleep. Then I'd go home, get some sleep, and go back to *All My Children* the next morning.

When I did *Annie Get Your Gun*, the director used to say to me that I was a perfectionist and that I needed to let that go. She was so right. I should let it go. I was somehow able to let it all go in *Annie Get*

Your Gun and I had the time of my life. However, when I did *Dancing with the Stars*, try as I might, I somehow wasn't able to give up those high expectations for myself. In a way, that proved to be very valuable to me. And at the same time it was extremely humbling. Oh my goodness, was it humbling. It was the first time I had taken something on where I didn't do well and it happened in front of millions of people—live! I advanced to a respectable level, but I would watch Warren Sapp dance so well with a great big smile on his face—which is how I usually dance, but not here. I was really challenged by the discipline and I couldn't find the freedom and the joy within that discipline.

Tony and I were voted off the show in week seven after eight individual dances and a couple of additional group dances that were new to the format that season. I felt very bad, but truth be told, it was time for me to go. I felt relieved because I knew my heart and it wanted and needed to be someplace else—back in New York with Liza and her baby.

When I called Liza that night to tell her we were eliminated, she said, "I know, Mom, and I'm glad. And I think you should know, I didn't vote for you these last two weeks." We both laughed.

"I understand, honey. I want to come home," I said. And I did. Still, looking back, I'd do it all over again.

A few weeks later, my dear friend and Liza's godmother, Patty; Liza's mother-in-law, Valerie; and I hosted a postbirth baby shower for Liza. Shortly after we encountered the deer on the dune, I decided to write down the details of that experience so I could keep the particulars fresh in my mind. I wanted to share this very special story with Brendan about the day he was born. The story just poured out of me and onto paper during my long plane ride home. I asked a friend in the art department at ABC to help me compile a bound book that would tell the story along with a few pictures from that day that I had gathered from family and friends. I presented the book to Liza at her baby shower. She said she couldn't believe what I had put together and it made me so happy to see how thrilled she was to have that keepsake. I was so glad to somehow find the right words about how unforgettable that day was and how it will remain in my heart forever.

*U*nder dramatic circumstances of a different kind, Liza's first son, Royce, was born in 2006 on my birthday, December 23. While he was the best gift I could ever imagine receiving, I was in Las Vegas at the time enjoying another unexpected gift.

Since I never really had birthday parties growing up, Helmut planned a surprise destination birthday party for me in Vegas with twenty of our closest friends. Liza was originally due in late December. Just before we left, Liza's doctor told her that she might have the baby a week earlier, maybe as early as December 22. Helmut questioned whether he should keep the plans to surprise me, but Liza insisted that he follow through with the trip.

"Don't tell Mom about my new possible due date," she said to Helmut. "You know she'll never go if you do." And she was right. So when Helmut and I flew to Las Vegas, not only was I in the dark about the wonderful surprise that waited for me there, I was completely unaware that my daughter might go into labor.

Helmut planned a perfect evening, taking our friends and me to see Tom Jones. Tom was fantastic, and even sang "Happy Birthday" to me during his show. The next morning, I called Liza to check in. This was a very normal thing for me to do. When we are traveling, I always let my children know we've arrived safely and call them to make sure they're well. That's when Liza told me she had known about Helmut's surprise birthday party plan all along.

"Mom, there's something I need to tell you. I've just gone into labor." This was the morning of December 22.

Unbeknownst to me, Helmut had chartered a private plane that was kept on standby just in case Liza did, in fact, go into labor. We continued to check in with her every couple of hours to see if there was any progress. We spent the rest of the day enjoying the company of our friends. By chance, a few of us stopped into a store and spotted a beautiful bracelet that had amethysts (Liza's birthstone) and turquoise (her baby's birthstone) all around it. I turned to my friends and said, "This is a sign. I have to get this for Liza. I want to bring this to her when we go to the hospital."

By the end of the day, the baby had not yet arrived. After dinner, we went to the casino with our friends, and by eleven forty-five, everyone was taking bets on whether the baby would come on the twenty-second or if would it be on my actual birthday, the twenty-third. One of our best friends, Frank, was looking up to the heavens and saying, "I don't want Liza to be in pain longer than she needs to be, but could she please wait fifteen more minutes so the baby can be born on her mother's birthday?" Of course, we just wanted her to be safe and for the baby to be healthy. By two o'clock in the morning, there was still no baby, and we all went to bed.

I woke up like a shot the next morning. It was *exactly* six A.M. in Las Vegas and in Los Angeles, where Liza was living. I still hadn't heard from her and her husband. I woke Helmut up and told him we needed to reach Alex right away. I didn't want to be one of those annoying mother-in-laws, but I felt certain that Liza had had the baby. When we phoned, Alex's voice mail picked up. I left a message asking him to call with an update whenever he had a moment. Twenty minutes later, our phone rang.

"How's Liza?" I asked before he could get a word in.

"Royce was born at *six o'clock* this morning."

Liza had been in labor for twenty-two hours, the exact amount of time I was in labor with her. When I spoke to my daughter, she sounded so peaceful and calm. I could feel the baby in her arms. I couldn't wait to get back to L.A. to be with my baby and her firstborn son—our first grandchild. Helmut and I showered, got dressed, and were on the plane within an hour of hearing the blessed news. When we got to the hospital, she looked like a radiant and beautiful new mom. She was more gorgeous than ever.

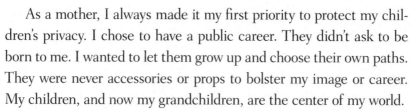

As a mother, I always made it my first priority to protect my children's privacy. I chose to have a public career. They didn't ask to be born to me. I wanted to let them grow up and choose their own paths. They were never accessories or props to bolster my image or career. My children, and now my grandchildren, are the center of my world.

But what would Liza's babies—my grandbabies—call me? When I was cast as Erica Kane, I thought I had been given the role of a lifetime—that is, until I discovered the greatest role of my life, becoming a mom. I didn't think there was anything in this world that could possibly top the love and warmth I have in my heart for my children until I discovered the joy and pleasure in taking on the best role ever—Grammie.

I read an article by Jamie Gregory in *Town & Country* magazine entitled "Do I Have to Be Called Grandma?" Jamie quotes different people from all walks of life about their experience of becoming a grandmother. Somehow that "label" calls up images of being old and gray and sitting in rocking chairs. As I've told you, I've never liked labels. As I look around, the grandmothers I see and know look nothing like that. Many are beautiful and vital young grandmothers like Jamie Gregory. The *reality* of having these children in my life is spectacular—it's the *label* that took a little getting used to. Besides, in our family, my mom has always been known as "Grandma" and my grandmother was called "Nana." Those names belonged to them, so I had to decide what I would be called.

There was a lot of discussion around the dinner table about it. All I wanted was for the children to feel warm and happy when they spoke my name. We went through a litany of possibilities, including Lulu, Mimi, Grandy—an adorable name my daughter came up with—and so on. We knew too many dogs names Lulu, so that was out. Liza didn't get Mimi, so that was out. Grandy was great, but not quite right. Somehow, I thought it implied grandness at arm's length. No thank you. That isn't how I wanted those children to think of me. And then I remembered my cousins often called my nana "Gram." Occasionally, Andreas refers to my mother as Gram, too. Whenever she heard that name, she would light up. That made me smile, too. I thought there was a nice ring to it, so I thought "Grammie" was a great name. It would be easy for them to say and something about the word just feels right to me.

I see those two little boys and I thank God for them in my life. I love when our family gets together for casual dinners. I look around the table, whether it's a Sunday pizza party or barbecue at the beach, and I soak in the sound of all of us gathered together, laughing and celebrating life. It's those moments in life that are such an important part of giving children a sense of who they are, who they will become, and a great sense of well-being. And that makes me so deeply happy.

And, as I write this book, my daughter, Liza, is about to have a baby girl. We are over the moon with happiness. Liza and I are looking forward to experiencing moments with her daughter that we shared together when she was a little girl—going to see the Nutcracker at Lincoln Center, tea time at the St. Regis Hotel, ice cream sundaes and frozen hot chocolate at Serendipity, her first shopping and lunch excursion at Bergdorf's, and her first tutu. Can you tell we're excited?

CHAPTER 16

Africa

In 2009, Helmut and I were asked to participate in a life-altering journey to Africa with Feed The Children, a nonprofit relief organization that cares for more than one hundred thousand children in Kenya's slums every day. Feed The Children delivers food, clothing, medicine, and other basics we so often take for granted to needy families in Nairobi and elsewhere in this African country. We were asked to go on this trip as part of a special television documentary produced by David McKenzie, a well-known producer of the Daytime Emmys among many other notable projects. David is a spectacular producer and a very warmhearted and caring human being. He was there to provide an up-close and personal look at Kenya and its wonderful people and the challenges they face every day. The special would also feature the extraordinary compassion of those who are saving abandoned babies from certain death, hunger, AIDS, and missing or dead parents. Several of daytime television's biggest names, including Montel Williams, Anthony Geary, and Kelly Monaco traveled with us, too, along with Christopher and Kyle Massey, Erik Estrada, and Devon Werkheiser. Our intent was to help raise awareness of the desperate situation faced by Africa's poor and of this very worthy organization's efforts.

We ventured out into some of the world's most impoverished cities to meet one-on-one with the people who live there. We spent time with the founders of Feed The Children, Larry and Frances Jones and their daughter Lari-Sue. Jones shared his philosophy with us: no matter what color or religion, a hungry child needs to be fed. In fact, his organization feeds eight hundred thousand meals every day to children in 112 countries around the world. He told us that he and Frances started the organization after seeing a story on the poverty in Africa and learning that the children there were not receiving the food donations they were supposed to be getting from other groups. Larry gathered his own resources and built a program that ensured the food he received in donations would be sent to the communities and families who so desperately needed it. I couldn't help but wonder how in this day and age there are still so many people starving in the world. I felt sad and angry about their circumstances, especially as the week went on, but I also felt relief that there were caring people like Larry and his family doing so much good to correct the situation.

One of the most moving experiences I had while we were there was visiting the various orphanages and schools that Feed The Children maintains all over the country. The primary goal of these homes is to reunite orphaned children with their families. Sadly, there is an AIDS epidemic in Africa, which impacts so many families that this goal is not always possible. Many children have lost one or both of their parents. Some have no other relatives who can afford to care for them. Oftentimes, it is the husband who contracts AIDS and infects his wife. In the worst of these cases, the husband's family disowns the wife. She can also be ostracized for her condition by the larger community, making it difficult for her to find work to support her children. There are even instances when the family takes all of her belongings and pushes her out into the streets. The heartbreak of the AIDS epidemic runs very deep.

David knew Africa very well, as did Lari-Sue, who has been traveling there since she was a little girl. Our first stop was Nairobi, where I met a little boy named Bernard whose mother agreed to let us take him to the local orphanage run by Larry and Frances for some much-needed medical attention. As heartbreaking as the decision to let him leave home must have been for her, I am certain she did it because she knew that this was his only chance for survival. You see, Bernard was two years old but could barely sit up. He was so malnourished that he couldn't even walk. My mind could barely comprehend the unimaginable suffering this innocent child had endured. I believe his mother's decision was the most selfless act a mother could take, as she knew the orphanage would feed her son, give him proper medical attention, bathe and clothe him—all things she could not do on her own. I felt for them both.

When we got Bernard to the orphanage, I was told that many of the children we were meeting would likely spend their whole childhood there because they were either discarded or they needed to remain there for their own good. After hearing that, I was curious to know if Bernard's mother would be allowed to visit her son. I simply couldn't imagine a mother giving up her child under those circumstances and not being able to see him whenever she wanted to. I was so happy to hear that not only could she visit with him, she was actually encouraged to do so. Feed The Children provides transportation for parents to get to and from the location. I hold great hope that after Bernard is treated and on the road to recovery, he and his mother will be reunited.

I played with all of the babies in the nursery for hours, holding, hugging, and kissing as many as I could wrap my arms around. It was so hard to leave them that we all actually broke down when it was time to go. Every motherly instinct I had made it near impossible for me to leave those babies behind. It was the most difficult thing I'd experienced in a very long time and something I will never forget.

While we toured the orphanage that day, I met a wonderful Italian woman in her eighties who periodically came there because she loved these children very much. I was told that she was a countess. Although she was obviously very wealthy and I was certain she had made substantial financial donations, she came specifically to cook homemade meals for these kids. She made spaghetti and tomato sauce from scratch and fed hundreds of hungry children and the staff members, too. The countess was terrifically inspiring. Seeing what she was doing made me realize just how much of a difference even one person can make in these children's lives.

After rescuing Bernard and spending some time with the other children at the orphanage, it was time to say our good-byes and move on to the slums and villages in the surrounding areas. The slums we saw were unlike anything I had ever seen or experienced. They weren't slums in the way we Americans often think of them. They were far worse. Families live in shantytowns composed of mud huts with thatched roofs or shacks with tin roofs. Many had no doors. In some cases, there was only a piece of fabric strung up where a door would have been. The people who live in these structures are the fortunate ones because they at least have a place to call home. There is no running water, no plumbing, and no electricity. Residents have to collect rainwater so they have "fresh" water for bathing and drinking. I was both shocked and devastated to see the children in these slums walking through the streets barefoot while sewage water ran on both sides of the road, leaving them even more prone to diseases from parasites absorbed through their feet. God only knows what is in the water that runs through the debris- and waste-filled streams, but it certainly isn't safe.

Education is not mandatory in the region. But the lucky children who get to attend school are taught to respect their teachers from a very early age. I learned that it only takes thirty-three dollars a year to send one child to school there. That money covers their education, uniform, supplies, a hot meal, and a pair of shoes. The schools are full of children from ages three to twelve. The schoolrooms aren't fancy. In fact, the ones we saw all had dirt floors. The teachers are assigned one age group that they teach every subject to. Some of the children share a single pair of shoes with their brothers and sisters. At lunchtime, there was no pushing or shoving. The children stood in line in a very orderly fashion and patiently waited for their meal, which was primarily a bowl of beans and corn. For some, this was the only meal they would eat all day.

When we arrived at the school, the children ran to greet us with a song. They were so full of energy. It warmed my heart to listen to their voices. Even though they have virtually nothing, they sang with complete joy. Despite the things they lack, you can see how bright their eyes are. Their smiles are big and full. Their hope is far from gone. I can't help but wonder where such resilience comes from.

When we visited the first school, I brought the children four brightly colored rubber balls, the size of soccer balls, to play with during recess. It was an easy gesture that was received with so much appreciation that the children lifted me up on their shoulders and carried me around like I was Pelé after a winning game. Earlier I had been asked to talk to the eleven-year-old children. Middle-school children in our country are often challenging to talk to, so I worried about whether these children would embrace my presence and open up to me or if they'd be shy. I wasn't sure what I would discover, but I was absolutely willing to find out. I asked the children if they thought about what they wanted to be when they grew up.

"I want to be a pilot," said a young fresh-faced girl.

"I want to be a doctor," another said.

The children were delightful and so full of hopes and dreams. There wasn't the attitude some kids their age tend to have elsewhere in the world. I asked if any of them liked to sing, dance, and per-form because that's what I liked to do a whole lot more than math or science! They laughed at my attempt at humor and then asked me to teach them an American song. Someone suggested I teach them "Somewhere Over the Rainbow." I sang a few bars and they learned it right away. Singing with those children was an unforgettable experience.

A friend of mine who had been to Africa several times suggested that I bring lollipops to give to the children we would meet along the way. It was something so simple yet so meaningful. I came across a beautiful little girl standing in a doorway, wearing the prettiest little cotton dress. Her mother must have found a way to press it because it didn't have a single wrinkle. When I handed her the lollipop, I could tell by the curious look in her eyes that she'd never seen one before. She didn't even know that she should remove the paper covering. So I unwrapped the lollipop and showed her how to eat it. It didn't take long for this precious child to understand that lollipops are yummy. As she stood in front of me eating her treat, her brother came over to see what we were doing. And then another little child showed up. Before I knew it, there were several more kids who circled around us, each wanting a lollipop of their own. Believe me, I was only too happy to grant them that simple wish.

Seeing the joy in these children's faces was one of the most fulfilling moments of my life. The producers of All My Children had written a trip to Africa into the script in the hope that while I was there I could shoot a scene for the show. Erica was supposed to speak directly into the camera. I was positioned near a trough, with streams of water running by me. I was standing on the dirt next to the water when I noticed a little boy walking by. He stopped to watch what we were doing. I motioned with my hand for him to come over to where I was standing. He came a little closer but still kept a good distance away. I could see that he was intrigued by the camera and wanted to be included, so I motioned for him to come even closer until he was finally standing right next to me. I started to do the scene with him in the shot. All of a sudden there were a few other children standing off to the side and across the stream. They also kept their distance until I motioned for them to come over, too.

The kids leaped over the stream, and before I knew it, there were *thirty* children in the scene. The producer and I decided this was a much better and more interesting shot than Erica speaking one-on-one to the camera.

When I look back on this experience, the overwhelming thing that has stuck with me is the openness and warmth of the children I met while touring Africa. They're not bitter about their circumstances because they don't know any other way of life. Their eyes aren't dead, the way that one might expect those of the poor and hungry to be; they're full of love, life, and light. They are bright and smiling all of the time. I keep a framed photo of Bernard in my dressing room so I can be reminded of him each day when I go to work. His smiling face brings a smile to mine. I look forward to a time when our eyes will someday meet again.

CHAPTER 17

Good-bye, New York

In January 2010, *All My Children* made an epic company move from our studios in New York City, where we had resided for forty glorious years, to our new home in Glendale, California. The decision to move the show was based on many factors, most of which were financial. Yes, even daytime television has had to make some adjustments in these challenging economic times.

I received the news shortly before a general announcement was made on the set. I was called in to the executive producer's office for a brief meeting. I could see Agnes Nixon through an open door, but I couldn't hear a word of what was being said. I had no idea what was happening or why, but it didn't feel like it was something good. Although I wasn't necessarily worried that the show might be canceled, I really wasn't sure what to expect when I walked in for *my* meeting.

All of the ABC network daytime executives were present, and each was dressed in very formal business attire. They basically gave me the news straight.

"We are moving the show to Los Angeles," Brian Frons, the head of ABC daytime, said.

They proceeded to lay out their reasons, all of which seemed logical and appropriate. When they shared this information, I automatically assumed that everyone associated with the show would be asked to make the move, meaning actors, executives, and crew. We were a family. I couldn't imagine doing our show without the entire team. In fact, the thought that they planned for only some of us to go never even entered my mind. The crews in New York were all so caring, hardworking, and considerate. It seemed impossible to me that we would make a company move without them. Sadly, the executives told me we would be getting an entirely new crew in Los Angeles. I felt terrible for all of the people I worked with—people I considered to be extended family. It didn't feel right.

I was very attached to many of the dedicated and amazingly talented members of our crew, especially my beloved hairstylist, Joyce Corollo, and makeup artist, Robin Ostrow. Joyce kept a quote up on the bulletin board in the hair and makeup room that read *When work is the focus of your life, your life is out of focus.* I liked that saying a lot. It was a daily reminder not to put all of your effort and energy into that one area of your life or everything else would end up out of balance.

Our New York crew was so committed and good at what they do—and they were *always* so wonderful to me. Walter, a former Marine and the type of guy who wears shorts in the dead of winter, was always so considerate and helpful. He and the rest of the crew always did their best to make me feel comfortable, especially when scenes required me to be in a more intimate setting. Whenever the script called for Erica to climb into a big bubble bath, for instance, our crew made sure that the water temperature was just right and that there were enough bubbles to cover me up. They'd want me to come a minute or two early to be sure the temperature wasn't too hot or too cold. And to be clear, this was a freestanding tub in the middle of a football field–sized studio in the middle of New York

City with no attached plumbing. The water was brought by hand, using buckets to fill the tub and trying to monitor the temperature. There was lots of heavy lifting involved here. As they were filling the tub, it was another crew member's job to blow the bubbles using an air hose, making sure that they were all just right. The bubbles had to rise to a certain level so that when I got into the tub they would cover me just enough without blocking the shot.

Our fabulous stage manager, Rusty Swope, made a point of being right there supporting us during our scenes, especially during these technically difficult and sensitive ones, from the beginning of the day until the last shot. Even if the director was screaming in his ear, Rusty never once brought his frustration to the actors who were in the scene. Rusty and Walter and the first-rate camera and boom operators, as well as the rest of their crews, were all so even-tempered. There was never a harsh word or raised voices among them in my presence or anyone else's that I had ever seen. There was such a great relationship among all of us. It was impossible to imagine that this rapport could be duplicated anywhere else.

Love scenes are often when the true professionalism of the cast and crew are evident. Although they can be highly sensual, the truth is, they're also highly choreographed. One thing is for certain: they're never private. There is a camera above you, next to you, and often one breathing down your neck. Sometimes the director might shoot a love scene later in the day so there are fewer people on the set, and on occasion, they may even clear the set of all nonessential people so the actors can have some privacy. Whether these types of scenes are shot in a semiprivate or not-so-private atmosphere, I could always count on the crew to be respectful and to make sure things went off without a hitch.

I've always enjoyed the physicality of my work, whether I am stuck in a hole twenty feet beneath the ground with soot and debris all over me or lying in bed with a handsome man. One of the most memorable scenes I ever shot had Erica making love to Jackson on a pool table after her plane crashed. It seemed so decadent and out there—even for Erica. I loved it. As it does in real life, physical contact in acting allows an actor to go to another place. It may not be the same kind of interaction you share with someone you love, but it still transports you somewhere else and that playacting is terrific. Fortunately, I have a husband who understands that love scenes are part of my job description and all in a day's work. Thank heavens my husband has always had a great sense of humor and a lot of self-confidence!

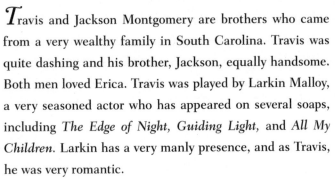

*T*ravis and Jackson Montgomery are brothers who came from a very wealthy family in South Carolina. Travis was quite dashing and his brother, Jackson, equally handsome. Both men loved Erica. Travis was played by Larkin Malloy, a very seasoned actor who has appeared on several soaps, including *The Edge of Night, Guiding Light,* and *All My Children.* Larkin has a very manly presence, and as Travis, he was very romantic.

Erica and Travis married twice. The first time, they had a daughter together, whom they named Bianca. When Bianca was diagnosed with Reye's syndrome, Erica and Travis remarried so that their child could have a stable family life. Bianca recovered, but Erica and Travis weren't meant to be. Erica began an affair with Travis's brother, Jackson, that turned into a tangled triangle for many years.

When Bianca walked in on her mother and Jack kissing in the living room, she realized that her mother was cheating on her father with her uncle. That was very hard for Bianca to take. She kept her emotions inside, acting out how she was feeling mostly through her dolls. She had an Erica doll and an Uncle Jack doll that she set on fire, accidentally burning down her family home. Travis was able to get custody of Bianca and ultimately took her away from Erica. Losing her child this way was very hard on Erica. She desperately wanted to kidnap Bianca. She went into an emotional tailspin and decided to move out of her house. As she was clearing out the safe, I discovered that the crew had placed twenty engagement rings inside! I couldn't react to it on camera, but after the director called "cut," I burst out laughing.

One of my favorite scenes with Travis was shot at a plantation in South Carolina very late at night. There were a thousand votive candles on the lawn outside and in the garden, where Erica and Travis waltzed in the candlelight. In another scene, shot very late at night, Erica was supposed to drive up to the plantation in a beautiful Rolls-Royce Corniche, a huge and gorgeous cream-colored car that I had never driven before. It was so dark out as we were filming the scene at two o'clock in the morning that it was very hard for me to maneuver the car. In fact, as I turned into the driveway and entered through the iron gate, I heard this horrible sound. I had scraped the whole length of the driver's side of the car from the front bumper to the back taillight! There was a soundman lying down on the backseat with a walkie-talkie, telling me in the most soothing voice, "Don't stop. Just keep driving. It's fine. Don't worry." There was a momentary pause and then, in his same ultrasoothing voice, he said, "Okay now, just back it out. We're going to do another take." And we did.

I knew I had just damaged a $250,000 car, but from the darkness in the backseat, the soundman had talked me through it, assuring me that "the owner won't mind!" Something told me that he might.

The decision to move to Los Angeles was a difficult one for me. I had a complete life in New York, which I wasn't ready to give up. My family and I love everything about living there, from the change of seasons to the electricity in the air. I struggled with the idea of leaving at first because New York is my home, and *home* is where I always want to be. To me, home is driving through Central Park on my way to work, passing Lincoln Center, racing along Broadway to get to my voice teacher on West Sixteenth Street, or meeting friends for dinner uptown and downtown and everywhere in between. New York is where my children and grandchildren live. My closest friends were mostly in New York or in other easily accessible cities on the East Coast, so I didn't want to make a decision that took me three thousand miles away without carefully weighing the pros and cons.

I was working so many hours at *All My Children* the year before we left for Los Angeles that admittedly my commute became one of the cons. It seemed to be growing increasingly harder for me to get anywhere at the right time or right place. I'd come home so late that I rarely saw daylight. I left in the morning when it was still dark and returned at night in the dark. I was living like a vampire! The drive to and from the studio each day totaled two hours. I always made good use of that time, studying my scripts and memorizing my lines for the next day, so I didn't mind the ride, but this factor had to be considered, too. (As luck would have it, once I got to Los Angeles, my commute was cut down to six minutes—seven minutes if there's traffic. At first I didn't think I would be able to memorize my scripts unless I had at least an hour in the car before work. Helmut jokingly offered to drive me around for an hour each day before heading to the studio if I thought that would help. After all of the stories I'd heard about life on the freeway in L.A., I never would have thought that my travel time there would become one of the pros in my decision.)

I also warmed up to the idea of moving when I stopped to think about the opportunities that existed in Los Angeles. Although I never wanted to leave New York for good, I thought it might be interesting to experience life and work someplace else, as long as I could figure out a way to come home on a regular basis.

Timing was the final factor. When I started out as an actress, I often dreamed of making the transition from television to film. Helmut and I contemplated moving to L.A. then, but once we had children, we chose to stay in New York, where we had roots in the community and we knew that our children could grow up with a sense of normalcy.

Even though things were going very well for me in those early days at *All My Children*, I had no idea that our show would become *breakthrough* television. I was pregnant with Liza when one of the tabloid newspapers crowned me the "Queen of Daytime." I liked the sound of that, but at twenty-seven years old, I hardly felt as if I had earned the title. Princess, maybe, but not the queen—not yet anyway. That tabloid story was a definite indication of how much attention the show and the part of Erica were receiving. It was also an incentive to stay. But suddenly the networks were proposing nighttime series written just for me; movie offers started coming in, and before I knew it, life got busier than ever. After examining the realities of doing a prime-time show, however, I came to the conclusion that the timing and circumstances just weren't right for me. I'm sure there are people who think that I made the wrong decision in passing up those opportunities, but they're wrong. When I discovered that shooting a nighttime show often allowed for only a limited hiatus during the summer months, I realized that I'd be away from my children more often than I wanted and that I'd also have less control over the other things I got to do in my career. Ultimately, it made more sense to stay in daytime television so I could be free when my children were off from school or whenever my family needed me. Although I did end up doing several movies for television, very few were filmed in California, so we never did end up making the move . . . until, of course, *All My Children* presented the opportunity to do so.

*R*ight around the time the networks were proposing creating a nighttime series for me, I was also approached about the possibility of playing drag car racer Shirley Muldowney in the autobiographical film *Heart Like a Wheel*. Shirley had wanted me to portray her in the movie version of her life, so Helmut and I flew to L.A. to meet with the film's director, Jonathan Kaplan. Some people think there is a risk in taking an actress from daytime television and crossing her over into film. Of course, I disagree. There are many people who worked on soaps over the years who have gone on to have great film careers. I was also told very early on in my career that playing a character such as Erica Kane could be detrimental to my landing other roles, so I was never very surprised when I didn't get a part. Though I was sometimes disappointed. Bonnie Bedelia was eventually cast as Shirley Muldowney. She did an excellent job and went on to win a Golden Globe Award for Best Actress in the motion picture drama category that year.

There's only one movie role I auditioned for that I regret not getting. I was up for a James Bond movie as one of the "Bond Girls." The producers were auditioning two parts at one time, so I wasn't sure which they were interviewing me for. I was told they were only seeing two actresses in New York and I was one of them. Helmut drove me to meet Barbara Broccoli, the daughter of legendary James Bond film producer Albert "Cubby" Broccoli. We met at her town house on the Upper East Side. It was a beautiful summer day, so we drove into the city with the top down. The butler opened the door to her home, which looked like a beautiful palazzo straight out of Rome. There was a beautiful marble floor and a large circular staircase. It was exactly what I fantasized her home might look like. As we walked through the door, Barbara was coming down the winding stairs. Although we had a lovely meeting, the role ended up going to Barbara Carrera.

Whenever I get some type of news that surprises me or that initially feels like an unexpected bend in the road, I often think of the lyric's to Johnny Mercer's song "Accentuate the Positive."

We all have choices in life, especially when it comes to how we respond to change. You can travel down the really dark path of wallowing in your discomfort or you can venture outside your comfort zone, learning, growing, and gaining as you go—something I've learned to do over the years. I've found myself, on occasion, in professional situations that test my patience, tolerance, and understanding of people who've taken the other path. I don't always comprehend the things these people say and do. In those circumstances, I can take other people's decisions personally and even feel bad about their comments and actions. But more often than not, I try to cut them slack, take them at their word, and go toward the light—it's a much better route.

Before I won my Emmy, I appeared on a talk show, and out of the blue, the hostess asked me if I was *bitter.*

Bitter?

We had been talking about my career when she lobbed this strange question my way. We weren't talking about not winning the Emmy or I think I would have understood where that question was coming from. So much went through my mind in the split second before answering. I just sat there on national television trying to deflect the question without really understanding what she meant. There was no place to go except to say, "No. I am not bitter." I thought about it for some time afterward and realized that she was definitely talking about my career—which she obviously viewed, by her own measure, as something to be bitter about.

The hostess was shocked by my response because I think she was truly expecting me to say that I *was* bitter. Instead, all I could think about was how grateful I was for all of the blessings and opportunities I had in my life as a result of playing Erica Kane and for the success of *All My Children*.

There was absolutely no point in trying to defend myself over something I didn't think warranted a defense. I didn't want to make things any more awkward than they already were. I wanted to give this woman the benefit of the doubt, with hope in my heart that maybe the question wasn't meant the way it sounded. It has taken me years to understand that people often project their own feelings onto others. More times than not, those types of statements aren't about you; they're about the person saying them. I learned that lesson a long time ago during the yogurt incident in the control room.

Looking back on my career, I believe that I kept my job for more than forty years because I truly love playing the part of Erica Kane. I recognize that it's a treasure and that a part like this doesn't come down the pike every day. And, as a result of my years on *All My Children*, I've been able to have a broader career—singing in night clubs, starring on Broadway, guest-hosting talk shows, dancing competitively, and so much more, all in addition to playing a part that I love.

In contrast to the opinion of that talk-show host, there are many people who would love to have a career and experiences like mine. We all have different ideas about what the ideal is when we first come to this business full of hope and ambition. Over time we experience surprises and our vision of the ideal changes. Few of us imagine our careers at the start being what they ultimately become. As grateful as I am for my career, without a crystal ball I could not have fantasized about it going exactly as it has. When most actresses truly allow themselves to dream, Meryl Streep's career is the one we probably all fantasize about. Although I've never met Meryl, she certainly represents an actor's actress. I remember seeing an interview with her when she was promoting *Out of Africa*. She was on a different continent for eleven months making that film. My husband was watching with me and could see the wheels turning in my head as I imagined what playing a role like that might be like. Who wouldn't love to work with the finest directors of our time, stand next to the most talented film actors and actresses, and have the opportunity to truly stretch their wings in that way? But before I could say a word, Helmut turned to me and said, "You're not cut out for that." And I knew he was right. At the time I hadn't even done a movie for television, let alone shot a feature film halfway around the world! Our children were very young. Liza was five and had just started kindergarten and Andreas was a baby. I could not have taken the separation from family for even a month, to say nothing of eleven. From everything that I've heard, Meryl Streep is a fantastic human being, a wonderful mother, and I subsequently read that she made plenty of provisions to be with her children throughout her career. But few people have the ability to give their all to both their craft and their family to the degree that she clearly has. While I remain inspired by so many other actresses' work to this day, I decided a long time ago that it was important to stick to my own path and make it the very best one it could be.

When I did film, I enjoyed the process very much. It was such a luxury to be able to do take after take until a scene was just right. Working in daytime doesn't allow that type of freedom because our shooting schedule demands that we cover so much material in a very short time. We shoot our scenes with three cameras in very limited space. I especially loved doing the film *Double Edge* because I got to play two characters. I was a police officer who was the ex-wife of a detective, played by the very handsome and talented Robert Urich. The other character I played in the movie was an assassin. The two women were not supposed to be related—they weren't evil twins; they were just two people who happened to look somewhat alike.

The director wanted to make sure they didn't resemble each other too much, though, so I spent a lot of time in hair and makeup changing up my look while developing different mannerisms and speech patterns for each of the characters. I thought we did a really good job of convincing the viewer that they were two different people.

Anastasia, the made-for-TV miniseries, was another very memorable movie experience. Amy Irving played the lead and I was cast in a supporting role as Princess Darya Romanoff, part of the Romanoff family who fled Russia before the revolution and relocated to New York. When I read the script, I was thrilled because I thought my scenes would be shot in New York. Since none of the other movies I had been in were shot there, I thought it was going to be a fun and different way to experience my own city. It turned out, though, that the producers didn't want to shoot the film there after all. No, they wanted to shoot all of my scenes in Vienna! I can't say that I was all that disappointed, because I love Vienna, and of course, my husband is from Austria, so it was a going-home of sorts for him.

I loved playing the princess. I did a lot of research on the Romanoffs before starting the movie. I wanted to understand the time period and the wardrobe. The costume designer shopped all over Europe to find the perfect vintage clothing for the cast. She had a wonderful eye and all of her choices were absolute perfection.

Amy Irving and I got along very well. We often ran our lines in her trailer between scenes. Everything about the movie was magical, from the camaraderie on the set to the location to the music that was created for the film. It was a wonderful experience that I will always treasure.

And speaking of treasures, a favorite souvenir from one of my first films for television is a black fedora given to me by the amazing Tony Curtis, who played my character's father, Sam Giancana, in the movie *Mafia Princess*. I loved making that movie. Tony was spectacular to work with. He was a *real* actor. He loved working on scenes, keeping them very alive and present. Each take was equal to the first take. And while each take might have been a little bit more nuanced, it was never anything less than everything.

Both of us were aged throughout the movie, which was really interesting and fun. I went from being fourteen to being in my mid-forties and Tony went from being a young man to an old man. Tony accomplished this using very little makeup. Instead he changed his hair and his hat, which somehow made him look older. The fedora he wore for most of the movie was synonymous with his character. When we wrapped, Tony signed the inside of the hat and presented it to me as a memento of our time together. I will cherish that hat forever, now more than ever since Tony passed away in September 2010.

Whenever I was on location doing a film, Helmut, who has a great feeling for architecture and detail, would find a reason to take on a new project in our house. I never knew about any of his undertakings until I returned home. It didn't matter if I was gone for three days or three weeks. When I got back, there was always something new. One of the most shocking of those projects was when Helmut decided to take every award, certificate of appreciation, magazine cover, and photo of me with famous people and friends, along with countless other mementos we had collected over the years and put them up on the walls in our basement. It was wild to walk down the steps and suddenly come face-to-face with a visual summary of several decades of my professional career.

As I stated earlier, I've never been one to look back at my work, admire my awards, or clip newspaper articles that mention my name, but I will admit that it was moving to see what Helmut had done. Looking at my nineteen Emmy nominations framed and nailed to the wall made that journey all too real. There was my People's Choice Award, the first ever given to a daytime actor, perfectly placed on a table beneath the Emmy nominations, which was right next to the *Soap Opera Digest* Award I received in 1993.

There was the award given to me from the American Academy of Achievement, an organization that puts together 350 of the top high school students in the country with leaders in their respective fields for a wonderfully informative and interactive weekend. Oprah Winfrey called me personally to urge me to do this event.

My children were at the kitchen table eating dinner one night when the phone rang. Liza answered the call. A moment later, she screamed, "Mommy! Oprah Winfrey is on the phone!" She was excited. And to be perfectly candid, so was I.

Really?

Oprah?

"For me?" I said.

It was really Oprah calling to say she had recommended me to the American Academy of Achievement and hoped that I would truly consider being a part of their event.

"Don't toss this one aside. It's a really good event for a very special cause. I did it last year and the people you will meet from every field are extraordinary," she convincingly said. And it turned out that she was right.

Audrey Hepburn, George Lucas, Martin Scorsese, Barbara Walters, Dizzy Gillespie, Oscar de la Renta, Calvin Klein, Colin Powell, and General Norman Schwarzkopf were all a part of the weekend gathering. One of the most incredible moments for me during this weekend was listening to Martin Scorsese speak about his career and influences. He gave so much generous commentary on his life. He is witty, articulate, and very down to earth. Dizzy Gillespie also spoke while reading from a yellow legal pad filled with notes. He didn't appear to be terribly comfortable at first. I have no idea if those were his own notes or if someone helped prepare them. He finally decided to put the pad down and just speak to us from his heart. As he began to open up his voice became like an instrument—one he played with such finesse and poise. He spoke in musical notes and although he expressed himself using those notes more than words, I understood everything. There was a fabulous mix of people who lectured and spent time with these kids, sharing their thoughts on their careers and hopes for them. I am so grateful to Oprah for thinking of me for this very memorable and special opportunity and even more so for encouraging me to attend, as I also had the chance to soak in the advice and messages of those who spoke.

As I continued to look around the basement, I had the chance to walk farther down memory lane. I saw all of the fantastic framed photos of celebrities I'd met over the years scattered around. Some even appeared on *All My Children*. Helmut framed one of my all-time-favorite keepsakes from the show—Tom Murphy and Warren Buffett's uncashed paychecks for appearing as guests. At the time Tom Murphy was the CEO of Capital Cities ABC, which was the parent company of our network. Agnes Nixon was friendly with him, so she wrote him into one of her scripts. Apparently, Warren Buffett is also good friends with Tom, and when he got wind that Tom was appearing on the show, he said that he, too, wanted to do it. So Agnes wrote more scenes and they both appeared as financial advisers to Erica.

There was also a beautifully framed personal photo of my television mother, Fra Heflin, who passed away on June 1, 1994. Fra's husband, Sol, had died from lung cancer two years earlier. He was a heavy smoker. Fra wasn't, but she was diagnosed with lung cancer, too. The only explanation was that she got sick from secondhand smoke.

Even when Fra was dying in her hospital bed at Sloan-Kettering in New York, she would call in to say she wasn't going to make it to rehearsals. She was just an incredible woman. When she passed, her daughter Mady gave me one of her mother's cameos, which I shall always treasure.

I remember going to Fra's funeral. Her family generously asked me to say a few words. I was matched up with Fra from the very beginning of *All My Children*. We played so many scenes together over the years. I literally grew up with her. I knew she would be missed, but I had no idea how hard it would be to go on without her presence on the set. When we had to shoot Mona's funeral scene for the show, my grief rose to the surface. Although my own mother was still alive, I really felt the loss of my television mother. I was missing Fra so much that I had a real and genuine source of emotion to draw on. Later that night I drove out to the beach house. My parents were there visiting for a few days. When I walked through the door, I remember throwing myself into my mother's arms, breaking down and crying. I was so sad that Fra was gone and so grateful that I still had my mother.

Also on the basement wall was a wonderful photo of Carol Burnett, who was a big fan of the show and the first major star to make a guest appearance on *All My Children*, joining the cast as Verla Grubbs, the long-lost daughter of Langley Wallingford. Carol was an avid watcher of the show who rarely, if ever, missed an episode. When Carol heard that several cast members were in Los Angeles to do a game show a few years ago, she invited us to her home before the taping. Ruth Warrick, Peter Bergman, and I decided to take her up on the offer.

The three of us were trying to find her house in the dark. We were New Yorkers. We had no idea where we were supposed to be going in L.A. This was long before the invention of mobile GPS units or even MapQuest, so we were relying on the limited directions we'd been given by the concierge at our hotel. We found a house that looked like it could be Carol's. It had a gate, but no address. We pulled up, buzzed the call box, and waited for the gate to open. When it did, we saw a man in the gatehouse scurry across the driveway and into another building.

Once we were inside, the gates closed behind us. It was a little eerie, especially when we noticed that all of the lights in the house were off, which seemed odd since Carol was expecting us. When we approached the front door, nobody answered. There were windows on either side, so we peeked inside. It looked magnificent. I saw several incredible paintings but nothing that made me believe we were at the right house.

We got back into the car and began looking for the gate man to let us out. He was nowhere to be found. We pushed several buttons, but none cleared the way for us. Ruth, who had lived in L.A., suggested turning on our headlights and pointing them directly at the gate. She thought it might be operated by light sensors. Sure enough, that worked. To this day, I don't know what happened to that gate man. We drove around the block one more time and finally found the right house.

When we arrived, Carol, Vicki Lawrence, and Carol's whole staff greeted us in the driveway wearing *All My Children* T-shirts. Each of them had a single letter on their shirt that, all together, spelled out the name of the show. Carol was lovely. She had drinks waiting inside, where we ended up having a wonderful time. Carol was an unabashed fan and certainly let us know it. She remembered every story line and detail of the show. She actually had better recall than we had. It was really fun to get to know her and a thrill when she eventually joined us on the set.

Helmut also framed a photo of Stevie Wonder, with whom I got the chance to sing "I Just Called to Say I Love You" during a scene at the Chateau. Erica Kane was promoting a "Don't Drink and Drive" campaign in that scene. There were also photos with Victoria Principal, Diana Ross, and Julio Iglesias at a nightclub in New York called Club A. I used to see them from time to time when Helmut and I went dancing there in the late seventies and early eighties. It was a very popular club during the height of the Studio 54 days, but much lower key. And there was even a photo of me with Danny Sullivan, who taught me how to drive an Indy race car.

There was the plaque commemorating my star on the Hollywood Walk of Fame, something I absolutely loved receiving. What made it so extra special is that my star sits right in the front of the Kodak

Theatre in Los Angeles, which is where the Daytime Emmys are now held, as well as the Oscars!

The Hollywood Walk of Fame is something every aspiring actor or actress grows up dreaming about. It was something I read about in the newspapers and magazines, but I never realized I would someday be a part of it. I was told that many fans had written in on my behalf, rallying behind me to get that star. Although I had spent pockets of time in Los Angeles making movies or doing cameo roles for television, I wasn't part of the Hollywood community. When I was told that I was going to receive a star on the Walk of Fame, I was very honored that Hollywood would embrace me in that way.

I didn't know what to expect on the day of the presentation. The ceremony took place on a drizzly afternoon in front of the newly built Kodak Theatre. I knew it wasn't going to be a good hair day, but it was very exciting to be there. Helmut, Andreas, Liza, and her husband, Alex, were with me, too. Agnes Nixon, who flew in from New York, and Bob Iger, then the president of the Walt Disney Company, and who was once the studio supervisor at *All My Children*, both spoke on my behalf before presenting me with the plaque commemorating my star. Several members from the cast of *All My Children* were also there to help me celebrate this milestone career event.

Agnes spoke first, saying generous and glowing things about my work as Erica Kane. When Bob Iger spoke, he recalled a story that I'd never forgotten—it took place in our old studio on Sixty-seventh Street in New York in the mid-70s. It was shortly after I had given birth to Liza. Since there were no telephones in our dressing rooms and cell phones had yet to be invented, I asked Bob if he would mind my using a vacant office in the studio from time to time to call home and check on my daughter. Much to my delight, he said yes. Bob Iger's speech was charming, and given his enormously busy schedule, he was exceptionally kind to agree to be a part of the ceremony.

The next day Helmut suggested we go back to look at the star once more before we left. I told him I thought it was a great idea.

"Where is it?" I asked. I wasn't being ditzy or coy. I just assumed that the ceremony took place in front of the Kodak, but that star was obviously moved somewhere else afterward.

"It's right where it was yesterday!" Helmut said.

I really had no idea they were going to keep my star where it was. That was very exciting because the location was almost as poignant for a television actress as having footprints in front of Grauman's Chinese Theatre would be for a classic film actor in the 1920s, '30s, '40s, or '50s. When we returned to Hollywood later that day, there were the usual tour buses lined up and down Hollywood Boulevard. As we got closer to my new star, there were actually people standing around it taking pictures. I didn't want to call attention to myself, so I patiently waited to take my turn. One of the bus drivers came over and tapped some of his riders' shoulders and pointed to me standing there. It was a very funny moment for all of us. A lot of jaws dropped and there were a few audible gasps before the picture taking began. It was a lot of fun to experience this moment with the fans.

The first time I attended the Emmys after receiving my star was a very special and memorable night. I had to smile, just a little bit, when I walked the red carpet and saw that they had cut the carpet where my star was placed in the sidewalk so it would be visible.

In life, you can bet that oftentimes things do come full circle. I was reminded of this when I saw a copy of a caricature of me hanging on our basement wall. The original, of course, hangs on the wall at Sardi's in New York. I never dreamed that my caricature would join all the other famous caricatures on the walls of that restaurant when I used to go there with my mother so many years ago.

And then there was the black-and-white photo of Sammy Davis Jr., Dean Martin, Shirley MacLaine, and me at the Friars Club testimonial dinner in honor of Dean Martin on September 13, 1984, at the Waldorf-Astoria. Frank Sinatra was the master of ceremonies. I had no personal connection to Dean Martin, so I was surprised but thrilled and honored to be asked to sit on the dais.

Helmut and I were at the cocktail reception before the ceremony. There was quite a large group in attendance, including Milton Berle, Red Buttons, Dick Cavett, who had been a guest on *All My Children*, Angie Dickenson, Lucille Ball, Brooke Shields, Joe Piscopo, and Shirley MacLaine, my father's favorite actress because she has red hair like my mother. I was so excited when I spotted Sammy Davis Jr. across the room. I have always considered him one of the great performers of all time. I suddenly noticed that Sammy was walking toward me. I automatically assumed he was heading over to speak with Frank, Dean, and Shirley, who were in close proximity to Helmut and me. But as he crossed the room, I realized that he was slowly coming closer and closer to me. I had seen Sammy on Broadway in *Golden Boy* many years before this event. I had always wanted to meet him, and now, I finally had my chance, as he was within earshot of me. As he got closer I could see that he was holding a briefcase in his right hand. He stopped right in front of me, put his briefcase down, held out his right hand, and introduced himself.

"I love your work," he said . . . to *ME*! I wanted to cry and tell him about the day I waited for him outside the stage door, but I didn't have the courage or the words. I was completely starstruck and tongue-tied.

"Would you like to meet Frank Sinatra?" he asked.

Of course I did. Sammy took me by the hand, walked me over to meet the Chairman himself, who I was certain had never seen a single episode of *All My Children*—and that was fine by me. Sammy began telling Frank all about me, my character, the show, going on and on, saying so many glowing things about my work to Shirley MacLaine, Dean Martin, and Frank Sinatra. I wanted to pinch myself to make sure this wasn't a dream and did my best to conceal my obvious blushing. This was a moment I will never forget.

I continued looking at all of the memorabilia Helmut had

collected. As I turned the corner and rounded the fireplace, I noticed numerous magazine covers I had all but forgotten about. There was one in that collection that was particularly memorable—the cover of *Cigar Aficionado*. The cover was shot after I won my Emmy in 1999. It was one of my all-time-favorite shoots. The photo shows me sitting in a bathtub holding a cigar, wearing a gorgeous diamond necklace and surrounded by perfect floating red roses. Although I've never been a smoker, I took a few puffs on the cigar that day. I didn't love the taste, so to help me out, No-No, my wardrobe mistress from *All My Children* who was with me for the shoot, helped me by smoking the cigar until the ash got to just the right place. Still, I thought the concept of that magazine cover was fabulous and the shoot had been an experience I adored being a part of.

When I stood in the basement and realized the vastness of my experiences, all of which came as a result of playing one single character, there was no way I could ever look back on my life and think, *Bitter*. Never.

So as the move to Los Angeles loomed over my head, I did what I always do—I accentuated the positive. I knew in my heart and soul that *All My Children* had always been a wonderful place to work. There were so many memories of shooting the show during its forty years in the Big Apple. Every story shared, every controversial subject tackled, every funny behind-the-scenes moment savored, and every opportunity to work with incredibly amazing people on-screen and off for those first forty years unfolded right there within those studio walls on the west side of Manhattan or some fantastic fairy-tale location I was lucky enough to film in. It seemed impossible that Los Angeles would have a fair chance to match those memories, but I was willing to give it a try.

CHAPTER 18

Looking Back
to Go Forward

There is a real ensemble feel on the set of *All My Children*. It's very hard to say what creates that among the cast. We are essentially a group of actors thrown together with the expectation of putting on a great show. But one of the wonderful hallmarks of *All My Children* is that it was created with characters representing every generation. The actors who play (and have played) these characters come from a variety of backgrounds, have lived in different times, and each has unique experiences that they bring to their roles. Somehow, that combination really makes things work on our set. I love when generations are mixed together and I think our audiences have loved it, too. As far back as I can remember, the fans embraced Ruth Warrick, Ray MacDonnell, James "Jimmy" Mitchell, Eileen Herlie, and Fra Heflin every bit as much as they embraced Michael E. Knight, Walt Willey, Darnell Williams, Debbie Morgan, and me. People tune in to watch characters who they can identify with and who they can become emotionally invested in. That wasn't accidental, as I am certain Agnes Nixon knew exactly what she was doing when she created the backstories for each of these unforgettable people.

There have been many times throughout my career when I've spent more time with the actors who have played the men, women, and children in Erica's life than I was able to spend with my real-life husband and children. But these amazingly talented and gifted people made that time fun, exciting, rewarding, and often very, very sexy.

I learned so much as an actor *and* as a person from these great professionals who were worldly, sophisticated, bright, and experienced. Jimmy, Ruth, Fra, Eileen, and others had so many interesting adventures to share. I was grateful for their insightful comments on life, political and social events, the arts, and on aspects of our scripts and the direction of the show. These were rich performers and rich beings who enhanced my life in ways I could never have imagined when I took the part of Erica Kane so many years ago.

I wanted, felt, and needed to believe that working in Los Angeles would bring together a new generation of actors who could enjoy that same camaraderie, but I also had to realize that some of the veterans of the show might not choose to make the move—or that those who did might not like the change enough to stay. One of those actors was David Canary, who played Adam Chandler. I have always loved working with David. Although he came out to Los Angeles when we began filming there in early 2010, he only remained with the show for a few short months. I had no idea how much I would miss him until we began to work without his company on the set. He has a very powerful presence on-screen and in person. David is such a wonderful actor. He played a fantastically complex character who shared a most complicated relationship with Erica Kane.

The first time I laid eyes on David Canary was when I used to watch him on *Bonanza*, as Candy Canaday. Suddenly, years later, he was on our show. I got to see David ride a horse in person for the first time when we shot on location up in Canada. He rode western and held his reins in one hand like an old pro. He was doing a scene that required him to ride along a rocky cliff, so the horses were slipping all over the place. Unfortunately, the director had no riding experience, so he had no way of knowing that he was putting everyone in danger. He asked David to do the scene again, only this time he wanted him to get even closer to the edge of the cliff. I stood off to the side watching as David did his scene flawlessly. But every time I looked at David on his horse, the only thing I could hear in my head was the theme song to *Bonanza*.

Later in the day, he and I were set to do a scene on horseback. Five actors on the show were riding in this particular scene. David was just behind me to my left while the others flanked us on either side. It was nearing sundown. The horses were tired and definitely ready to head back to the stable. The scene called for a helicopter to capture some aerial shots. I was once told that when a horse gets spooked, it will sometimes suck in its stomach. If it does that, the girth can loosen and slip. As I mounted my horse, the stage manager began counting down to the scene. I wasn't quite ready when the horses took off like a shot. My horse's girth slipped, which made my saddle fall sideways. I had lost my footing in the stirrups and was holding on to the horse's mane. As I was hanging off the side, I kept thinking that if I let go, I wasn't that far from the ground. What I hadn't considered were the four other horses that were stampeding close to my head. My horse was in a full gallop, and I was scared. Out of the corner of my eye, I could only see the other horses' hooves, so I knew I had to hold on or I would be trampled. The next thing I knew, the wife of the horses' owner came running out and somehow grabbed my reins. She miraculously got the horse to stop before I was seriously injured. As I climbed down, David rode up and said, "Thank God you didn't let go. I knew what you were thinking!" And he was right.

One of the reasons it was so much fun to work with David was that Adam and Erica had such a long and tumultuous relationship. Adam came to Pine Valley in 1984. He was the producer of the movie based on Erica's autobiography, *Raising Kane*, written with Mike Roy, Erica's ghostwriter. Mike was played by Nick Surovy, who had a definite worldliness about him. Nick, by the way, was very charming and very well traveled. His mother was a famous opera singer, Risë Stevens. He once gave me tickets to his mother's box at the Metropolitan Opera in New York so I could take my children to see their first opera—*Hansel and Gretel*—on New Year's Day. It was very nice of him to do that for my family.

Anyway, Erica and Mike discovered that they had developed feelings for each other during the process of writing her book. I believe he could have been the real love of Erica's life. It was an unexpected pairing. He was a journalist and a no-nonsense kind of guy, hardly the type our audience would think Erica would fall for. He had no clue who Erica was, and when he found out, he could have cared less. She was completely outraged that he didn't know anything about her. He teased her often and knew how to push all of her buttons. Erica loved that Mike was so irreverent with her. It took Mike a while to realize there was more to Erica than met the eye.

When Adam and Erica met for the first time, he did everything he could to get Mike out of the picture so he could pursue Erica. He wanted to become Erica's fourth husband. Adam somehow figured out a way to send Mike off to Tibet to work on a story assignment. Once Mike was gone, Adam could pursue Erica without any distractions. Erica was very unhappy that Mike left her to do the assignment all the way in Tibet. She felt abandoned and alone.

And although Erica had achieved her own success by the time she met Adam, she knew he could open even bigger doors for her than she'd been able to do for herself. Erica began to play with the big boys when she started her relationship with Adam Chandler, taking her to a different league than she'd ever been in before.

Adam was ruthless and manipulative. He wanted to possess Erica. Although she wasn't in love with him, Adam convinced her to marry him by promising to take her to Hollywood and to financially back films that would make her a star. In 1984, Erica married Adam on the rebound from Mike and out of revenge for Mike's leaving her.

I believe there was always a great love between Adam and Erica, but they were never meant to be husband and wife. To test her love, Adam faked his own death. When she believed he was dead, she realized that she was still in love with Mike Roy. She had her marriage to Adam annulled so she could be free to marry Mike when he returned to Pine Valley. When Adam turned up alive, he forced Erica to choose between his money and her love for Mike. It was an easy decision for Erica because she genuinely loved Mike and knew she was not in love with Adam.

Mike was unexpectedly shot and killed doing an undercover story for Brooke English, played by the fabulous Julia Barr. Erica made her vows to Mike as he lay dying in her arms. Unfortunately, the marriage was not valid because at the time, she wasn't actually divorced from Adam.

Adam did not leave the picture entirely, but at this point, Erica, who was terribly distraught over the loss of Mike, decided to go to Tibet, a place she knew Mike loved. There she would scatter his ashes. And there she would learn that Mike had once saved the life of a monk. Erica was beside herself, worried that she would never be able to live without Mike. While she was in Tibet, Mike's spirit came to her and told her she had to return to Pine Valley because there was someone wonderful waiting for her there. When she returned, she took a job as editor in chief at *Tempo* magazine, where she met a handsome man named Jeremy Hunter, who had arrived to do some artwork for the magazine. Erica didn't know that Jeremy was the monk Mike had saved in Tibet, but there was a very strong connection between them. Erica and Jeremy were instantly attracted to each other and fell deeply in love.

Jeremy was played by Jean LeClerc, a French-Canadian actor who was very handsome, charming, and extremely experienced. Jeremy's character was a monk, so he was very pure in his heart and his mind. Erica faced a challenge with Jeremy's vow of celibacy. She set out to change his pure heart and intentions. And although she never succeeded, they came very close—very, *very* close.

When Jeremy was arrested for murdering Earl Mitchell, a jealous husband whose wife had been having an affair with Erica's brother Mark, Erica didn't think she could live without him. Erica's brother was played by a wonderful actor named Mark LaMura. Mark had a headful of gorgeous curly hair, big blue eyes, adorable dimples, and a beautiful smile. He is a classically trained Shakespearean actor whom I loved working with. Mark and I see each other in New York or Los Angeles from time to time. Before Erica learned that he was her brother, the two of them had been on the verge of becoming lovers. Mona and the audience knew the truth and that they had to be stopped, but Mark and Erica didn't have a clue.

Jeremy was severely beaten in jail, which upset Erica so much she decided she had to marry him, even if he was in prison. Naturally, she had another plan, too. She wanted to secretly break him out of jail during the ceremony, so she staged a prison break.

The climactic helicopter escape was shot on location in Connecticut. It was freezing cold outside. We got there very early in the morning, just before dawn. When I got to the set, I approached the director, Jack Coffey, who told me how he wanted to shoot the scene. He explained that while dressed in a wedding gown and high heels, Erica was supposed to climb up a thirty-foot ladder through an opening in the roof. When she got onto the roof, they would yell "cut." The next scene called for Erica to run as fast as she could across the top of the roof, over pebbles and debris, and on toward a ladder that would be hanging from the hovering helicopter. They would yell "cut" once again, and then my stunt double, a woman dressed just like me, would take over and grab the rope, climb that ladder, and fly away over Connecticut. None of this was especially out of the ordinary, nor did it seem like it would be hard. Once I had my direction, I was good to go. (I just wished it would stop snowing.)

When they opened the hatch in the ceiling, snow was falling through the roof. When I got to the top, I ran down the length of the building, as expected. After doing it the first time, I was so pumped up with adrenaline that I thought to myself, *I can grab that rope myself. I can dangle off the helicopter and they won't have to stop the scene.* I thought I was doing a good thing and making the scene better as I began to climb up the rope to the helicopter until I felt the producer and director throw their bodies on top of me to pull me down and stop me from being lifted into the air.

"Are you crazy?" one of them yelled as they threw me to the ground. That's when I came to my senses and realized that hanging from a chopper hundreds of feet above the ground was probably not a great idea.

The stunt double came over to me afterward and said, "You don't want to do that. It's a dangerous stunt, Ms. Lucci." She was wearing gloves that looked similar to mine, but I later found out that they had special grips on them so she wouldn't fall. It was very cold, and the higher up she went, the colder it got. My fingers would have frozen and I would have definitely lost my grip.

Jeremy didn't end up accompanying Erica that day. He refused to escape because of the consequences of getting caught. Although he was eventually cleared of Earl's murder, Erica never forgave him for not going with her. Although they never married, she loved him very much—at the time.

*D*imitri Marick, played by the very handsome Michael Nader, whom I had admired from his work on *Dynasty,* was one of Erica'a most successful love interests. Michael was wonderful to work with, very experienced, and extremely funny. I knew him before he came to *All My Children* in 1991 because we shot a made-for-television movie together in 1988 called *Lady Mobster.* I was very excited that he'd be joining the cast, all the more because he was to be one of Erica's love interests and future husband.

Michael's character on *All My Children* was a Hungarian aristocrat known as Count Andrassy. Erica and Dimitri actually married twice. Their first wedding was on June 22, 1993, and their second on December 30, 1994, a traditional Eastern Orthodox ceremony that took place at a beautiful chapel on the grounds of Wildwind, Dimitri's Gothic estate. I had never seen anything like that ceremony, as it was quite beautiful in imagery as well as staging. There was a moment when two crowns were held above our heads while the wedding party marched around us three times. The exchange of vows was very moving. I suddenly felt like I was part of a thousand-year-old tradition.

We went on location to Budapest shortly after the Berlin Wall came down. That was my first time in Hungary. The architecture in Budapest was gorgeous, but after years of Communist control, it was also in great need of repair. The people there did their best for our crew, but there simply was no money in the country. The buildings needed cleaning and there were few flowers and very little food in the city. The countryside was breathtaking, with rolling hills, but it was also desolate. The vines had all dried up on the farms, there were no animals—everything appeared to be deserted. Our driver told us that the farms had been taken over by the Communists and had been used as military bases and housing. The Hungarian government was doing what it could to return the land to its rightful owners, but it would take at least three years to start making progress in that endeavor.

As I said before, Erica and Adam's relationship was complicated. The two married for a second time on December 13, 1991. Erica surprised Adam by becoming the ideal wife—sort of. She was doing her best to kill him with kindness. Knowing he was someone who always needed to be in control, Erica began turning Adam's world upside down by changing everything that was familiar to him, including his home. She redecorated Chandler Mansion, a once-masculine home, into a softer more feminine estate. Her plan to drive Adam crazy succeeded, and by the end of 1992, Erica and Adam were once again headed for divorce—*War of the Roses* style. He realized that no matter how hard he tried, he would never win Erica's love. He gave her the divorce she so desperately wanted.

One of my all-time-favorite scenes with David was also one of the funniest I have ever shot on *All My Children*. It was a thirteen-page food and pillow fight! Erica is in her hotel suite in New York City hoping Jackson "Jack" Montgomery, played by the one and only Walt Willey, is coming to meet her. Walt is quick on his feet, not just funny but hilarious, and as everyone in the audience could see, extremely easy on the eyes. Not only is he big, blond, and beautiful, he is a really great dancer. And, oh . . . did I mention those blue, blue eyes? He's got a wonderful spirit, is always prepared, and wants to get the most out of his scenes. He is an absolute doll to work with, as he is always respectful of everybody around him.

*I*n 2010, *Soap Opera Digest* named Erica and Jack "Best Couple" in all of Soapdom. The truth is, all of the actors I've been paired with over the years have been hot men— and that's intentional. We have great chemistry, and we are supposed to. That is what makes people tune in and watch and what makes the romantic story line sizzle. That magic is due to the tremendous instincts and fantastic eye of our casting director, Judy Wilson, who has won several Emmy Awards for her work on our show.

A wonderful new additional to our cast and, lucky for me, in Erica's life, too, is the fantastically talented and highly regarded actor Michael Nouri. Michael is tall, dark, and handsome and has the broadest shoulders ever. He is warm, creative, and absolutely hilarious. He does the best Richard Burton imitation ever and can play every role in *South Pacific* by himself! He is truly a one-man show. I love working with Michael, just as I have loved working with each of the men, men, men I have had the PLEASURE of working with over the years.

Our fans have been very passionate about Erica's relationship with Jack. I personally think they're better being divorced than married. When they were married the first time, their children needed both of them too much for the marriage to work. They couldn't be present for their children and there for each other, too. Their blended family just wasn't blending. In fact, it was actually tearing them apart.

The second time Jack and Erica got married, they promised each other that they would never let the children interfere in their relationship again. Jack took Erica to a boathouse, played some music, and danced with her as a symbol of his love and devotion. Unfortunately, circumstances in their lives are always dire. Sometimes Walt Willey and I will read our scripts and say, "But the kids are grown!" Still, the events that surround their lives are always huge and require more from Erica and Jack than they can give while they're in each other's lives.

So, when the bell to her hotel room rang, Erica was surprised to find Adam there instead of Jack. Adam was in the wrong place at the wrong time!

When Erica realized it was Adam and not Jack, she simply couldn't control her anger or disappointment, so she took it out on Adam through a highly choreographed scene created by renowned stage-fight director B. H. Barry. The scene opened with Erica throwing things and ripping open a pillow, which sent endless amounts of goose-down feathers flying everywhere in the room but was ultimately not very satisfying. Oranges were thrown, bread went flying, and walnuts were launched at Adam like missiles. Erica eventually got so frustrated that she grabbed a huge bunch of grapes from a bowl on a table behind Adam and just squeezed them over his head, letting the juice run down his hair and onto his face.

David and I rehearsed the food fight for the entire day prior to shooting the scene because we all definitely wanted to get it in one take. We wound up shooting that final scene at nine-thirty in the evening. Everyone from the crew to the cast had already put in an extremely long and full day. Most of us had worked straight through lunch to get it right. By the time we set up the shot, we were all ready to get it in the can and go home. Thankfully, we did end up getting the entire scene in one take so that was a wrap. The scene was so well received that it is archived in the Museum of Television.

David and I have been through so many experiences together, but my all-time-favorite story line between them was when Adam kidnapped Erica and their plane crashed on a remote island. The scenes were shot on location in Canada, north of Toronto, in an area called Stone Lake. Erica was trying to escape from Adam to get off the island. She ran to the edge of a cliff where she came face-to-face with a large grizzly bear. The bear could have backed her off the cliff, but instead, Erica decided to confront it.

"Get away from me, you disgusting, disgusting beast! You may not do this! Do you understand me? You MAY NOT come near me! I am Erica Kane and you are a filthy beast!" Erica goes on to growl at the bear before it turns away and leaves.

When I read the scene for the first time, I went to Jackie Babbin, who was our executive producer at the time. Although I had always been ready and willing to try to rehearse whatever was written on the page, I asked Jackie if she thought the script had gone just a little too far this time? I really didn't think the scene could ever work, but Jackie assured me it would, and if I played it right, everyone would love it. I said I would try, of course, but I felt like Erica confronting a bear was more than our audience would ever buy into. Jackie insisted the scene would play great, so I said okay and did it with every fiber of my being believing this could really happen.

It was a very hot July day when we shot this scene. When the wrangler brought the bear to the set, the animal was so hot that all he wanted to do was go swimming in a nearby stream. When it was time for the bear to come to the set, he didn't want to get out of the water. He let out several grunts and cries while we were shooting just to let everyone know how hot he was. (Don't we all wish we could do that from time to time?)

I didn't want to be the one to argue with a hot and tired grizzly bear in an unscripted scene, so I gave it my all on the first take. Thankfully, everyone loved it and the bear was able to return to his stream. Looking back on that day, I wish I had been given another crack at the scene. I was fighting so hard to find the reality there, I would have liked the opportunity to make it work even better.

That scene has become *All My Children* legend. In many ways, it epitomized who Erica Kane is. She can do things and get away with stuff that the rest of the people in this world cannot. She has an unending fighting spirit in her. You cannot keep Erica Kane down. A lot of people wish they had that type of spunk when their back is against a wall. Everyone fantasizes about standing up for themselves and winning. And that is part of what makes Erica so lovable.

Speaking of lovable, when I heard that David Canary and Julia Barr weren't going to make a permanent move to Los Angeles, I felt a sense of tremendous loss. I couldn't imagine *All My Children* without either of them. And to be completely honest, I didn't want to imagine it. I am sure there is a noticeable loss on camera, too, as our audience must miss them dearly as well. Their story has been left with Brooke and Adam leaving Pine Valley together. I can only hope and pray that they will someday return.

There was so much trust between David and me. We had many scenes over the years that involved a lot of verbal sparring and snappy repartee. All of the scenes were extremely well written, which made them fun and exciting to play. We shared a mutual respect for each other, as did our characters, which I think was always underlying their verbal jousting. Erica and Adam were rivals who really respected each other underneath all of their sarcastic remarks. As for Susan and David, there was no sarcasm between us at all. There was only and always will be love and mutual admiration.

Julia Barr played Brooke English, a character who had a wonderful, rich relationship with Erica over the years. Julia is so down-to-earth, candid, and very funny. She is a genuine delight to be around and to have on the set. She has positively impacted all of the people with whom she has worked. She and I had wonderful chemistry together that lasted for many years. Erica and Brooke were archrivals and had some of the best woman-to-woman scenes in daytime. The audiences loved those scenes almost as much as Julia and I did. Our characters threw some unforgettable verbal punches and one-upped each other frequently over the years. These scenes were the most fun to play. As time passed, Erica and Brooke found a fondness for each other, taking their rivalry from an envious one to a friendly one, so that whenever one of us was really in trouble, the other knew well enough to put a lid on it for a while. But the knock-down, drag-out scenes in the ladies' room became classic. These were the scenes we all begged to have more of.

Not only did Erica lock horns with Brooke English in the ladies' rooms of Pine Valley, but Erica's best friend, the zany Opal Cortlandt, played by the charming Jill Larson, often jumped into the fray. I usually can't take my eyes off of Jill. She used to be a model in Paris, but when she is in character as Opal, she wears more layers of jewelry and hair adornments better than anyone on the planet and somehow manages to pull it off! Her comic timing is unbeatable and she is just a pure delight. I am so glad they cast her as my best friend. When Opal married Palmer Cortlandt, she became the unlikely lady of Cortlandt Manor—a role she embraced wholeheartedly, having given up her former occupation as the owner of the Glamorama, Pine Valley's local beauty salon. Although Cortlandt Manor made the move to Los Angeles, the Glamorama didn't. And boy, do I miss it!

And finally, no discussion about those who will be *very* missed in Los Angeles would be complete without mentioning the spectacular, wonderful, legendary, charming, and handsome Jimmy Mitchell, who played Palmer Cortlandt since joining the show in 1979. While Jimmy did make the move to Los Angeles, he died on January 22, 2010, from chronic obstructive pulmonary disease complicated by pneumonia.

Jimmy was a highly skilled and trained dancer. And, he was a great one! He performed on Broadway in *Brigadoon, Paint Your Wagon*, and other musicals, played Curly in Agnes DeMille's iconic ballet scene in the musical version of *Oklahoma*. He also danced with the American Ballet Theatre. He was so talented, funny, and very well versed in both film and theater. He was so bright and always so full of life. And he was also very flirtatious in the most wonderful way.

He had a great big presence on camera as Palmer Cortlandt. I used to love when he opened the door to Cortlandt Manor and you could hear his "Doberman" guard dogs in the background. Of course, the barking was done with sound effects, but they so perfectly accompanied Palmer's larger-than-life image.

I was doing a concert version of *One Touch of Venus* at the New Amsterdam Theatre. Leroy Reams was playing the barber, Peggy Cass was playing my mother, and I was playing the bratty fiancée. The only way I could make those rehearsals while doing *All My Children* was to run like crazy during my lunch breaks from the studio to the conductor's apartment on the Upper West Side. I'd rehearse my dance with Leroy for thirty or so minutes, and then run right back to the set of *All My Children* in time to rehearse for the show. I remember waiting to do one of my scenes and noticing Jimmy standing behind the set of Cortlandt Manor waiting to do his. There was some sort of camera breakdown, so we had a little downtime. All of a sudden and out of the blue, Jimmy strolled over, took me in his arms, and started to dance with me. I thought to myself, *I will never forget this!* Dancing with Jimmy Mitchell behind the sets!

I knew life in Los Angeles and at the show was going to be different. It would take some adjusting, but it would all be for the greater good. The state-of-the-art HD studio they built for us is three times the size of the one we had in New York. With all of that extra space, the cast imagined we were going to be getting larger dressing rooms, too. I had always heard about the fabulous spaces other television actors had while doing shows in Los Angeles. Some had two rooms with enough square footage for exercise equipment, a small kitchenette, and even a private bathroom with a shower and tub. When my daughter, Liza, was doing *Passions*, she called and told me all about her palatial accommodations. She knew I had something a little larger than a broom closet in New York. In fact, she had a private bathroom with a shower and a separate living room—and a television set, too! She said that all of her coworkers knew I still used the public bathroom back on the set of *All My Children* and felt very bad about it. I tried to convince Liza that New York is a vertical city, which means space is always going to be limited and that my lack of space didn't really bother me. From the very beginning of my career, I never had any of those perks, so I didn't really know what I was missing. Still, I had hoped for something a *little* bigger when we got to L.A.

I had the furniture from my New York dressing room shipped to the new one so I could decorate it exactly the same. It was my way of keeping a little piece of New York with me in our new surroundings. And besides, I liked my dressing room furniture and wanted to keep it. I'd think about how to fill all of that extra space once I got there. But the irony is that my new dressing room is actually smaller than my old one, though I do have a window—something I never even thought of having back in New York. Thankfully my furniture shimmied into the space well, and it looks great, like a little jewel box. I have a series of beautiful black-and-white framed cityscape shots on the walls so I can be reminded of the place we all left behind when we moved to L.A.; pictures of my husband, children, grandchildren; mementos from *Annie Get Your Gun* and *Dancing with the Stars*; and that beautiful framed picture of Bernard from Africa. And, just in case you're wondering, I still don't have my own bathroom. That's showbiz!

I never thought we'd find a crew that was as good as the one we had in New York, but somehow, Julie Hanan Carruthers, our fantastic executive producer, and her team were able to put together yet another incredible group of professionals. I consider myself inordinately lucky to have this experience a second time in my career. Having such close contact and working with such great people twice is an extraordinary luxury. Although I miss everyone who didn't make the move with us, I hope they know how much they are loved and appreciated for all of the years of hard work, dedication, and commitment they put in helping me and everyone at *All My Children* do the very best work we could do.

People often ask me what my plans are. It's a funny question because when I took the part of Erica Kane, I didn't plan on playing her forty years later. I've had a great opportunity, which is both a rarity and a gift. I don't know many people who have held a single job spanning more than four decades, let alone many people who still feel as passionate about their work and their role as I do. Every time my contract came up for renewal, I would reevaluate my options. I'd ask myself, *Am I happy? Do I want to continue this?* For me, the answer has always been yes. Erica Kane would be a lot to walk away from for many reasons. For one thing, she is not a normal run-of-the-mill character. The role of Erica has allowed me so much range and room to play in and has garnered such a great response from the public that I wholeheartedly believe it is the reason so many people were willing to take a risk on me outside of daytime. I have enjoyed and cherished every one of my experiences. Erica has given me opportunities I'm not sure I would have otherwise had.

If I had not been given the freedom to play other parts in movies, or been able to pursue my interest in Broadway, to perform my nightclub act, or to develop products for HSN, I would have had to leave because I personally don't think you can be an actress if you only play one part, no matter how great a part it may be. But I've been blessed to have *both* the part I love to play *and* the chance to expand my career!

When my contract comes up for renewal, it forces me to be conscious of my commitment to *All My Children*, and even more, to be conscious of my commitment to my own family. Many years ago, Helmut and I toyed with the idea of me leaving the show and moving to Vermont, where we would open a quaint inn. He'd take care of the kitchen while I ran the dining room. It would be just like old times. That thought lasted about two and a half seconds after

Helmut told me that there was no place in Vermont that we could buy with big enough closets for all of my clothes and shoes.

So, as I look toward the future, I feel fantastic. My children tell me they're proud of me. And my husband, God bless him, has remained by my side all this time. Helmut is a visionary with great life and business experience and he is a realist, too, while I am all about the arts. His creativity has helped us build franchises outside of *All My Children*, which keeps things interesting and fun.

As for me? Well, I will continue doing what I love most— acting—while being the best wife, mother, daughter, grandmother, and friend I can be.

> *I was only supposed to be on every other Tuesday. But thanks to you, I am here and I promise I will try my best to never let you down. I'm going back to that studio on Monday and am going to play Erica Kane for all she is worth!*
>
> —FROM MY EMMY ACCEPTANCE SPEECH, 1999

CHAPTER 19

A Fan Letter to My Fans

After taking a look back at my life and all of the experiences I've had in my career, I realized that there is one more fan letter that I feel compelled to write—and that is to you.

All my life, I wanted to be an actress. It's one thing to dream about it as a little girl and another to make it a reality. You were there for me from day one. There has never been a moment in my professional career when I haven't felt your presence and your loving applause, whether appearing live onstage or coming to you from Pine Valley as Erica Kane. I truly believe that my career has been the stuff that dreams are made of, and none of it would have been possible without you. So for that I want to say thank you, from the bottom of my heart. Your continued support means the world to me. I look forward to doing what I love to do for many more years and to having you come along on this joyous ride with me.

Wishing you as much love and happiness as you've given me.

Susan

MY FAVORITE THINGS

T rying to narrow down my five favorites of *anything* was extremely challenging for me because I don't even like to give one birthday card to people! I like variation, choices, and options. So forgive me for giving you a few extra favorites here and there!

Five People I Admire Most
1. Oprah Winfrey
2. Meryl Streep
3. Tina Turner
4. Sophia Loren
5. Maya Angelou

Five Secrets to Perfect Skin
1. Using Youthful Essence-Hydration exfoliation and nutrients
2. Drinking hot water with lemon (honey optional)
3. Drinking lots of water and eating foods that internally hydrate, including cucumber, lettuce, blueberry, salmon, and avocado
4. Applying sunblock with a minimum of 15 SPF daily or 30 SPF when spending time outdoors
5. Maintaining a disciplined cleansing and hydration (moisturizing) routine. (Always take off your makeup!)

Bonus secret:

Getting a good night's sleep (sleeping on your back is especially good for your skin)

Five Secrets to Keeping Fit

1. Practicing Malibu Pilates
2. Eating balanced low-fat, low-carb meals full of fresh fruit, vegetables, and fish
3. Staying active and playing sports you love, i.e., I love to walk, play tennis, ski, and ride my bike
4. Remaining in motion—my work definitely keeps me moving. There are lots of ways to be active, whether it's through your work or running after your children. It doesn't matter, as long as you move!
5. Getting regular check-ups, including a stress test, mammography, etc.

Five Secrets to Aging (While Kicking and Screaming All the Way!)

1. Do what you love to do and don't be afraid to take on new challenges
2. Take care of yourself—physically and emotionally, nurture your spirit
3. Stay close to the people you love
4. Spend time with friends
5. Be grateful and give back

Five Secrets to Keeping Romance Alive in Your Relationship

1. Remember why you fell in love in the first place and never lose track of that . . . and never take a moment with each other for granted
2. Make time just for yourselves
3. Give credit where credit is due freely and often
4. Make love (I'd like to say freely and often, but I know life happens. Just try to make this happen whenever you can.)

   5. Laugh, listen, celebrate, and sprinkle life with sexy surprises

Five Ways to Look Taller (Or No-Fail Ways to Fake Your Height!)
1. Wear high heels, preferably stilettos and platforms that blend with your skin tone
2. Stand up tall
3. Find the best tailor or dress maker you can (remember, we are dealing with millimeters here!)
4. Dress in linear and monochromatic clothing
5. Try to keep your weight down. Proportion is everything!

Five Favorite Types of Music
1. Brazilian jazz
2. Motown
3. American jazz
4. Standards-American songbook
5. Broadway

Favorite Artists on my iPod (These are just some of many!)
Elton John, Stevie Wonder, Ella Fitzgerald, Barbra Streisand, early Sinatra, Rolling Stones, Ray Charles, Rod Stewart, Andrea Bocelli, Fergie, Pink, Steven Sondheim, Leonard Bernstein, Gershwin, Irving Berlin, Aretha Franklin, Aaron Copeland, Smokey Robinson, Quincy Jones, Peggy Lee, The Three Tenors, Brazilian jazz artists, including Antonio Carlos Jobim and Jiau Gilberto

Five Favorite Must-Have Items When I Travel
1. Simple, comfortable, yet stylish clothes that I wear in cozy layers
2. Easy on/off shoes for airport security
3. Lightweight pashmina or sweater coat
4. Extra moisturizer for lips, eyes, and hands
5. Scripts, magazines, and a good book for pleasure, pleasure,

pleasure

Five Favorite Meals
1. Veal meatballs with rigatoni and a side of broccoli rabe or rapine
2. Simple grilled wild salmon with lemon wedges, steamed spinach, and a green salad with cucumbers
3. Roasted chicken with grilled asparagus or steamed broccoli and a big mixed green salad
4. Breakfast—I love Kashi cereal with blueberries, skim milk, and coffee. Or another refreshing alternative is a yogurt parfait made with low- or nonfat Greek yogurt, berries, and a sprinkling of granola on top
5. Thanksgiving dinner! I especially love stuffing with gravy, mashed potatoes with gravy, and gravy with gravy

Five Favorite Vacation Spots
1. U.S.—Deer Valley, Ut; Vail, CO; Palm Beach, FL; Pebble Beach, CA; Hamptons, Long Island; Saratoga Springs, New York, and the Adirondacks, Vermont. Of course I love NYC, too—even if you live in New York, it so much fun to stay in a hotel and take in all the sights as if you were discovering the city all over again! The Wynn Hotel in Las Vegas is also a favorite.
2. Austria—The Alps, especially Lech, Ischgl, Zurs, Vienna, and Innsbruck
3. Paris and the South of France, especially La Reserve, outside of Monte Carlo
4. Italy, Sardinia, Capri, and Rome
5. Amanpuri in Phuket

Five Meals My Husband Taught Me to Cook
1. He taught me NOT to cook frozen pot pies and cheerleading

tuna casseroles
2. Weinerschnitzel, German potato salad, pressed cucumber salad
3. Chicken breast Milanese with rice pilaf
4. Veal meatballs
5. Kippferl—Viennese crescent cookies

*I still want to learn how to make Knodel—these are Austrian dumplings . . . ready when you are Helmut!

Five Things No One Knows About Susan Lucci

1. I sleep on the right side of the bed.
2. I like to put my left shoe on first. I didn't know this until I did *Annie Get Your Gun,* when the wardrobe helper backstage asked me which foot I prefer to put in first. Without thinking about it, I said, "My left." For some reason, it just feels better to me.
3. Ever since my children went away to college, I keep the lights on in my children's rooms in the house at night to feel their presence.
4. I can't stand the smell of cigarette smoke.
5. I don't like scary movies—I've felt this way ever since my brother took me to see *Simba: Terror of the Mau-Mau* when I was a little girl.

My All-Time Favorites:

Color: Red

Movies: *To Kill a Mockingbird, Gone with the Wind, Dr. Zhivago, A Man and Woman,* the James Bond movies, *Roman Holiday, To Catch a Thief, The Easy Life, And God Created Woman, An American in Paris, Bringing Up Baby, Pat and Mike, The King's Speech, The Lives of Others, Inglourious Basterds, Nine, It's Complicated,* and *Road to Perdition,* just to name a few.

Books: *To Kill a Mockingbird, Gone with the Wind, The Secret Life* of Bees, Nightfall, *The Lion's Game*, *The Girl with the Dragon Tattoo*—again, only a few of favorites but all so powerful.

American designers: Donna Karan, Ralph Lauren, Michael Kors

European designers: Jean Paul Gaultier, Dolce and Gabbana, Versace, Chanel, Yves St Laurent

Makeup: Clé de Peau, Koh Gen Do

Shade of lipstick: Clinique—Think Bronze, Sugared Grapefruit; Chanel—Ipanema, Crazed, Violet Diamond, Lover; Guerlain—Delit de Fuchsia, Rose Malicieux

Nail polish: Manicure—Essie Limo-Scene, Pedicure—Essie Spaghetti Straps, UPS, Fishnet Stockings, and Bermuda Shorts; OPI Vodka and Caviar

Shoes: Jimmy Choo, Manolo Blahnik, Prada, Louboutin

Fragrance: Susan Lucci Invitation—I really do wear this every day; Clive Christian-X for Women

Ice cream: Vanilla and chocolate, chocolate chip, Starbuck's java chip, pistachio

Dessert: Ice cream profiteroles with dark chocolate sauce, affogato (my favorite is vanilla and chocolate ice cream with hot espresso poured over the top), and baked Alaska—which I think is nothing short of a dessert miracle

Meal: Thanksgiving

Car: Mercedes or Ferrari

Piece of jewelry: Wide gold bracelet that Helmut gave me for my first mother's day

The Best Advice Anyone Has Ever Given Me Was:
"Study with the best." This is the advice my father gave me when I was young and it was reiterated during my studies at Marymount. "If you want to make it as an actress in New York, stay in New York." Robert Dale Martin

The Worst Advice Anyone Has Ever Given Me Was:

"Never trust anyone over thirty!" My generation grew up on this advice.

If I weren't an actress I'd be a: I y'am who I y'am. . . . But if I had to choose anyone else, I'd be Beyoncé.

My mantra: Live and let live . . .

ACKNOWLEDGMENTS

To Helmut, Liza, and Andreas—without each of you my story would not be nearly as rich or meaningful, not even close. Without you all my life wouldn't be as full and my smile as wide.

To Royce, Brendan, and our new baby granddaughter who have added immeasurable joy to my life.

To Laura Morton, thank you for your intelligence, wit, patience, and being so darn hip and with it. And for making this process so much more enjoyable than I thought it would be. You've been there guiding me every time I called, texted, e-mailed, and you never once flinched or yawned. And to Laura's fantastic assistant, Adam Mitchell, the behind-the-scenes guy who helped us seamlessly move through this process at breakneck speed.

To Mel Berger and Kenny DiCamillo who were the first to encourage me to write this book and then put the wheels in motion. I wouldn't and couldn't have done this without you. And to Graham Jaenicke for all of your hard work and assistance along the way. To Fran Curtis, who can and does make miracles happen.

To Hope Innelli, for being my editor extraordinaire, for bringing your experience, elegance, blood, sweat, and tears—no one could have helped me tell my story and share my vision better than you.

To Lisa Sharkey at HarperCollins and to Carrie Kania and the entire team at IT Books. What most comes to my mind is the song, "It Had to Be You . . ." I knew from the moment we met that you were the right publishing partners. I'm really glad you felt the same way and were so enthusiastic about being a part of this journey.

Many thanks to Kevin Callahan, Michael Barrs, Alberto Rojas, Joseph Papa, Kim Lewis, Joyce Wong, Robin Billardello, Amanda Kain, Amy Bendell, Lisa Thong, and Susan Amster.

To Agnes Nixon, there are no words to tell you what an extraordinary presence you've been in my life and how grateful I am every day to have been put into your hands. Your wisdom and example helped shape my life and your words on the page made me feel I could fly.

To everyone at *All My Children* for your invaluable help in so many ways, especially Julie Hannan Carruthers, Nadine Aaronson, Enza Dolce, David Zyla, and Judy Wilson, all of whom I greatly admire and respect and who were kind enough to make the time to brainstorm with me; Sallie Schoneboom, who is no longer at *All My Children* but was such a big part of my life there for many years and continues to be such a good friend; Michael Cohen for his ever-present energy and warm smile; Ann Limongello, Marisa Dabney, and all of the staff and crew in New York and Los Angeles, who make going to work a pleasure and who take that creative ride with me every day.

To Shawn Gough for the magic of your music and for taking such good care.

To Helene LiPuma, our longtime personal assistant and director of mission control.

To Yolanda Perez and Martin whose photography is as beautiful as they are.

To Joyce Corollo, Robin Ostrow, and Michael Woll who always make me look and feel my best.

To Frida and Lina who hold down the fort and keep our house feeling like home.

To Kathleen DiCamillo for your warm encouragement to tell my story.

To Pat Johnson, for being my best friend, for all the love and laughter and always saying it like it is. . . .